Comedy and Conscience
after the Restoration

Comedy and Conscience
after the Restoration

JOSEPH WOOD KRUTCH

COLUMBIA UNIVERSITY PRESS

NEW YORK

DEDICATED TO MY MOTHER

Preface to the Second Printing

THIS STUDY was originally published as a Columbia dissertation in 1924 and has long been out of print. It has been cited or quoted in a sufficient number of subsequent works to create a demand for copies, which had become very difficult to obtain. For that reason it is now being republished.

The text, the bibliography of seventeenth-century critical writings, and the bibliography of the Collier controversy are reproduced exactly as they originally appeared. The book now has, however, two additions: an index, and the bibliography of relevant modern discussions of the immediate subject, prepared by Professor G. S. Alleman of Rutgers University. Professor Alleman is at present engaged in the compilation of a general bibliography of material relating to the literature of the period, and he has very generously selected from his collections this list of books and articles bearing directly upon the subject matter of the present study. The list does not include studies of individual dramatists and is confined to those works which are immediately relevant to the special purpose of this book.

Since *Comedy and Conscience* was first published, the drama of the Restoration and the early eighteenth century has been extensively studied and our knowledge of it enormously increased. The author feels that for this reason, and because this book was written when he was a young student, it could not be revised without being to a large extent rewritten. Minor revisions would suggest that no others were necessary to make the work what he would now have it; and since that would be far from the case he has decided to let it stand, in the hope that it contains enough material not else-where available to make it still useful. As a glance at Pro-fessor Alleman's bibliography will show, its central subject has not often been investigated as a whole in subsequent studies. No work surveying the same field from the same points of view seems to have superseded it.

Professor Alleman has pointed out to me two errors which should be corrected. (1) I should never have implied that Charles II was personally responsible for the attack on Sir John Coventry, even though that attack was supposed to be in retaliation for an insult to him. (2) The once general be-lief that the Earl of Rochester arranged for the beating of Dryden in Rose Alley has at least been called in question in an article by J. Harold Wilson in the *Review of English Studies* for July, 1939.

Attention should be called to the fact that D. C. Taylor's *William Congreve* (Oxford, 1931) makes some few additions to the bibliography of books and pamphlets which constitute the Collier controversy. *The Critical Works of John Dennis,* edited by E. N. Hooker (Baltimore, 1939) dates more pre-cisely a number of pamphlets of which only the year of pub-lication is given in the present study. Mr. Hooker's review in *Modern Language Notes* for May, 1929, of Sister Rose Anthony's *The Jeremy Collier Stage Controversy 1698–1726* gives reasons for attributing to specific authors two works listed in my bibliography as anonymous.

J. W. K.

REDDING, CONNECTICUT
FEBRUARY, 1949

Foreword

THE following book was completed in the Summer of
1920. Various circumstances which have arisen have
made it impossible for me to publish it before now and,
though I have grown increasingly sensible of its defects,
the pressure of other work has prevented me from making
any revisions since its completion.

When I first began my investigations it was my intention simply to study the controversy which arose over
Jeremy Collier's attack upon the theater but I soon discovered that this attack was not an isolated phenomenon
and was led further and further afield until I was compelled to trace the various influences which led to the
decline of the Restoration Comedy and the rise of the
Sentimental Comedy by considering the general social and
literary history of the times. The present book is, therefore, an account of several more or less separated movements in literature and morals which converge towards a
single point.

As is usual in the case of such a book, there are too
many indebtednesses to be mentioned; but in addition to a
general acknowledgment of the services of the authorities
of Columbia University, the British Museum, and the
Public Records Office in London, I wish to tender thanks
to the following persons: to Professor W. P. Trent, whose
enormous general knowledge of the seventeenth and eighteenth centuries is matched only by his tolerance of people
who know little, for much counsel; to my friend Professor
Mark Van Doren, both for specific information and for the

effect of his contagious enthusiasm for the writers of the Restoration; to my brother Charles E. Krutch, for continuous interest and encouragement; and to my wife, for much help including the reading of the proofs.

New York City.
April, 1924.

Contents

CHAPTER I

THE DEVELOPMENT OF THE RESTORATION COMIC TRADITION

" I WILL answer for the poets, that no one ever wrote baudry for any other reason but dearth of invention," said the Spectator, but he was speaking as a moralist, and no one who reads fairly the comedy of the Restoration period can fail to see that men such as Congreve succeeded frequently in being supremely witty and outrageously indecent at one and the same time.

As immoral as it was brilliant, is the conventional characterization of Restoration comedy; and as we wish to approach the subject first in its most superficial aspect, we can do no better than accept this conventional judgment, insisting only that sufficient emphasis be provided for both of the adjectives. A reader may be blinded by its brilliance, as Lamb was, and see only the wit; or he may be a Puritan and see only the immorality, but both elements are there to a degree seldom matched elsewhere.

It is by no means impossible to take exception to the Elizabethan drama, especially if one include under this term some of the later plays of Fletcher and Shirley, which, in fact, contain the germ of the later comedy. The latter's " Changes " as we shall see later is loose enough, and yet considering as a whole the drama before and after the Commonwealth, one cannot but feel immediately the difference in the atmosphere. There is much that is naïve in the earlier drama, but sophistication and super-sophistication characterize that of the Restoration. Eliza-

bethan plays were much occupied with vice, it is true, but
vice was still, theoretically at least, "a creature of hideous
mien," while the Restoration dramatist, in spite of all
protests of a satiric intention, often looked upon it toler-
antly or, at best, cynically. There is a good deal of faith
in human nature in the Elizabethan drama, especially in
its earlier period, but after the Restoration such faith is
almost dead. That society is wholly base, the dramatists
seem ready to admit, whether they accept this fact with
heartless calmness as Etherege did, or fulminate with what
seems to me the genuine bitterness and disgust of Wycherley. There is corruption enough in the Elizabethan drama,
but there is also an abundance of "chaste maids" and
other models of virtue sadly lacking in the drama which we
are about to discuss. Here the pursuit of women is regarded as the regular occupation of most men, and a faithful wife or a "chaste maid" are decided exceptions.

The Restoration Comedies belong almost exclusively to
one type — what we call "society comedy" or the "comedy
of manners." The scene is usually London, and the chief
persons, with few exceptions, members of high society.
If the country or any city besides London is introduced, it
is only for the purpose of ridicule. "The country is as
terrible, I find, to our English ladies, as a monastery to
those abroad; and on my virginity, I think they would
rather marry a London gaoler, than a high sheriff of a
county, since neither can stir from his employment," says
one of the characters in "The Country Wife," and the attitude is typical. The scene moves usually in a restricted
circle: the drawing room, the park, the bed chamber, the
tavern, then the drawing room again, through which
scenes move a set of ever recurring types — the graceful
young rake, the faithless wife, the deceived husband, and,
perhaps, a charming young heroine who is to be bestowed

in the end on the rake. Shadwell (who himself sometimes wrote very much the kind of thing he complained against) described the type in a preface to " The Sullen Lovers." " In the plays which have been wrote of late," he says, " there is no such thing as a perfect character, but the two chief persons are commonly a swearing, drinking, whoring ruffian for a lover, and an impudent ill-bred tomrig for a mistress — and there is that latitude in this, that almost anything is proper for them to say; but their chief subject is bawdy and profaneness."

This characterization is but little different from the description given by Jeremy Collier in his " Short View of the Immorality and Profaneness of the English Stage." " A fine gentleman," he says, " is a fine whoring, swearing, smutty, atheistical man. These qualifications it seems complete the idea of honor. They are the top improvements of fortune, and the distinguishing glories of birth and breeding! This is the stage-test for quality, and those that can't stand it, ought to be disclaim'd." Says Farquhar: [1] " A play without a beau, cully, cuckold, or coquette, is as poor an entertainment to some palates, as their Sunday's dinner would be without beef and pudding "; and the same author, this time in the prologue to his " Sir Harry Wildair," sums up better than is to be found anywhere else the aim and practice of the Restoration dramatist.

> " From musty books let others take their view,
> He hates dull reading but he studies you.
> *   *   *   *   *   *   *   *
> Thus then, the pit and boxes are his schools,
> " Your air, your humor, his dramatic rules.
> Let critics censure then, and hiss like snakes,
> He gains his ends, if his light fancy takes
> St. James's beaux and Covent Garden rakes."

[1] Preface to *The Twin Rivals*.

It is not merely the looseness, but also the hardness of the dramatic heroes which disgusts one. The world is usually pretty willing to forgive the young rake, if he is represented as gay and thoughtless, but the absolute brutality of some of the so-called heroes is appalling. Take the case of Etherege's " The Man of Mode," which Steele, writing over thirty years after its original production, acknowledges to be still regarded in his time as " the pattern of genteel comedy." When the play opens, Dorimant, the hero, is entangled in three love affairs belonging to the past, present, and future. He is seeking to break off the old affair with one Mrs. Loveit by interposing his present love Emilia, while at the same time his imagination is fired by the sight of Harriet, whom I have described as the future love. In one act, Emilia, who is a girl of his own social position, is seen leaving his room; in the following he arranges marriage with Harriet. When Emilia reproaches him, Harriet takes his part and exclaims feelingly to Emilia, " Mr. Dorimant has been your God Almighty long enough. 'Tis time for you to think of another."

If any excuse is to be made for the men, it is that the women are as eager to be pursued as the men to pursue them. Says Lady Fidget in " The Country Wife " : " We think wildness in a man is as desirable a quality as in a duck or a rabbit. A tame man! Foh! "

Another type of character which belongs, more or less exclusively, to the Restoration drama, is the so-called false ingenue, whose characteristic is ignorance but not innocence. Mrs. Pinchwife in " The Country Wife " and Miss Prue in " Love for Love " are good examples. Vanbrugh has two, Hoyden in " The Relapse " and Corinna in " The Confederacy." The type, no doubt, was derived from " L'École des Femmes " of Molière. Sometimes it is very amusing, but it is indicative of the sophistication of the times, which substituted the highly seasoned piquancy of such indelicate characters for the simplicity of a Miranda.

It would be rash indeed to accuse any age of exceptional immorality because it made fun of marriage, since all ages apparently have done so; but one can at least say that the dramatists of the Restoration worked this ever popular field more completely than had been done before. Since praise of marriage came to be one of the favorite themes of the later and reformed comedy, attention may be directed to the reverse here. If the pursuit of women was the principal business of life for the characters of these comedies, marriage was the most dreaded calamity, and that love was strong indeed which would submit to it. Heartfree, in Vanbrugh's "The Provoked Wife," breaks out with this passionate declaration of his passion: "I could love you even to matrimony itself, a-most, egad," and though many comedies end with the marriage, no happy married couples figure on the stage. Young Maggot in Shadwell's "A True Widow" is afraid to marry for fear that this would cause him to lose his reputation as a wit, and the sacredness with which the marriage ceremony was held is revealed in the speech with which the father in "Sir Fopling Flutter" orders the priest to perform the ceremony over his daughter, asking him to "commission a young couple to go to bed together i' God's name." One more quotation, and we are done with this phase of the matter. It is from Dryden's "Marriage a la Mode." Rodophil is tired of his wife, though she is young, amiable, and beautiful.

"*Palamede:* But here are good qualities enough for one woman.

Rhodophil: Ay, too many, Palamede. If I could put them into three or four women, I should be content."

Before attempting to define or analyze any more closely the characteristics of the later seventeenth century comedy, it will be as well to attempt to trace its development, and to find out when and by what stages it differentiated itself from the comedy of the earlier part of the century. Let it be remembered also that to say that such-and-such a famous work is the first novel, or the first novel of character, or the first comedy of manners, is, ordinarily, to display ignorance rather than knowledge. Types do not leap into being full formed, but are ordinarily foreshadowed by a series of works in which peculiarities of the developed form show more and more plainly. Thus the plays of Wycherley, or Farquhar, are obviously a distinct species, recognized immediately as belonging to their kind, not to an earlier one, yet it is impossible to say that anyone invented this type. It is possible, however, to watch the gradual emergence of the characteristics which distinguish it, as they appear in plays related on the other hand to another species. Sir George Etherege, being the first author to attain very great reputation as a writer of comedies of manners, is sometimes given credit for their invention. Yet Etherege learned much from others, and his own three plays offer in themselves a remarkable example of the evolution of a type, the first being an uncertain feeling out, and the last a finished performance. But it must be remembered that in the years that intervened between his first and last play, others from whom he learned much were also experimenting.

Before examining the works of some of the less distinguished playwrights, it will be necessary to define the Restoration Comedy of manners — a task which will not be difficult after what has been said. They are, briefly, comedies depicting realistically and in a sinister spirit the life of the most dissolute portion of the fashionable society of the city. The hero is ordinarily a man pursuing the pleasures of drink, play, and love, with a complete disregard for the well being of others; and the heroine is a woman whose scruples, if she has any, are based on prudence rather than virtue. Great emphasis is laid on repartee for its own sake, and upon epigrams propounding an elaborate and systematic code of immorality.

This highly sophisticated offspring was derived from the union of certain elements of the old comedy of Humours with certain elements in the romantic plays of the same period. From the former it took its realism, and from the latter hints in the handling of dialogue, while it intensified the tendency to coarseness often observable in both. Ben Jonson had given a picture of the bottom of society, so that we might call his plays comedies of bad manners. Fletcher had elaborated the play of courtly characters, but chose usually to lay his scenes in remote or imaginary countries. The writers of the Restoration borrowed from both, presenting a picture as realistic as that of Jonson, but of a society as cultivated as that in the imaginary courts of Fletcher. Their characters might be no more decent than Jonson's, but they were more refined. They gave their rogues the manners of gentlemen, and, be it added, apparently thought that they were gentlemen. As Voltaire put it more wittily and cynically [1] when speaking of Congreve, "The language is everywhere that of men of honor, but their actions are those of knaves; a proof that he [Congreve] was perfectly well acquainted with human nature, and frequented what we call polite company."

The relationship between Jonson and the Restoration Comedy has not been sufficiently emphasized. A play like "Love for Love" may seem a long way from one by Jonson, but by the aid of certain intermediary forms

[1] *Letters Concerning the English Nation.* 1733.

(to be discussed later) the relationship may be more
easily detected. Both are realistic portrayals of contemporary manners, the one of low life, and the other of high.
The tricks practiced in the later plays are not those of
ignorant rogues, but of wild gallants; the oaths are the
fashionable " igads " and " stap my vitals " instead of the
camp terms of the soldiers; and the verbal battles are the
contests of wit by accomplished conversationalists, instead
of vituperative battles between low bullies and swaggerers;
but both are realistic. The element of " humor " in the
technical sense generally dies away, but in certain authors,
notably Wycherley, it is still generally evident. Dryden's
" Wild Gallant " has at least as good a claim as any
other play to be called the first Restoration Comedy, but
Sir Timorous, a bashful knight, is irresolution personified;
and True, the tailor, with his mania for jesting, might have
stepped from a Jonsonian comedy. Even in the best plays,
where this somewhat crude technique has been abandoned,
the descriptive names remain, as in the case of Wycherley's
" Horner," Congreve's " Lady Wishfort," or Farquhar's
" Lurewell."

The Restoration did not, then, invent realistic studies
of manners, but it gave them a new development by com-
bining two old elements. Similarly, the wit combats, which
formed so important a part of Restoration Comedy, are
also a modification of an old tradition. The presence of
dialogue which exists for its own sake and without reference
to the situation, has always been remarkable in English
comedy. The enjoyment of talk for and in itself is seen
everywhere in Elizabethan plays, even in the best tragedies
of Shakespeare. But in the Jonsonian comedies, the point,
to speak paradoxically, lies in a vehement and exuberant
bluntness, in the grotesque oaths of the Miles, the copious

but meaningless jargon of the Puritan, or the boisterous vulgarity of the denizen of Bartholomew Fair. The wit combats of the later plays are related more to the courtly tradition emanating from Lyly, but it is to be constantly borne in mind that the realistic spirit is derived rather from Jonson. The court comedies from Lyly to Fletcher are as essentially Elizabethan in their constant tendency to escape into the land of fancy as the later plays are essentially Restoration in the refusal of the dramatist to leave the familiar haunts of London, even in imagination.

An excellent example of the comedy of manners that had not yet freed itself from romance is found in Shirley's " Changes: or Love in a Maze " (1632). The scene of this play is called London, but there is little or no local color. Young Caperwit, the poet, and Sir Gervais Simple, the 'Squire, are " humorists "; but the serious characters are not so much London youths as denizens of one of those fanciful courts whence came the tradition of polite comedy. The opening situation in which the sisters confess their love for the same man is realistic enough; but when this too fortunate lover finds that he loves both, and invites a friend to relieve him of either, and when all this is done not cynically but romantically and sentimentally, one knows that he is in no real London. Before the play is over, lovers and mistresses are handed about from one to the other as though Puck had squeezed into their eyes the juice of Love-in-Idleness, and manners have been lost in romance. The Restoration Comedy borrows the sparkling dialogue of such a play as this, but treats it in a spirit of realism borrowed not from Fletcher but from Jonson.

During the twelve years from 1630 to the closing of the theaters, realistic comedy was extremely popular, and there are many plays, notably those by Shirley, Brome, Glapthorne, Cartwright, Nabbes, Marmion, and others, which, in the broadest sense of the term, might be called comedies of manners; but very few of them in any way approximate our definition of the Restoration form of light comedy. Studies of low life are more common than attempts to depict good society, and nowhere, not even in Shirley, who more than any of the others anticipates the style of our period, does one find realism, polish, and refinement combined with complete cynicism. Brome concerns himself almost exclusively with the vulgar, and with his plays may be placed Marmion's " Holland's Leager " and Cartwright's " The Ordinary." [1]

Returning to the plays performed during the twelve years before the closing of the theaters, we find that Nabbes' " The Bride " deals with respectable society, but that it is really a bourgeois drama like some of Heywood's, or even like a problem play such as Middleton's " A Fair Quarrel." The ethical side of the question (the right of a son to steal his father's bride!) is seriously discussed. " Covent Garden " (also by Nabbes) sounds more promising. High and low life are mingled, but the manners of the wild gallant smack rather of the tavern than of the drawing room, and the perfect gentleman declaims with stiff propriety and little ease. The gallant of the Restoration would have considered one as low, and the other as

---

[1] The relative lateness with which true comedy of refined manners develops may be due, in part, to the oft repeated definition of the critics, who said that comedy consisted in stories of the vulgar class. Dryden notices this belief, for instance, in his preface to *An Evening's Love,* and as late as 1698 Congreve (*Animadversions on Mr. Collier's,* etc.) pointed out that when Aristotle said that comedy was the imitation of the worst sort of people, he meant worst in manners or morals, not worst in quality. This however was denied by Congreve's opponents, who objected that men of quality should not be exposed to ridicule on the stage.

formal, and taken them as new proof that the true *savoir faire* was not known in England until the King returned from France.

Other comedies of this period by more or less obscure authors might be discussed; but they are mainly either somewhat romantic like Quarles' " Virgin Widow " or they contain foreign scenes like " The Knave in Grain," or they repeat the features described in plays of Brome, Nabbes, and Shirley. Passing reference may be made, however, to Cartwright's " Wit in a Constable," as a clean and fairly ingenious comedy of polite society, and to Killigrew's " Parson's Wedding." In considering the influence of the court on the development of the new style of wit, it is interesting to remember that Killigrew was close to Charles, both during his exile and after his return. The " Parson's Wedding," though acted before the closing of the theaters, was not printed until 1664. If the passages following actually appeared in the original production, then Killigrew was a Restoration wit before the Restoration. One character says, " I grew so acquainted with sin, I would have been good (for variety:)," and another remarks, " That wife is a fool that cannot make her husband one." During the Restoration the technique of wit becomes that of rationalizing debauchery into a philosophical system and producing a great corpus of mock casuistry whose fine points are expounded with a zeal worthy of a theologian. Killigrew was in close connection with the court and he early caught its spirit.

From our point of view, Shirley is the most interesting of the dramatists before the civil war. He has not the Restoration cynicism, but with him the play of polite manners has in some cases detached itself from the Fletcherian tradition of romance, and real London characters of the upper class appear in a real London setting. " Hyde

Park " is perhaps the best example of a play of this sort, as it is a completely developed comedy of manners. It differs from the later plays chiefly in the relative cleanness of its moral tone. The grossness of some of Shirley's pieces shows that taste was already pointing downward, and his frequent compliance with that taste in the matter of language, in spite of his own evident preference for at least the appearance of decency, is another proof that the public and not the dramatist ruled. But in spite of the grossness which he permitted as a sop to his audience, his prevailing tone is ostensibly healthy, and in his plays virtue usually triumphs and has the sympathy of the author.

His " Gamester " has been singled out for especial reprobation, but at least the Elizabethan pretense to virtue is kept up. The opening situation in which the hero, Wilding, makes love to his wife's kinswoman, Penelope, is corrupt enough; but one does not have to read more than a hundred lines to see that it is intended to give a moral thrill to a taste jaded with Jacobean horrors and not merely to arouse cynical laughter. In the end Wilding is hurriedly and unconvincingly reformed, in a manner strongly suggestive of that employed by Cibber. Obviously, such a play, in making a study of the manners and morals of an upper class, represents a step towards the Restoration tradition; but equally obviously, the new spirit of cynical *abandon* and immorality had not been developed.

To transform Shirley into Congreve it would be necessary first of all to sharpen the edge of his wit, and then to inspire a spirit of cynical indifference to the carelessness and the selfish indulgence of society as he saw it. It was not that the Jacobeans found coarseness unpleasant — the authors of the low life comedies had no reserves — but that they did not draw those elegant and accomplished rakes so characteristic of the Restoration. And they did not draw them chiefly, perhaps, because these gentlemanly scoundrels were the product of Restoration society. Though Shirley, as was pointed out, presented the rake as the central character, he did not, like the authors of the Restoration, present him unblushingly as a hero. On the contrary, the theme of the rake reformed was a favorite one with him, being used in " The Witty Fair One," " The Wedding," " The Example," and, with the substitution of an extravagant woman for a rake, in " The Lady of Pleasure."

In view of the close relationship which, in spite of differences, did exist between Shirley and the best writers of the succeeding age, it is rather hard to understand his complete loss of reputation — a loss so absolute that he came to be regarded as almost a stock example of a bad playwright. A reference to him in this light in " MacFlecknoe " is familiar, and " The Play-House. A Satire," speaks of " Shirley! The very Durfey of his age."

A careful examination of the plays produced in the years immediately preceding the closing of the theaters shows conclusively that though the Restoration tradition was foreshadowed, the plays were no more than a foreshadowing. Plays of realism and plays seeking to represent the spirit of a polished society are abundant, and the elements of cynicism are common enough; but in order that these tendencies should be fused together into the Restoration tradition, there was necessary the influence of the peculiar social conditions of the next age. The credit for the brilliance of the plays of the time of Charles and William belongs largely to the genius of the writers. The perversity of their tone must be charged to the spirit of the age.

We must turn now to an examination of the plays which appeared immediately after the re-opening of the theaters. The records of these early years as collected by

Genest are very imperfect, but it is evident from what is known that neither author nor manager knew just what was going to be required to suit the taste of the new age, and accordingly they revived and imitated the old dramatists almost indiscriminately, until experience and observation taught them how to hit more accurately the taste of the time. When the theaters were reopened, the tragedies, comedies, and tragi-comedies of Beaumont and Fletcher, Shakespeare, and Jonson, were again brought upon the stage, as well as the works of lesser writers like Brome and Suckling which were also rather indiscriminately revived.

The first new comedy of which we have record is Cowley's " Cutter of Coleman Street," made over from his " Guardian " and acted in 1661. It was a comedy of intrigue with a scene laid in London in 1658, but in no sense anticipated the Restoration Comedy. Rather it is a story of true love temporarily frustrated by cruel parents and by the unjust suspicion of the lover. Mr. Puny, the coxcomb, belongs more to the old age than to the new, and the hero actually thinks of abandoning his mistress because she seems to show unseemly ardor for him. One is not surprised to find that Cowley was not the man to hit Restoration taste. Next comes Wilson's " The Cheats " (acted in 1662), a somewhat Jonsonian comedy of soldiers, a hypocrite, and an astrologer, though perhaps somewhat looser in tone than Jonson would have written it, and with somewhat more emphasis on the amorous intrigue. It attracted lasting popularity, but is by no means a polite comedy. Some attempt is made, though feebly, to express the cynical spirit of the new age. For example:

> " Those married men are like boys in the water,
> Ask 'em how't goes. Oh! Wondrous hot, they cry,
> When yet their teeth chatter from mere cold."

This is not a very successful epigram, but it is the kind
of remark that Congreve learned how to turn into a glittering phrase.

Two other new comedies appeared in 1663. One of
them, " The Adventures of Five Hours," a play by Sir Samuel Tuke, with a plot taken from the Spanish, we can pass
over and then come to Dryden's first and much neglected effort, "The Wild Gallant." Here a very pretty, but not completely solvable problem arises. After a rather unsuccessful
appearance, " The Wild Gallant," which Pepys says was
badly acted, and " so poor a thing as ever I saw in my
life almost," [1] was not printed, but remained in manuscript
until after its more successful revival in a revised form in
1667. As it stands it is not great literature, but in its
theme and spirit it is a typical Restoration play, and if
we could be sure that the revisions were not material,
then to Dryden could surely be given the credit for having
first seized completely the essentials of the coming tradition.

Sir A. W. Ward in the " Cambridge History of English
Literature " [2] says that the play has no other claim than
that it was Dryden's first " to be singled out among the
comedies, at the same time extravagant and coarse, in
which the period of dramatic decline abounds; though
there are some traces of the witty dialogue, often carried
on by a flirting couple, in which Dryden came to excel."
Yet this last reservation is extremely important, for just
that witty dialogue between a flirting couple is one of the
most characteristic features of the Restoration Comedy that
was to follow, and, in conjunction with certain other characteristics to be mentioned presently, gives " The Wild
Gallant " its important place. Such bits as the following

[1] February 23, 1662-3.
[2] Vol. VIII, chap. I.

are the very quintessence of the Restoration manner and spirit. The second might be from Congreve himself.

> *Isabelle:* (To a suitor). — " but he I marry must promise me to live at London: I cannot abide to be in the country, like a wild beast in the wilderness, with no Christian soul about me."
>
> *Frances:* " I hope you intend to deal by my husband like a gentleman, as they say?
>
> *Lovely:* Then I should beat him most unmercifully, and not pay him neither."

To read the *Dramatis Personae* with its Lord Nonsuch, an old rich humorous lord, and Sir Timorous, a bashful knight, etc., one might expect a conventional comedy of humors, but these two characters are only of minor importance and the hero, Lovely, is just the irresponsible reckless spark that swaggers his ruthless way through the plays of Etherege, Wycherley, and Congreve, or, in the actual persons of Rochester, Sedley, and Grammont, through the court at Whitehall. Already the pursuit of women had come to be recognized as the chief occupation of a gentleman, and " The Wild Gallant " would be the best possible general title for the plays of the Restoration, for he is almost without exception their hero.

The prologue to the 1667 version gives some clue to the changes which were made. From it we learn that the scene in which the hero holds revel with the company of prostitutes on the night before his marriage was introduced late, so that his principles would be (in a sense the reverse of the usual) unquestionable. " I swear not, I drink not, I curse not, I cheat not," says he, " they are unnecessary vices. I save so much out of these sins and take it out in that one necessary vice of wenching."

The two prologues are themselves highly instructive. In 1663 was spoken the not very witty but clean one which consists of a dialogue between two astrologers; but in 1667 the play was provided with the brilliantly written verses in Dryden's mature style which begin as follows:

> " As some raw *'Squire* by tender mother bred,
> 'Till one-and-twenty keeps his maiden-head,"

and proceed thus to apologize for the comparative cleanness of the rakish hero of the earlier versions of the play, and boast that the author has increased the extent of the wild gallant's transgressions.

> " Our unfledged author writ a Wild Gallant.
> He thought him monstrous lewd, (I lay my life)
> Because suspected with his landlord's wife;
> But, since his [i.e., the author's] knowledge of the town began,
> He thinks him now a very civil man;
> And, much ashamed of what he was before,
> Has fairly play'd him at three wenches more.
> 'Tis some amends his [the author's] frailties to confess;
> Pray pardon him his want of wickedness."

Nothing could show better not only the taste of the time, but also the fact that in 1667 this taste was known and could be counted upon in a way that was impossible in 1663, when playwrights were still experimenting. By 1667 the tradition that the more debauched the hero was, the more completely he was a hero, had been firmly established. In the four years between 1663 and 1667, the Restoration spirit had been developed and recognized. One hesitates to give special importance to a play as universally neglected as " The Wild Gallant," but it seems clear that if the earlier form was substantially the same as the latter, then Dryden wrote the first real Restoration Comedy. Nor should this conclusion be surprising, for Dryden showed no characteristic more marked than his ability to give the people what they wanted.

The next important play to come after Dryden's maiden

effort was written by Etherege. His three plays furnish an
interesting study of the evolution of the type. The first,
" Love in a Tub " (1664), is as coarse as " The Wild
Gallant," but its material is more old fashioned. The title
is taken from a farcical situation in which Defoy, a dis-
eased French valet, has his head thrust through a tub, the
other chief comic material consisting of a Middletonian
story of the guller gulled at play and almost married to
a mock widow, while that portion which deals with the
better part of society is a romantic love story told partly in
rhyme, with occasional touches that have a certain genuine
prettiness. It might have been written before the civil
war. In " She Would If She Could " (1668), rhyme has
been discarded, and also the scenes of low life, so that one
gets nearer to the newer comedy and is concerned with a
series of polite intrigues. In " Sir Fopling Flutter " (1676),
the emphasis is shifted from incident to character, and we
have in Sir Fopling that type of Restoration fop whose
follies are so polished as to cause him to be mistaken by
some for a wit. As Dryden has it:

> " Sir Fopling is a fool so nicely writ,
> The ladies would mistake him for a wit;
> *   *   *   *   *   *   *   *   *
> True fops help nature's work, and go to school,
> To file and finish God A'mighty's fool."

But before this last play was produced, comedies had
already been written which preceded Etherege's final efforts
in the Restoration type. Wycherley had produced all of
his plays. He had shown that it was possible to base a
play not on impossible situations or intrigue, but purely
on contemporary manners, just as Dryden had shown the
extent to which cynicism could be made popular. Etherege's claim to be the originator of Restoration comedy
cannot rest on " Sir Fopling Flutter," which came too late,

and must fall to the ground if based on his other plays, for they are but experiments.

Returning to glance rapidly at the other comedies produced in the years immediately following the Restoration, we find several minor dramatists trying various styles. Sir Robert Howard's " The Committee " (pub. 1665) is a not very successful satire on the Puritan domination; Lacy's " The Old Troop " (1665) is a rough comedy laid in the same period. Skipping one or two insignificant plays, we come to Dryden's " Sir Martin Mar-all " (1667), an adaptation from Molière, and then to " Mulberry Garden," a fairly good comedy of manners which shows its author, the rake Sedley, to be more decent than the respectable hack, Dryden. The latter professed, at least, that he had no genius for comedy, and in fact his plays are never absolutely first-rate. But though they are often foreign in scene and built upon borrowed plots, they show the author a clever journalist who knew how to employ his powers of pointed assertion in those dialogues of cynicism and obscenity which the audience demanded. Probably they were written in cold blood and without enthusiasm, but " The Assignation, or Love in a Nunnery " (1672) and " An Evening's Love " (1668) are as outspokenly depraved as any of the comedies of the time. The tone of the former may be judged by the fact that the nunnery is referred to as the " seraglio of the godly."

Dryden's early plays are particularly important as early embodiments of the typical spirit of the Restoration. But he has a fondness for something approaching romance rather than realism. The later Restoration plays are remarkable not only for their looseness of tone, but also for their desire to represent the actual manners of the times, and to show real characters in a familiar setting. In this connection attention should be called to James Howard's

"The English Monsieur" (1666) and to "The Morning Ramble" (1673), by Nevil Payne, for in them the chief emphasis is on the mere exhibition of familiar character and the presentation of familiar scenes. The former is a feeble satire on Frenchified Englishmen, and the second a series of pictures in the life of a town rake of respectable birth who arouses the sleeping citizens with his nocturnal serenades and scoffs the authority of the constable, the lr'tter being a procedure considered by Restoration gallants as an excellent exhibition of *esprit*.

Thomas Shadwell, whom, in spite of his substantial merits as a dramatist, Dryden, by his mere genius for vehement assertion, succeeded in persuading the world to take for a dunce, produced his first play in 1668. In time he became one of the most successful playwrights of the age, but he was constantly railing at the taste of the times. Jonson, whom he resembled in size, petulance, and self-esteem, was his god, and his witty contemporaries his aversion. "A comedy of humor that is not borrowed is the hardest thing to write well," he said, and he boasted that he had never written a comedy without a new humor in it. Those of his contemporaries who loved repartee for its own sake he called men of little understanding. He despised the "Tittle-tattle sort" of conventional conversation, partly perhaps because his mind, unwieldy like his body, was not equal to it. He set up, too, as a moralist and a lasher of the vices of his age which, it is true, he did satirize with a more scrupulous realism than did any of the others. But whatever his moral basis, either the love of representing life as it was or the pressure of public taste made his plays coarse enough, and his wild gallants were wild enough to please his audience and his moralizing not insistent enough to trouble them. "The Sullen Lovers"

(1668) and "The Humorists" (1671) are dull, and it was not until " Epsom Wells " (1673) that he produced his first really excellent play. He was at his best when, as in the last-mentioned play, in " The Squire of Alsatia " (1688), and "Bury Fair " (1689), he selected some particular locality and caught the essence of the life there. Perhaps because he had little imagination, his plays seem more literally true than those of his more brilliant contemporaries, and give somehow the impression of being fully documented. In " The Lancashire Witches " (1681), indeed, he assures his readers that all the phenomena are substantiated by the authority of standard works on witchcraft.

In the seventies Wycherley ran his brief and astounding career as a dramatist, and in the much abused " The Country Wife " (1673) produced the most powerful comedy of the Restoration. It has not been customary for many years to admire the " manly Wycherley," as he was called by his contemporaries, but as a dramatist he was the greatest genius who appeared during the century following the civil war. The theme of " The Country Wife " is perhaps inexcusable, but its *raison d'etre* is neither its obscenity nor its wit. It is a moving drama, the result of a realistic imagination as powerful almost as Ibsen's.

Since this chapter does not aim to give a history of the drama, but only to trace its evolution to the point where the tradition of comedy was fully established, it is not necessary to go further, for nothing strictly new appears to have been introduced between Wycherley and the beginning of the sentimental comedy at the end of the century. With " The Country Wife " (1673), every distinguishing feature of the Restoration Comedy had appeared in definitely recognizable form. Its development had been rapid. Before the

civil war nothing more than the beginning of the tradition
could be found; in a few years scattered elements had
been fused into a new and definitely recognizable type.
Dryden hit first upon that peculiar cynical perversity
which dominates its tone. He, too, first laid predominant
stress upon the witty give and take of dialogue existing
for its own sake. Working upon the hint of a few
previous writers, Shadwell first showed what could be
done with prosaic and literary realism used to replace
the more or less fanciful elements of Dryden. Etherege led
the movement for the study, long continued, of the fop.
Wycherley showed how the familiar material could be
treated with a withering scorn in place of cynical indifference or approval. Beyond this, nothing new was added;
there could be only increased effectiveness. And the other
dramatists were, in a way, mere followers. Mrs. Behn
could out-do even Dryden in lusciousness, and Congreve
could surpass all the rest in polish of dialogue, but neither
was an innovator. If the latter is the most read dramatist
of the Restoration, it is not because he added anything new
in spirit or incident. He simply gave the familiar material
the highest polish that it could bear, and by the perfection
of his workmanship raised it to an intellectual plane where
perverseness of spirit is lost in perfection of manner.

In conclusion, some attention should be called to the
literary influences upon the development of the Restoration
tradition. As might be supposed, a society centering about
a court lately returning from exile in France, and looking
to France as the center of fashionable life, was not un-
affected by the works of the great contemporary genius
across the Channel. In fact, Molière may be said to have
come in with Restoration Comedy, for Davenant's " Play-
House to Let," one of the first plays to be performed
after the reopening of the theaters, owed a part of itself

to Molière. The latter's influence has been the subject of an exhaustive study,[1] and here it will be necessary only to observe that in spite of many borrowings from his plays, his influence was not so significant as one might expect. From him Etherege, Wycherley, and others may have received an additional impulse to the study of contemporary manners and a tendency to greater regularity and constraint in construction; but his spirit, the very reverse of the bitter and cynical, was profoundly different. Many dramatists ransacked his plays for the bare bones of situation, but from our point of view (the discussion of the dramatists' attitude toward life) his influence is of very little importance.

If much that came from France was too correct to meet exactly the demand of the English, a more congenial spirit was found in a section of the classics. No poet was so much translated as Ovid, and there was much in Ovid's thought that was congenial. Other of the less severe classical authors — especially Petronius and Lucian — were read and imitated. The Elizabethan age had got from the ancients chiefly the sterner side, and the days of Rome and Athens appealed to them as the age of strict ideals; but the more sophisticated Restoration found a lighter side to classical literature and recognized its own kinship with the decadent writers of antiquity. Consequently it translated and absorbed them. From Ovid, especially, it derived all that it could not invent of the animal tradition of love. To him at times, as to them always, love was the chief business of life, and love had none of the " seraphic part." Congreve's most characteristic line is but a translation and amplification of a well known phrase in Ovid's " Elegies ": " *casta est quem nemo rogavit.*"

[1] Miles. *The influence of Molière on Restoration Comedy.*

CHAPTER II

THE DRAMA AND SOCIETY

In the preceding chapter we have been concerned with a literary evolution; but this literary evolution was only an accompaniment of a social evolution. The sophistication of society tends naturally to produce a comedy of manners, and the peculiar characteristics of the Restoration Comedy of manners were the result of the peculiar characteristics of the sophistication of the times.

Jeremy Collier and his kind charged the drama with having caused the corruption of the times, but as his opponents pointed out, to make such a charge was to put the cart before the horse, for it would be much more fair to attribute the corruption of the drama to the times. In the first part of this chapter I wish to show that the atmosphere of the plays corresponded very closely with the atmosphere of a portion of society, that their heroes were drawn from the characters of such persons as Sedley, Rochester, and Charles himself, and that however shocking the incidents and speeches might be, they are to be matched in dissoluteness by what is to be found in the histories and memoirs. John Dennis protested that the comedies were but a faint representation of actuality, and that one might hear more profanity in one evening in a tavern than on the stage in a year. Similar protests are frequent.

Speaking broadly, the extraordinary debauchery which succeeded the Restoration was the result of the reaction. When Charles and his companions, whom Trevelyan calls the merriest troop of comedians that ever stepped upon

English soil, returned from exile, they determined to enjoy
to the full the pleasures that had been denied them before
and were now so abundantly offered. They were received
amid the greatest possible rejoicing, and their natures were
so little averse to merry-making that they threw themselves unrestrainedly into pleasure and even their partisans
were sometimes shocked. Thus Bishop Burnet[1] puts it
rather mildly when he speaks of " the general joy which
overran the whole nation upon his majesty's restoration,
but was not regulated with that sobriety and temperance,
that became a serious gratitude to God for so great a
blessing."

They wished to make the time to come in every way the
reverse of the time that was past, and the sin of regicide
of which the preceding generation had been guilty made it
seem a sort of piety to reverse all that had been done;
to pull down all that had been set up, and set up all that
had been pulled down; to hate all that had been loved and
love all that had been hated. The Puritans had tended to
regard all pleasure as sinful, and they determined to regard no pleasure as such. The Puritans had condemned
the May-pole and ordered that Christmas should be kept
as a day of fast; so the courtiers of Charles determined to
carry pleasure and gallantry even to divine service, and
Charles himself ordered that church music should be such
as he could beat time to. Instead of whipping actors at
the cart tail, they received the women as mistresses; and
instead of forbidding all plays however innocent, they encouraged all however indecent. As to language, we learn
from Halifax:[2] " The hypocrisy of the former times inclined men to think they could not show too great an aversion to it, and that helped to encourage this unbounded

[1] *Life and Death of John Earl of Rochester.*
[2] *A Character of King Charles II.*

liberty of talking, without the restraints of decency which were before observed." To be debauched was the easiest way of clearing one's self of suspicion of disloyalty. Thus Dryden makes one of his characters in "The Wild Gallant" say: "He has been a great fanatic formerly, and now has got a habit of swearing that he may be thought a cavalier."

Sometimes the effect of reaction was observable in the careers of individuals. Macaulay cites the case of Philip, Lord Wharton, whose father was so severe a Calvinist that he forbade not only plays, poems, and dancing, but even hunting, in his household, with the result that his son early acquired and "retained to the last the reputation of being the greatest rake in England." [1]

Clarendon [2] tells the story of Charles having fallen in his youth into the hands of the Scotch Presbyterians, who made him listen to interminable prayers and sometimes as many as six sermons in a row, from which, not unnaturally, he developed a distaste for piety of any sort. Of Charles among the Presbyterians Burnet says: "He was not so much as allowed to walk abroad on Sundays, and if at any time there had been any gaiety at court, such as dancing or playing cards, he was severely reproved for it." It must not be forgotten, however, that under the Restoration debauchery was often combined with extraordinary genius, as in the case of Rochester; or with genuine political ability, as in the case of Wharton, who, in the intervals of dissipation, was a power in the state for many years.

In the carnival which they were holding, the courtiers were but little restrained by the teachings of the English Church which they gave themselves so much credit for hav-

---

[1] Macaulay. *Hist., Chap. XX.*
[2] Book XIII.

ing reëstablished. A writer in Traill's "Social England"[1] says that there perhaps has never been a time since the fifteenth century when the clergy exercised such an influence as they enjoyed between 1660 and the death of Queen Anne. But assuming that this is true, it must, so far as the court during the early part of this period is concerned, be understood to mean political influence. Under Charles, the church as an institution was exalted, partly because the Puritans had pulled it down, but chiefly because it was royalist, many of its leaders holding the doctrine of divine right in its extreme form, and some maintaining that the King could, literally, do no wrong. But however much the courtiers were willing to honor the church, they had no mind to listen to its precepts, and, according to Burnet, Charles himself took care at his devotions to let people know that he took no interest in the affair. His courtiers did not scruple to go to sleep in the royal chapel, as is evidenced by the amusing story of the great preacher who begged the noble not to snore so loudly lest he should waken his majesty. Pepys, too, has his evidence. After attending service at the Abbey, he writes:[2] "There I found but a thin congregation already. So I see that religion, be it what it will, is but a humour, and so the esteem of it passeth as other things do."

It was on such a court that the destinies of the theater were dependent more closely than they had been at any previous time. Before the civil war there is but one instance, that of Henrietta Maria, of a sovereign witnessing a performance at a public theater,[3] but Charles took the greatest personal interest in the stage, and attended public

---

[1] *Rev. W. H. Hutton,* Vol. IV, Chap. XV.
[2] October 2, 1660.
[3] Cunningham. *Nell Gwyn.*

performances.[1]   When in 1662 he gave patents for the two
companies of actors, he himself acted as patron for one, and
the Duke of York for the other.   Nor was Charles' interest
a merely formal one.   The taste for French plays is attributed largely to him, and he was ready to make specific
suggestions to playwrights.   Thus Crown (preface to " Sir
Courtly Nice ") remarks on the King's preference for comedy, and says that he was often commanded by him to
write it.

From the court in general then, and from Charles in
particular, our comedy took its tone.   What that tone was
likely to be is evidenced by Charles' character as it was so
well described by Clarendon, Halifax, Temple, Evelyn,
and other contemporaries.   Gay, witty, polished, amorous,
pleasure-loving, unscrupulous, and cruel, he was a very
wild gallant on a throne.   The famous epigram which
charged him with never having done a wise thing is fair only
if " wise " be interpreted in the highest sense, for politically
he was astute enough.   Still, on the lighter side of his
character he was simply the beau idéal (except in the
matter of personal beauty, which he certainly did not
have) of the man of fashion of his age.   His religion,
Halifax says keenly, was that " of a young prince in his
warm blood," and he adds that in the library of such a
prince " the solemn folios are not much rumpled, books of
a lighter digestion have the dog's ears."   The sharpness
of his wit is too well known to need illustration, and Halifax remarked his tendency to make " broad allusions upon
anything that gave occasion."

From Fuller we learn that at his birth " The star of
Venus was not only visible the whole day, but also during
the two which followed," certainly a fitting prodigy to

---

[1] Anne returned to the habit of witnessing plays only when performed at court. Strickland. *Queens of England.*

signalize the birth of the amorous prince whom Louis
understood well enough to send to him the subsequent
Duchess of Portsmouth when he wished to cajole him dip-
lomatically. But it was Halifax who analyzed best this
side of his character. "It may be said," Halifax wrote,
"that his inclinations to love were the effects of health
and a good constitution, with as little mixture of the
seraphic part as ever a man had." As little mixture of the
seraphic part as ever a man had! Volumes could not furnish a better comment on the gallantry of the Restoration
life or Restoration plays. Like the best dramatic authors,
Charles "had a very ill opinion both of men and women;
and did not think there was either sincerity or chastity in
the world out of principle." [1]

As in the case of the heroes of comedy, it is necessary,
if we are to judge him favorably, to allow his graces to
blind us to the essential viciousness of one side of his character. When his subjects perceived the affability of his
manners, they were willing to forget everything else; but
it must be remembered that he was capable of forcing on
his Queen the shameful humiliation of honoring one of his
mistresses in her own household, and that he hired thugs
to waylay a member of Parliament. When in 1669 it was
proposed to tax the players, the move was opposed on the
ground that the players were part of the King's pleasure.
Sir John Coventry asked if the King's pleasure lay among
the men or the women of the company, and in revenge
Charles caused some blackguards to waylay him and cut his
nose to the bone. But his fashionable subjects forgave him
because of his brilliant manner, just as they forgave the
contemptible Dorimant, hero of "Sir Fopling Flutter," and
exasperated Steele because they insisted on considering
the former a fine gentleman though in spite of his outward

[1] Burnet. *History*, Part II, Chap. I.

perfection he was capable of complete baseness. Like
Charles, Dorimant broke the Ten Commandments but kept
the ten thousand. Restoration men, whether in real life or
on the stage, were gentlemen in everything — except
essentials.

Estimates of Charles' character varied much with the
political opinions of the writer, but his greatest admirers
could do no better by his personal habits than to turn
looseness into a virtue, as Dryden had done in " Absalom
and Achitophel " when he wrote:

> Then Israel's monarch after Heaven's own heart,
> His vigorous warmth did variously impart,
> To wives and slaves; and, wide as his command,
> Scatter'd his Maker's image thro' the land."

When, in 1662, Charles gave to Killigrew and Davenant
grants to establish companies of players, he enjoined that
" they do not at any time hereafter cause to be acted or
represented any play, enterlude, or opera, containing any
matter of profanation, scurrility or obscenity." [1]   Yet
certainly had this injunction been obeyed, none of the
spectators would have been more disappointed than Charles
himself.

The rest of the court imitated Charles' vices assiduously,
and his graces as well as they could. In an anonymous
pamphlet of 1675 called the " Character of a Town Gallant " the type is thus described: " His trade is making of
love, yet he knows no difference between that and lust —
he is so bitter an enemy of marriage that some would
suspect him born out of lawful wedlock." Reasonably
sober men, though no Puritans, could not but cry out
against the corruption of all kinds which flourished. Pepys,

[1] Printed in *The Dramatic Records of Sir Henry Herbert,* Edited
by Joseph Quincy Adams.

though timid, was not particularly averse to gallantry, but he was honest, and could not help exclaiming: [1] "But, good God! what an age is this, and what a world is this! that a man cannot live without playing the knave and dissimulation; " and similarly, he was shocked by the dissoluteness of the court, and ashamed of what he heard of Charles' debauchery. The famous Lord Rochester was an illustration of how not only wit but genius could be united with the extreme of debauchery, and Sir Charles Sedley, a wit and a very model of fashion, was morally so bad that when Pepys [2] wants to damn a man he calls him " worse than Sir Charles Sidly," and from Pepys, too, we get one of Sedley's bon mots which might have come from a play by Mrs. Behn. Having heard a character in a play comfort himself for the loss of his mistress by saying that, though the other had possession of her body, it was the speaker who deserved her, Sedley burst out, " But what 'a pox does he want? "

Go as low as you will in the farces of the time, even down to " The Morning Ramble," no extravagance will be found worse than the exploit alluded to by Pepys and described by Johnson in his life of Dorset. A convivial company was at the " Cock " in Bow Street. " At last, as they grew warmer, Sedley stood forth naked, and harangued the populace [Pepys says, July 1, 1663, that there were 1000 people] in such profane language, that public indignation was awakened; the crowd attempted to force the door, and being repulsed, drove in the performers with stones, and broke the windows of the house." For this misdemeanor they were indicted and Sedley was fined. According to Pepys (Oct. 23, 1668), Sedley again disported himself nearly naked.

[1] September 1st, 1661.
[2] November 16, 1667.

The extraordinary coarseness of language, too, was no mere literary tradition, but a fact of life. To be vile in language was fashionable. Motteux, who claimed to keep his " Gentleman's Journal " refined, tells how he saw a young gallant look at a copy and describes his reaction thus: " A young sport, whose pockets seemed better furnished than his head, yet had wit enough to adorn his outside, conscious perhaps that there was but little within, read some of it with an audible voice; at last, here take your book Mr., said he, there is not a word of baudy in't. How in the devil can it be a journal fit for a gentleman? " Nell Gwyn, apparently, had no objection to owning the most unequivocal Anglo-Saxon word descriptive of her position, and when her carriage was mistaken by a mob for that of Lady Castlemain, she is said merely to have informed the mob good humoredly that she was the Protestant not the Catholic whore. Yet it was she whom Dennis called " one of the most beautiful and best bred ladies in the world," [1] and whom he represents as addressing Wycherley, whom she did not know, from her carriage window in language which few other ages would have attributed to a model of good breeding.

Nor were the cruel and unscrupulous tricks which often formed the plot for plays unmatched in life. When the Earl of Oxford failed in his attempt to seduce a beautiful actress, he deceived her with a false marriage, and when she appealed to the King he gave her none but a monetary redress. If we are to believe another story, the dramatist Farquhar allowed himself to be caught by so theatrical a trick as a fake heiress, whose inheritance he discovered to be fictitious only after he had married her. The ordinary principles of decency and honor were no more essential to the fine gentleman in real life than they were on the stage.

[1] *Some Remarkable Passages of the Life of Mr. Wycherley.*

Anthony Hamilton, for instance, described complacently how the Count de Grammont attempted to repair his fortune by cheating at cards, and had not, apparently, the slightest feeling that such an action detracted anything from the count's claim to be regarded as the very model of a fine gentleman.

In the theaters themselves all pretense of order and decency was abandoned. During the early years of our period respectable ladies came masked and sat in a box, while the pit was filled with prostitutes. This is not denied by even the most determined defenders of the stage, and if we may believe the satirist, even ladies of quality sought adventure there. Says Robert Gould [1]

"How often, Cl(evelan)d, hast thou here been found
By a lascivious herd encompass'd round."

The young gallant, apparently, disregarded the play and devoted himself to conversation with the orange girls or the prostitutes. He came more to be seen than to see. Advancing to the middle of the pit, he produced a comb for his wig, called for an orange girl, and having bought some fruit, presented an orange to the nearest mask. After this, he fell asleep and only waked to start up at the end with an oath and loudly damn the play which he had not heard.[2]

It was a mark of wit to make loud-voiced comments on the play, and apparently no one had a right to object if his neighbor's conversation happened to drown out the voice of the actors. Pepys [3] is thus deprived of the pleasure of a play, but is quite reconciled because the disturber

[1] *The Play-House. A Satire.* 1689. These quotations are from the revised versions of 1709.
[2] *Character of a Town Gallant.* 1675.
[3] February 18, 1667.

is no less a person than Sir Charles Sedley, and his conversation with a mask at his side as diverting as that on
the stage. Brawls commonly interrupted performances,
and Gould, in the satire quoted above, describes the scene
vividly thus:

> " A harmless jest, or accidental blow,
>   Spilling their snuff, or touching but the toe,
>   With many other things too small to name,
>   Did blow these sparks of honor to a flame:
>   For such vile trifles, or some viler drab
>   'Tis in an instant damn me, and a stab."

In reading the memoirs and history as well as the plays
of the time, it is not so much the looseness which impresses
a modern reader as the terrible brutality. Between 1660
and 1700 much was done in reforming laws or administra-
tion to make human life less cruel, but during the early
part of this period there was much that was savage both
in public and private life. It was not only possible for
Titus Oates to send blameless men to execution, but also
possible to punish him with almost equal barbarity.
Politics was still a game played for heads, and you might
send your opponent to the block by fair means or foul.
The employment of thugs was almost a recognized manner
of avenging injured honor, and the case of Charles and Sir
John Coventry which has already been mentioned was only
a single instance. Others may be added. Rochester (again
be it noted a very fine gentleman) had Dryden beaten because he suspected that the latter had helped Mulgrave
with his " Essay on Satyre," which contained an attack on
Rochester, and Sedley took a similar revenge on the actor
Kynaston for burlesquing him on the stage. To us it
would seem that the disgrace would attach to the man who
took so cowardly a revenge, but contemporaries seemed to
think that the shame stuck not upon Charles, Rochester,

or Sedley, but upon Sir John Coventry, Dryden, and Kynaston.

If one turns over the records of social or political history, one sometimes turns sick at the hopeless tangle of intrigue and corruption, barbarity and baseness, which oft-times tainted even the best causes and the best men. Violence was familiar. Not only criminals, but also the more bigoted fanatics were punished with a revolting cruelty, as in the case of the pamphleteering Whig clergyman Samuel Johnson, who for his conscience suffered himself to be flogged like Titus Oates, from Newgate to Tyburn, without a murmur because, he said, he remembered how patiently Christ had borne the cross on Mount Calvary. With life as it was, it is no wonder that audiences at the theater were less sensitive than we to treachery and heartlessness, and were often moved only to laughter where we should be shocked. As spectators of life as well as of the stage, their feelings were necessarily less sensitive, and they were compelled, in self defense, to develop stomachs stronger than ours.

One might go on indefinitely citing illustrations and making comment and comparison, but enough has already been pointed out to show that no character or incident in the plays was unwarranted by life, that the dramatists were not perverse creatures creating monsters to debase the auditors, but that they were merely holding the mirror up to nature, or rather, to that part of nature which was best known to their fashionable auditors.

It is not to be supposed, of course, that England was exclusively made up of Rochesters and Sedleys, and that honor and decency were dead. Even among the wits there were no doubt many meetings like those described by Dryden,[1] where he speaks of " our genial nights, where our

[1] Dedication to *The Assignation.*

discourse is neither too serious nor too light, but always pleasant, and, for the most part, instructive; the railery, neither too sharp upon the present, nor too censorious on the absent; and the cups only such as will raise the conversation of the night, without disturbing the business of the morrow." Men like Evelyn and Pepys (though the latter was somewhat given to gallantry) would be gentlemen in any age, and the names of the Earl of Clarendon and Sir William Temple are enough to remind us that not all politicians were base. As for the ladies, the delightful and eccentric Duchess of Newcastle proves that one of them, at least, might be a wit and no prude; be beautiful, and yet faithful to her husband.

When one comes to the middle class, too, there is, no doubt, another story to tell. Many a Puritan still lived, and certainly the great majority of the people looked with horror upon the life of the fashionable set. While the gallants considered adultery as a sport, there were not wanting people to argue that it should be punished by death [1] and who, instead of being drunk for five years together, like Rochester, urged the prohibition of the importation of brandy. [2]

To realize what a numerous class the pious were as compared to the others, one need only study the bibliography of the period. In his preface to the Term Catalogues, Professor Arber says, " We must largely reverse our ideas as to the general character of English Literature during the Restoration Age — the general tone of its books was deeply religious; mingled with much philosophical inquiry, and deep research into nature — as this contemporary bibliography clearly shows — all those shilling plays put together

[1] See Pamphlet published 1675 and reprinted in the Harleian Misc., Vol. III, p. 93.
[2] Harleian Misc., Vol. III, p. 569.

do not form two per centum of the total English books of
the times; whether as regards their printed bulk, or their
prices. It was the religious people first, and the scientists
next, that made the fortunes of the London book trade.
They often subscribed as much for the folios of a single
writer, like Tillotson or Rushworth, Baxter or Ray, Man-
ton or Bunyan, as would have bought a complete set of
all the plays of that time." [1]

Far from being debauched, the middle and lower class
was permeated with a spirit of somewhat crude and narrow
piety. We are more familiar with the obscene fugitive
pieces and tracts, but the British Museum has, in addition
to such pieces as are reprinted in the " Poems on State
Occasions," an interesting collection of religious broadsides,
bearing such quaint titles as " The Young Man's Warning
Piece, or The Extravagant Youth's Pilgrimage and Progress
in this World " (1682), or " Divers Examples of God's
Severe Judgment upon Sabbath Brakers, etc." (1672).
The latter is adorned with truly horrendous woodcuts depicting a collection of stiff youths breaking through the
ice on which they had been disporting themselves at foot-
ball, unmindful of the desecration of the Sabbath. Whitehall and the Puritan populace were far apart, and not all
the nation had joined in the unrestrained carnival following
the Restoration.

But it must be remembered that this great body of
respectable Englishmen, who were not interested in *belles
lettres*, does not concern us, because the theater, to an
extent probably never true before or since, was the affair
only of the court and of the fashionable class. In the
time of Elizabeth, it belonged to the people almost as much
as the " movies " do today; but under Charles and James,
the great middle class neither frequented the theater nor

[1] *Term Catalogue.* Vol. III.

was represented upon the stage, except, perhaps, as an object of ridicule. That this is true there is abundance of evidence. We know that to attend the theater and be able to discuss the latest plays was part of the regular business of the man of fashion, and we know also that a small number of theaters were sufficient to supply the demand, and that hence it must have been only the people of fashion who attended. We have no complete record of the play-houses under Elizabeth, but it is probable that as many as seven were in operation at one time. When Charles settled theatrical affairs in 1662, he gave license for only two, and in 1682 it was discovered that there was not enough business to justify both of them, and so the companies were united. From that time until 1695, when Betterton seceded, London, which had six or seven theaters in Elizabeth's time, needed only one, in spite of the fact that the city had greatly increased in size.

In this connection, the anonymous dialogue called " Historia Histrionica," attributed to James Wright, contains an interesting passage. One of the speakers expresses surprise at the decrease in the number of theaters, saying that while there were a number before the Commonwealth, two are now hardly able to exist. His companion replies that in former times the price of admission was less and that, moreover, plays were then innocent diversions, but that of late they are no longer instructive, and the play-houses so " pestered with vizard-masks and their trade " that many of the more civilized part of the town shun the theater as they would a house of scandal. In 1706, at a time when only Drury Lane and the Haymarket were open, Congreve wrote that he did not believe that the play-houses could go on another winter,[1] and Cibber dates the beginning of the prosperity of the stage at 1711.

[1] Letter to Kealley in Berkley's *Literary Relics*.

Another indication that the theater was an affair of the fashionable world is to be found in the persons of some of the people who wrote for it. Of the five great comedy writers, Etherege, Wycherley, Congreve, Vanbrugh and Farquhar, four were distinguished men of fashion, and two were, in addition, knights; so that, if we may reverse the famous phrase, it may be said of them that they " for fame not money winged their airy flight." If the success or failure of a play had depended upon any but people of fashion, it is not likely that they would have risked their reputation before an audience. Briefly then, the Restoration stage was a fashionable entertainment where the most reckless of the upper class saw their follies and vices wittily and realistically presented.

From this it is evident that certain of the characteristics of the Restoration drama were inevitable. In the first place, since " the drama's laws the drama's patrons give," any dramatist who had written idealistically would have been neglected for some one who knew better how to meet the taste of the audience. In the second place, any comedy of manners which depicted the actual life of the upper class of the times had to be in one sense corrupt if it was to be true. It could not picture the times and be pure. It is not strange that under the circumstances people of the times should not have been shocked by this drama as its modern readers have been shocked, because the people for whom it was written were familiar with open corruption in a way that most modern readers are not. Dorimant and Mirabel may seem to some mere creatures of fancy, but the audience at the Restoration theater not only knew that they existed but had come into personal contact with them. This audience was not likely to resent on the stage what it knew to exist openly. Nor is there anything in this which need damn the dramatists as men. They had no deliberate intention of encouraging vice, which, being men of sense, they no doubt hated.

The material, then, of Restoration Comedy was inevitable; but there remains the question of the dramatists' attitude toward it. Those who attacked the stage came, as will be seen later, to object to the representation of impurity in any way, but it was also charged that the dramatists not only represented the corruption of the time but sympathized with it and encouraged it. The writers of sentimental comedy depicted faulty characters in order to show them in the end unsuccessful, and justified themselves on this plea. Certainly the Restoration writer did nothing of this sort. His heroes, however debased and however careless, found only greater success at the end of the primrose path. We are faced, then, with the task of discovering the attitude of the dramatist, of finding out what he was trying to do and what he regarded as his function. Did he consider himself a satirist, opposing vices and follies that they might be scorned and corrected; did he in the main sympathize with the society which he pictured; or, finally, was he merely indifferent, presenting life as it was and caring but little whether it was virtuous or vicious? To help us, we have statements from many of the dramatists themselves; for the literary art had become a manner of fashionable interest, and the writer found it worth his while to discuss for the benefit of his public the principles of his craft in a way that would have had but little interest for the general public in preceding centuries.

One well-known critic of the present day has been so rash as to assert that Jeremy Collier was the first man to propose a moral test for comedy. On the contrary, no critical question concerning it is older. Comedy, like other forms of literature, has endured because it pleases; but philosophers have ever been loth to accept a hedonistic justification, and comic poets, when driven to defend themselves, have usually chosen to claim a moral function, and to say that if they did not always, like tragic writers, punish vice, they at least discouraged it by making it ridiculous and by putting laughter on the side of virtue. The great Rapin represented a common opinion when he wrote in his " Reflections on Aristotle's Treatise of Poetry ": [1] " Comedy is an image of common life; its end is to show on the stage the faults of particulars, in order to amend the faults of the public and to correct the people by a fear of being ridiculous." This, which may be called the orthodox idea of the function of comedy, is the one most commonly stated by the Restoration dramatist; but it should be remembered that it was merely an orthodox opinion, and like the 39 articles of the Church of England was accepted as a matter of policy by many who had no intention of doing more than giving a formal assent.

Thomas Shadwell was more fond than any of the others of proclaiming the moral intention of his comedies, and though it is certainly hard to imagine any one's moral standard being raised by witnessing that excellent comedy " The Squire of Alsatia " (though he might learn some lessons of prudence), it would only be fair to Shadwell to say that probably few of the dramatists of the Restoration were as honest in their intentions as he, and so he may be allowed to speak first. In the preface to " The Humorist " he writes: " My design was in it, to reprehend some of the vices and follies of the age, which I take to be the most proper, and most useful way of writing comedy." He objects to the idea that comedies have no other purpose

[1] Translated in 1674 by Thomas Rymer.

than to entertain, and adds: " Methinks the poet should never acknowledge this, for it makes him of as little use to mankind as a fiddler, or dancing-master."

All this sounds well enough, but to what extent was the theory borne out in practice? Such protest of the sincerely satiric intention was the conventional attitude of the dramatist when he thought that he ought to defend himself, and some modern writers like Mr. Bernbaum [1] seem disposed to accept it at its face value. The latter quotes from several of the dramatists passages in which they proclaim such intentions; but he only succeeds in proving that satire was the ostensible theory on which they wrote. To establish his contention, he selects passages like the following, the first being from Dryden, and the last two from Congreve: " Comedy presents us with the imperfections of human nature — [it] causes laughter in those who can judge of men and manners, by the lively representation of their folly and corruption." " I designed the moral first, and to that moral I invented a fable." " Men are to be laughed out of their vices in comedy — as vicious people are made ashamed of their follies or faults by seeing them exposed in a ridiculous manner, so are good people at once warned and diverted at their expense."

If it were a question merely of what the dramatists said they did (especially when they felt the necessity of defending themselves) rather than a question of their actual practice, then still more protestations of the kind given above could be cited, but the plays themselves are more significant than anything which their authors say about them, and it would take a good deal to convince one that Congreve, for instance, wrote his plays for the sake of anything but amusement, or that if he had a moral it was anything but a cynical one. Moreover, Dryden himself,

[1] *The Drama of Sentiment.*

whom Mr. Bernbaum quotes, is not noted for the consistency of his critical utterances, and in the preface to " The Mock Astrologer " he flatly repudiates any responsibility of the dramatist to point a moral. The statement of his case is so unequivocal that it is worth quoting: " It is charged upon me that I make debauched persons (such as, they say, my Astrologer and Gamester are) my protagonists, or the chief persons of the drama; and that I make them happy in the conclusion of my play; against the law of comedy, which is to reward virtue and punish vice. I answer, first, that I know no such law to have been constantly observed in comedy, either by the ancient or modern poets — the chief end of it (comedy) is divertisement and delight: and that so much, that it is disputed, I think, by Heinsius before Horace's ' Art of Poetry,' whether instruction be any part of its employment. At least I am sure it can be but its secondary end: for the business of the poet is to make you laugh." Here is the true spirit in which the Restoration dramatist worked, whatever may have been his professed theory.

Mrs. Behn is equally clear when, in the preface to " The Dutch Lovers," she writes: " In my judgment the increasing number of our later plays have not done much more towards the amending of mens' morals, or their wit, than hath the frequent preaching, which this last age hath been pester'd with, (indeed without all controversy they have done less harm) nor can I once imagine what temptation anyone can have to expect it from them; for sure I am no play was ever writ with that design — as I take it comedy was never meant, either for a converting or conforming ordinance: In short, I think a play the best divertisement that wise men have." Yet Mrs. Behn was perfectly willing to fall in with the prevailing pose when there was occasion for it, as may be seen from her dedica-

tion to " The Lucky Chance " where she quotes Richelieu
and D'Aubignac on the moral and political value of plays.

Any attempt to regard the Restoration drama, as a
whole, as satiric in an austere sense is doomed to failure.
This is not, of course, to say that the method was not that
of satire. The method is that of picturing things in such
a way as to cause them to be laughed at, and this is, in
one sense, satire. But if, on the other hand, the term
implies also an attempt to promote moral improvement,
then the Restoration drama was not satiric. The dramatist
did not inspire to virtue, because he had no great faith in
it. He hated foolishness, cant, and all that was not easy
and graceful, and all these things he satirized. He satirized pretense, foppery, and failure, but not graceful vice.
Thus Sir Fopling Flutter is ridiculed, but there is no satire
for Dorimant, the graceful rake of the same play. In
" The Country Wife " there is a satire of the foolish husband, but no satire of Horner, who takes advantage of him.
Worldly wisdom is the ideal, and he who has it escapes
satire just as surely as he who lacks it falls under ridicule.
Virtue has nothing to do with the matter. The dramatists
cynically admire nothing but success, and satirize nothing
but failure — failure to be graceful, failure to be witty,
and failure in *savoir faire*, but not failure to be virtuous.

The truth of the matter seems to be that the poets were
not interested in morality either one way or the other.
They were not, as Collier tried to prove, actively engaged
in any systematic attempt to destroy it; but neither were
they engaged in any attempt through the employment of
satire, or by any other means, to recommend it. They
wished their plays to be realistic, to be witty, to be polished,
and, above all, to be penetrating; but they were expositors
rather than preachers, and they set forth the ideas of the

time without attempting either to improve or to debase
them. It is true that certain minor wits, including Dryden
and Mrs. Behn, did pander shamefully to the lust of
the audience, but that cannot be charged against Wycherley, Congreve, or Vanbrugh. The worst that can be said
of them is that they were cynical, and that they accepted
life as they found it without any attempt to make it better.
Dryden, Wycherley, and Mrs. Behn were each cynical for
a different reason: Wycherley because he had no faith
that human nature, bad as it was, could be made better;
Mrs. Behn because to refuse to be bound in any manner
by morality gave her freedom to devise those amorous
intrigues which she loved; Dryden chiefly, it seems, because it paid a writer to be so.

These men were more definitely than most literary men,
perhaps, a part of the life they depicted. The best writers
were themselves men of fashion and wit; and hence members of the same class as their characters, whom they therefore saw from within rather than from without, and whose
ideas they expounded, and, to a certain extent, whose
limitations they shared. They were almost too much a
part of the life to have an attitude towards it, and they
shared its limitations too much to be able to criticise
them. Consequently they express rather than criticise or
advocate the Restoration manner and thought. They did
not exactly advocate sexual looseness, but they held no
very high standard of sexual purity, for neither they nor
their contemporaries practiced or much regarded it. Purity
was perhaps an ideal, but they never expected either themselves or others to live up to it. Scruples of honor and
faith in the other relations of life were also, no doubt,
beautiful, but hardly customary; for, although they made
an additional ornament to character, they were so often

lacking that they were not regarded as necessary to the
heroes of drama any more than they were to the great
in public life.

Within these general limits, most of the Restoration
writers may be confined. They were the very opposite of
idealistic, and the differences between them consist chiefly
in the degree of frankness with which they acknowledged
the facts and the extent to which they disapproved of them.
One would judge from Mrs. Behn's plays that she thought
the world of restless amorous intrigue the best of all
possible worlds. Wycherley accepts it as frankly as she
does, and seems to have as little hope that it might be
better, but he recognizes its ugliness. The cynicism and
ferocious vigor with which he depicts the vices of the age
imply a genuine and savage disgust at its baseness.
Macaulay refers to him as " the most licentious writer of
a singularly licentious and hard-hearted school," but this
is hardly fair. His plays are obscene, perhaps, but not
licentious. He recognizes the ugliness of vice, as Mrs.
Behn, for instance, does not, and is to that extent a moralist, though he neither urges nor expects a reformation. An
upright character is a curiosity, and must be content like
Manly in " The Plain Dealer " to purchase personal
rectitude at the price of being himself deceived. The
successful man is the one who like Horner in " The Country
Wife " can play upon the weakness of his fellows. Wycherley's whole philosophy is summed up in a speech made by
Manly when an acquaintance remarks that, as for him,
he speaks well of all men. Manly replies that his friend
thereby does the greatest possible injustice to the few who
really deserve it.

Congreve's estimate of the world is not different, but it
is less bitter. No more than Wycherley does he believe
in faith or honor. But he is less savage. He would,

perhaps, admire virtue and truth, but they hardly exist. One may if he likes lead a blameless life, but he need not expect others to do so. Nor is it necessary to get excited over the matter. Congreve watches the corruption of society with an amused detachment, and is resolved to be content if it is only graceful. Wycherley sums up his philosophy in the bit of dialogue just quoted. Congreve summed up his in a light song which ends:

> " He alone won't betray in whom none will confide:
> And the nymph may be chaste that has never been tried."

The judgments of the two men are closely akin, but where one finds indignation the other finds only amusement.

It is evident that such a drama was too much a part of the spirit of the age wholly to please any other time. As manners improved, the plays would seem not like truths but like libels, and when idealism returned, moralists would insist also that plays must in some measure inspire as well as depict, and the drama would change.

We are to be concerned with this change. Before proceeding with the drama, it will be necessary to glance at the development of literary criticism, which was preparing a weapon to overturn the critical theories of the Restoration dramatists.

CHAPTER III

CRITIC AND AMATEUR

In the preceding chapter, attention was called to the fact that it was possible to cite the testimony of the playwrights themselves concerning their attitude toward their art. This fact is extremely significant, and indicates one of the greatest differences between the Elizabethan and the Restoration ages. In the former it was the exception when the dramatic author talked about his works to the public. The earliest dramatists never did so. But the habit grew during the seventeenth century, and by 1700 had become customary. This fact illustrates especially an increasing interest in literature, consciously thought of as such, on the part of the general public. No doubt artists had always been in the habit of discussing their craft among themselves, but the general public was not interested. It heard its ballad or saw its play, but cared nothing for the principles of literary criticism, or very much for the personality of authors. When we reach the seventeenth century, however, sophistication has advanced to such a point that literature has taken a prominent place in fashionable life, and become a thing not merely to be enjoyed, but also to be discussed. The principles of the art are in everyone's mouth, the dilettante has become fashionable, and the author a public personage. He tells the public of his ideas concerning literature, he publishes his letters, and after he dies some one presents an account of his life. Thus we are not very far from the modern tradition where everything that concerns an author, down to his taste in food, is a matter of public interest and is "written up" in the magazines.

The present chapter is an attempt to trace the growing importance of literary criticism, both formal and informal, and of this general public interest in authors and authorship which increased so much between 1660 and 1700. Nor is this subject at all foreign to our general topic. The decline of Restoration Comedy and the rise of Sentimental Comedy were accompanied by a great deal of discussion, oral and written, over literary questions. Marlowe gave but a brief warning that he was about to replace the early Elizabethan jiggings with poetry. Jonson introduced his style of comedy with somewhat more explanation and protest, but neither change was accompanied by anything like the amount of public discussion that attended the "reform" of the English stage about 1700. Every one was conscious of this change. Every one discussed it from one point of view or another. The whole movement was intensely self-conscious, and one of its chief protagonists, Steele, was a theorist more than he was a playwright. As to the Jeremy Collier controversy itself, it was, as Spingarn points out, really a critical controversy. Collier was principally a moralist, but borrowed some of his weapons from the critics, and indeed based some of his arguments on purely critical grounds. Moreover the controversy raged not only around questions of abstract morality, but also around the moral function of the stage and how it could best fulfill this function. No previous critical discussion had produced such a bulk of writing, and it is unlikely that the discussion would have taken the turn which it did had it not been for the previous development of criticism here to be discussed. And, inversely, it seems extremely probable that the amount of attention which the

Collier controversy attracted encouraged succeeding writers of criticism.

The debt which the reform movement owed to the critical development of the latter part of the century was a double one. This development gave currency to several theories about the function of the stage which, if put into practice, would necessitate a reform; and, second, by popularizing criticism it made these theories seem no longer merely academic propositions but live issues. It inspired the moralists to demand that they be put into practice, and it encouraged the dilettante to wish to see the experiment tried. It is the purpose of this chapter merely to show the growth of interest in criticism itself, and of the following one to set forth such of the ideas developed as are significant in our discussion.

Criticism is a late birth. In its earliest form it is likely to be learned, and prodigiously heavy; or, if popular, to confine itself to the bestowal of epithets such as the " honey-tongued Shakespeare " and the " mellifluous Ovid." For some decades after the close of the fifteenth century there was not a single critical treatise on the English language or literature existing in the English tongue. We find a little later that Hawes' " Pastime of Pleasure " (1517), discusses poets, that Wilson's " Art of Rhetoric " (1553), deals with the old technicalities, and that Ascham's " Toxophilus " (1545) and " The Scholemaster " (1570), attack " books of feyned chivalry " and the novella, but that Gascoigne's " Certain Notes of Instruction concerning the Making of Verse " is the first separate book of English criticism.[1]

In Sidney's " An Apologie for Poetrie " (1595), Elizabethan criticism produced one work which towers far above all other English criticism before the time of Dryden. Between Sidney and Jonson the principal critical writers, the

[1] Saintsbury. *History of Criticism.*

Gossons, the Googes, and the Webbes, were concerned with attack and defense of literature in general, or with technical questions, especially that concerning rhyme versus quantity, but with Jonson we have the first Englishman to devote sustained effort to criticism. He was the first [1] to furnish a preface to a play, and in taking this means to put before the reader his theory of comedy, and his likes and dislikes, he set a precedent of enormous importance in the development of popular as opposed to academic and pedantic criticism. Moreover he translated that, for seventeenth century critics, most sacred of sacred writings, Horace's " De Arte Poetica," and in his " Discoveries," if he did not as was formerly thought show great originality, he did at least give proof that he preceded the classicist or pseudo-classicist of the latter part of the century and read not only Aristotle, Seneca, Quintilian and other classical writers, but also the humanists, including the two Scaligers and D. Heinsius.

Yet in spite of Jonson's interest in the subject and the interest also of Bacon, criticism does not bulk large during the first half of the seventeenth century, and it is not too much to say that it was the later seventeenth century that gave it its place in the popular mind as one of the branches of literature. The Restoration age made the critic a recognized figure like the poet or dramatist, and so caused almost every successful work to be accompanied by critical discussion. Rymer felt this change keenly. Speaking of the early part of the century he says: " At this time — Ben Jonson, I think, had all the critical learning to himself; and till of late years England was as free from critics as it is from wolves, that a harmless well-meaning book might pass without any danger. But now this privilege, whatever extraordinary talent it requires, is usurped by the most ignorant; and they who are least

[1] Gregory Smith. *Ben Jonson.*

acquainted with the game are aptest to bark at every thing that comes in their way." This increasing tendency to discuss literature is important in our subject because it is paving the way for the controversy over the stage, and because it was not until such discussion should become familiar that a Steele, for instance, could use criticism to influence public literary taste as he did.

Speaking of the " great names " of Jonson, Bacon, Milton, and Hobbes, Spingarn says:[1] " It is doubtful whether any of these four justified one of the most significant of the critic's functions by interpreting a poet to his contemporaries, or by making an unknown name a real possession of English literature. Not a single author was better understood because of any light shed by them." What this means is that criticism, which interested only a few scholars and neither the general public nor many of the popular authors, was as yet cold, pedantic, and half alive. The later seventeenth century, on the other hand, loved to talk about literature; and from this talk sprang a style of criticism which was a sort of free and easy running comment on the writings of the day and by its close connection with living taste helped to mould it. " In former times," wrote D'Urfey,[2] " a play of humor or a comedy with a good plot, could certainly please; but now a poet must find out a third way, and adapt his scenes and plot to the genius of the critic, if he'd have it pass." What Steele said about his plays had perhaps as much to do with establishing the Sentimental tradition as did the plays themselves, but this could not have been true had not the years between 1660 and 1700 prepared the way by arousing public interest in criticism.

Hamelius, Saintsbury, and Spingarn have traced the de-

[1] Camb. Hist. of Eng. Lit. Vol. VII, Chap. XI.
[2] Preface to *The Banditti*.

velopment of the principal critical ideas during the seventeenth century. My purpose in the present chapter is somewhat different. Many of the ideas are not in themselves pertinent to our subject. What I want to do is to demonstrate by means of a bibliography and a discussion the growth in extent and variety of popular interest in critical literature, and the increasing prominence of the critic, so as to show how it was that by the end of the seventeenth and the beginning of the eighteenth centuries people were as open to influence from talks about literature as I shall later prove them to have been. The Sentimental Comedy was an artificial product and it was born and nourished partly as the result of talk — talk about morals in general and about those of the theater in particular. That a general purification of language and manners should take place was inevitable from social changes, but the change in the drama went deeper than this. There was a change in method from the satiric to the sentimental, and this change took place partially through the operation of critical theory.

We may divide seventeenth century criticism into two streams, the formal and learned treatises in pseudo-classical theory and the informal chit-chat of the coffee house. Between the two came literary mediators, king of whom is Dryden, who gave to formal criticism some of the ease of conversation. We shall discuss the formalists first.

It was on the classical writers that all the formal criticism was ostensibly based, but it was from the commentators on classical writers that the influence really came. Translations from Longinus appeared in 1652,[1] 1680, and 1692; Roscommon printed his verse translation of Horace's "Art of Poetry" in 1680; and another translation

[1] This date is wrongly given as 1662 in the British Museum catalogue.

by Oldham appeared later (1681). The "Poetics" of
Aristotle appeared in English dress in 1705, but it was
to the French that the English looked most often for
critical guidance. The noise of the controversy over the
"Cid" had reached England, and it was probably from
Corneille that Dryden got the idea of prefixing critical discussions to his plays. With the English, René
Rapin was an especial favorite. No less than six of his
critical works were translated in our period, beginning with
"The Comparison of Plato and Aristotle" in 1673 and
ending with "Comparison of Thucidides and Livy" in
1694. Boileau's "Art of Poetry" was translated in verse
in 1683 and Hédelin's heavy volume called "The Whole
Art of the Stage" in the following year. Other translations from the French may be found by referring to the
Bibliography.

In France criticism was already alive, and Hédelin tells
us that so great was the interest in formal criticism that
not only did the players scarce discuss anything else than
the value of the unity of time, but even the ladies in their
ruelles undertook to defend it. Hédelin himself was not
a mere theorist, as he had been made by Richelieu a sort
of overseer of the stage and so should have been a "practical man of the theater." He demanded, however, the most
rigid adherence to the rules, and would not purchase success at the cost of violating one of them, so that even in
France where the unities were much more revered than
in England, his regular but dull play was the subject of
satiric comment.

The honor of having written the first formal critical
treatise on the stage published in England after the Restoration must be given to Flecknoe. It is doubtful if
even Marvell's satire would have kept alive Flecknoe's
name had that name not been taken over by Dryden to

stigmatize Shadwell, and, accordingly, our unfortunate
critic may be said to owe such fame as he has, not to the
direct damnation of Marvell but to the reflected damnation
of Dryden. He was a by-word for bad poetry whom Langbaine described thus: " His acquaintance with the nobility,
was more than with the muses; and he had a greater
propensity to rhyming than a genius to poetry." Though
only one of his plays was ever acted, he amused himself by making lists in which suitable actors were arranged to various persons of his dramas. His " A Short
Discourse on the English Stage," published in 1664 as
a preface to a pastoral-tragi-comedy, " Love's Kingdom,"
is interesting in that it presents immediately the doctrine
of the moral end of all drama, which was so often presented by Restoration critics, but which somehow was
not taken seriously by the dramatists or the public
until the end of the seventeenth century. Aside from this,
Flecknoe can have but little interest. He was too well
recognized as a stock figure of a dunce for anyone to have
the hardihood to quote him, and so he can have had but
little influence.

The first Englishman to acquire a substantial reputation
solely as a critic was Thomas Rymer, now honored mostly
as an antiquarian for his collection of State Papers called
" Foedera," published comparatively late in his life (1704–
1713). Most people now remember only Macaulay's remarks about " Rymer whom we take to have been the
worst critic that ever lived," but though violently attacked
in his own time, he nevertheless commanded considerable
respect, for Pope called him " on the whole one of the
best critics we ever had,"[1] and we learn from the *Gentleman's Journal* (Dec. 1692) that his " Short View of
Tragedy " was " expected with much impatience."

[1] Spence's *Anecdotes*.

Rymer borrowed his ideas from the French, and his first critical effort was a preface to Rapin's " Reflexions sur la Poétique en General " which he translated under the title of " Reflections on Aristotle's Treatise of Poesie " (1674). Rymer was an uncompromising neoclassicist, who held the rules absolute, not because they had the support of authority, but because (as Rapin had put it) they were founded on reason and good sense, and poetry could not be profitable and delightful in defiance of them. In his own preface, Rapin had remarked that Lope de Vega [1] was the only man who had dared to attack the rules, and that he had succeeded so ill that this piece was not deemed worthy of inclusion in his collected works. In the " Tragedies of the Last Age " (1678) Rymer developed the doctrine of Poetic Justice, and in " A Short View of Tragedy " (1693), he damned himself so far as futurity was concerned by analyzing " Othello " as an example of a bad play and remarking that " Gorboduc " (because it was according to the rules) would have been a better model for Shakespeare and Jonson to follow than were those which they chose. In this respect he was only following Sidney, who could give even qualified praise to " Gorboduc " alone among contemporary plays. Sidney however saw only the beginning of the great drama, and, had he known Shakespeare, might not, like Rymer, have execrated him. Rymer recognized the genius of the English poets, but lamented their irregularities, so that he is inclined to regard them as Voltaire did Shakespeare — that is, as barbaric geniuses.

He was replied to in his own age, notably by an anonymous attack on " Tragedies of the Last Age " in the collection of " Miscellaneous Letters and Essays " edited by Charles Gildon in 1694, and by John Dennis, who objected

[1] See *The New Art of Writing Plays*. Trans. W T. Brewster.

to " A Short View of Tragedy " in " The Impartial Critic "
(1693). It would be unprofitable for us to inquire as some
moderns have done whether Pope or Macaulay was nearer
right in his estimate of Rymer. It is sufficient to say that,
granting him his premises, he was logical enough, and that
if consistency to principles which would have ruined the
stage is enough to entitle a man to the title of a " good
critic," then Rymer was one. Jeremy Collier himself
could not have insisted more firmly on the obligation of
the stage to teach morality; and this phase of Rymer's
system will be discussed in the next chapter, as it bears
directly on the principal subject in hand.

The great difficulty with such a critic as Rymer was
that he went at the matter from the wrong end. The rules,
formulated *a priori* from reason, must be right, he said,
for reason could not be wrong. And, accordingly, if a play
written according to the rules failed, then it must be the
fault of the audience. His own " Edgar " (1677) was a
complete failure, but that did not matter. Better to fail
with Aristotle than succeed with Shakespeare. Dryden, on
the other hand, was not that sort of man. He was a
dramatist first, and if some of the rules seemed to make
for bad plays, then he was more ready to suspect that
there was a flaw somewhere in the " reason " which supported the rules than that bad plays had been proved to be
good ones. Consequently, he felt, one had best re-examine
the reason. For instance, the pseudo-classicists " proved "
that it was absurd not to maintain the unity of place for,
said they, is it not ridiculous to suppose that the same spot
is in one scene Rome and in the next Athens? Dryden
saw that much better plays could be written if the playwrights were allowed liberty in this respect. He examined
the reason which supported the rule of the unity of place,
and shrewdly observed through the mouth of one of the

speakers in his "Of Dramatick Poesie" (1668), that it is
no more absurd to imagine a place Athens after having
imagined it Rome than it was to imagine it Rome in the
first place. Thus is the light of common sense let into
criticism, and through the device of the dialogue in which
the essay is written, occasion is given to submit even the
sacred rules to the ordeal by question, and hence to facili-
tate the arrival at truth and the clearing away of rubbish.
So through all his magnificent series of prefaces, Dryden
acts as mediator between critic and playwright. No playwright could follow Rymer and be successful, and Rymer
demanded that he be followed implicitly. Dryden assumed
no infallibility. He brought forth the classical doctrines,
held them up to the light of day and said, "Let us see
what there is in all this which is of value to us." Thus
he did more than any other man to bridge the gulf which
separated playwright and critic, and to make criticism a
living force.

Most of Dryden's criticism appeared in the form of
prefaces, and nothing is more significant of what we are
now trying to illustrate, namely the growing rapport between popular literature and criticism, than the rise of the
critical preface, which gradually became a recognized institution. Here we have critics who do not, as Sidney and
Rymer had done, stand off from dramatic literature and
unintentionally subtract from the effect of their criticisms
by pronouncing practically all that had been written and
admired basically at fault, but actually come to grips with
popular literature.

Beljame suggests [1] that the genesis of the preface was
an economic necessity, and that prefaces were written
primarily to give some good reason why a person who had

[1] *Le Public et les Hommes de Lettres en Angleterre au Dix-
Huitième Siècle.*

seen a play acted should buy the printed copy. Doubt-
less there is something in this, but the real reason goes
deeper, and lies in the need which the author felt of a
mediator between his play and the audience; the need,
in other words, for interpretative criticism. As has been
remarked, Jonson was the first to use the critical preface,
but, be it added, he was not the first to feel this need.
Even the reserve of Shakespeare is somewhat broken in
the famous prologue in which the audience is besought to
use its imagination to transform the wooden O; Marlowe
gave the audience due warning of his momentous innova-
tion in a few lines; and other playwrights had come before
their audience in prologue or in " Induction " to explain
their plays. But in spite of Jonson's example, the preface
did not rise to much importance before the Civil War.
Dekker has a few short epistles, and in " The Whore of
Babylon " (1607), lets us into his theory by remarking:
" and whereas I may, — be critically taxed, that I falsify
the account of time, and set not down occurents, according
to their true succession, let such (that are so nice of
stomach) know that I write as a poet, not as an historian,
and that these two do not live under one law." Marston
has one or two short addresses " To the Reader," and
Webster, in the " White Devil " (1612), protests against
being tried according to the rules. On the whole, however, these dramatists did not offer much apology for
their plays; but after the Restoration it became much more
common to do so, and the prefaces of Cowley, Dryden,
Shadwell, Mrs. Behn, Vanbrugh, and many others furnish
us with most valuable information. By this time criticism
had become fashionable. The new play was sure to be
technically discussed, and the playwright was fain at once
to protect himself and to furnish material for talk by
writing a preface.

If Rymer was the first man in England to be known definitely as " a critic," John Dennis was the first to make a living as one. It is true that he did some other literary work, and true also that his financial returns do not seem to have been very large; but he was a professional critic, and the fact that such a profession, which had never existed in England before, had come into being, was again an indication of the increasing importance of criticism in the popular mind. Dennis, though of infinitely smaller abilities, was, like Dryden, somewhat of a mediator. His principles were orthodox and founded on those of pseudo-classicism, but his method was to submit modern works to judgment in accordance with his views. His " Remarks on Prince Arthur " (1696) is sometimes called the first book review, though it is not quite clear to me why this title might not better be given to " The Censure of the Rota on Mr. Driden's Conquest of Granada " (1673), in which the new play is pulled to pieces and its absurdities revealed. Dennis was on the constant lookout for copy. Besides formal treatises like " The Advancement and Reformation of Modern Poetry " (1701), he seized every opportunity of criticism or reply, as in his retort to Rymer in " The Impartial Critick " (1693), and in the " Remarks on Prince Arthur." Moreover he printed letters from Congreve, Wycherley and others. Most of his work, however, lies beyond 1700.

A glance at the bibliography will show that in addition to the more or less formal treatises such as those mentioned, the impulse to criticism was seeking expression in various other ways. There is, for instance, the strange compilation " De Re Poetica " by Sir Thomas Pope Blount (1694), a sort of symposium on literature. It is divided into sections, " Concerning the Antiquity of Poetry," " Concerning Tragedy," etc., and the method is to proceed

by a series of quotations introduced by phrases such as
"Aristotle says," "Mr. Dryden tells us," "Milton observes," "Vossius says," etc., and thus to present a con-
sensus of opinion for the use, perhaps, of amateur critics
who wished to appear widely read at the cost of but little
effort.

The critical essays in verse furnish another class of
compositions which became almost a fad. The Earl of
Roscommon turned Horace's precepts in favor of moderation, judgment, and harmony into English, and published
them in 1680. Two years later the Earl of Mulgrave proclaimed that "nature's chief master-piece is writing well"
and offered what he thought was a sort of Horace brought
up to date, in which modern faults were corrected, abuses
regulated, and obscenities censured. Boileau's "Art of
Poetry" was translated by Soame, to whom Dryden, it is
said, lent his aid in adapting it to English conditions by
substituting the names of native writers for the Frenchmen
whom Boileau had used in illustration; and, finally, Mulgrave, aided possibly by Dryden, printed his "Essay on
Satire" in which, in addition to satirizing some of his
contemporaries, especially Rochester, he laid down what
he considered were the general laws of the game. These
essays are not to be confused with more or less fugitive
verse satires. They were serious attempts, not so much to
establish new principles as to phrase the old ones more
aptly, and to give final form to generally accepted doctrines. They were taken seriously by men of taste, they
were often quoted as authority in published criticisms, and
the epigrammatic phrases were no doubt much in the
mouths of the talkers. It is perhaps a little difficult for
us to understand the amount of interest which was taken
in these repetitions of familiar dicta, but it must be remembered that in no previous age had it been so nearly

regarded a literal truth that nature's chief masterpiece is
writing well and that, in addition, there was an increasing
belief in the necessity of conscious art to achieve good
writing. Without it, genius was thought to be of no avail,
and apparent naturalness was believed to be, if successful, only well hidden art. As Mulgrave put it:

> " Read Homer once, and you can read no more,
> For all things else will seem so dull and poor,
>
> *   *   *   *   *   *   *   *   *
>
> Had Bossu never writ, the world had still
> Like Indians, view'd this wondrous piece of skill;
> As something of divine the work admired,
> Hoped not to be instructed, but inspired."

Another type of critical publication never heard of before began to appear in the form of little pamphlets
devoted to the criticism of single new plays. They were
not at first very dignified or important. Thus the amusing
" Censure of the Rota " (1673) describes the meeting of
an imaginary club in which Dryden's " Conquest of
Granada " is discussed and damned. On a similar plan is
" A Description of the Academy of the Athenian Virtuosi,"
published in the same year, and attacking the same play
which, moreover, receives a serious defense in " Mr. Drey-
den Vindicated etc." (1673). These pamphlets, I believe,
furnish the first instance of a separate publication of a
criticism on a current play, but the custom became established. Another group centered around Settle's " The
Empress of Morocco " (published 1673). " Wit for Money;
or Poet Stutter, a dialogue — containing reflections on some
late plays and particularly on Love for Money; or, the
Boarding School " (1691) is an attack on D'Urfey. Two
friends invite Stutter (D'Urfey) to a tavern. In conversation they attack his bungling revisions, his thievings, and
his habit of writing now on one side and now on the other.

His fecundity is satirized by the statement that he has made "some 7,953 songs, 2,250 ballads, 1,956 catches, besides madrygals, odes, and other lyrick copies of verses ad infinitum." The dedication is signed "Sir Critic Cat-Call." D'Urfey also had the honor of receiving another separately published criticism on one of his plays. It had the complimentary title of " Poeta Infamis; or a Poet not Worth Hanging — With a Letter to the Author of ' The Marriage Hater Matched.' Written by a Friend " (1692), and was a satire on a letter of Charles Gildon's praising D'Urfey's " Marriage Hater Matched," which letter had been prefixed to the play. After 1700 such pamphlets became more important. Minor controversies raged around Addison's " Cato," Steele's " Conscious Lovers," and others.

Further public interest in authors is indicated by the publication of various familiar letters from well-known authors.[1] Interest in literature on the historical side was evinced by Sprat's " Life of Cowley," prefixed to the 1668 edition of the latter's works, by Fuller's " Worthies " (1662), and by the Bibliographical and Biographical Dictionaries represented by Philipps' " Theatrum Poetarum " (1675), Winstanley's " Lives of the Most Famous English Poets " (1687), and Langbaine's " Momus Triumphans " (1687) and his " An Account of the English Dramatick Poets " (1691), the latter being used as a basis for other works.

Finally, note should be taken of the appearance of literary criticism, especially in the form of book reviews, in journals. Motteux's " The Gentleman's Journal; or The Monthly Miscellany," which ran from January, 1693, to October, 1694, is a precursor of the monthly magazine. Besides original stories, poems, and the like, it contains

[1] See Bibliography.

short notices of new plays and a critical death notice of Shadwell. John Dunton's "The Complete Library: or, News for the Ingenious," which began in 1692 and ran at least until April, 1694, was more definitely a "review" and contained articles on such things as Gildon's popular collection of epistles called "The Post Boy Rob'd of his Mail," Temple's "Essays," Rymer's "Short View of Tragedy," Sir Thomas Pope Blount's "De Re Poetica." This sort of thing, like the other forms of criticsm, continued to increase after 1700 and criticism became a familiar journalistic feature.

We may also notice the increasing frequency with which the critic figures in contemporary satire, which again illustrates the growing consciousness on the part of the public of the existence of this new personage in the literary commonwealth. Suckling in his "A Session of the Poets" borrowed an idea from the Italian and started a fashion in literary verse satire, but in his poem the critic does not appear. In the anonymous "A New Session of the Poets" (1700) the poets put in their claims for the laurel left by Dryden, but the critics also appear. One paragraph may be quoted for its illustration of the satirist's attitude towards them:

> "D'Ur—y withdràwn, a brace of criticks came,
> That would by others' failure purchase fame:
> This peevish race will take a world of pains,
> To show that both the Arthurs [1] had no brains:
> And labor hard to bring authentic proof,
> That he that wrote Wit's Satire [2] was an oaf.
> Like Bedlam curs, all that they meet they bite,
> Make war with wit, and worry all that write:

[1] *Prince Arthur* and *King Arthur*. Both by Sir Richard Blackmore.
[2] Also by Blackmore.

Thus while on Shakespeare one with fury flew,
T'other his pen on well-bred Waller drew;
Writ on, and vainly ventured to expose
The noblest verse, and most exalted prose:
To both these bards heaven gave so little grace,
As of Apollo to demand the bays.
After a pause — bright Phoebus silence broke,
And with a frown to both by turn thus spoke:
How darest thou, Caitiff, Shakespeare to asperse,
Thou wretchedest Rymer in the universe!

*   *   *   *   *   *   *   *   *

Revere the dead, the living let alone,
But if, in spite of me, you must write on,
Leave others' works to criticise your own.
Critics, cried he, are most of all unfit,
To fill the peaceful throne of awful wit."

Similarly Dennis is introduced in the " Battle of the Poets " (1725), and, of course, the critics play a part in the " Dunciad." By that time no satire on the literary world could leave out this newly important class.

This increased interest in printed criticism was evidently accompanied by a great deal of talk on similar subjects. To the " wit " the satirist now added the " critic " in his gallery of town characters, and nothing is more frequent in prologues than an appeal to these pretended critics who make criticism a new and fashionable foppery. Sedley, for instance, in his prologue to " The Mulberry Garden " (1668), complains of:

" The cruel critick and malicious wit,
Who think themselves undone if a play hit."

So fashionable had literary criticism become that the Beau, if he had not taste, was obliged to counterfeit it. This may be illustrated by a story which is not, I believe, very well known. It was said that a certain man, anxious to shine in this respect, discovered that the Earl of Dorset

turned down the edge of pages containing passages which
he liked, and that the pretender, who had access to Dorset's
books, achieved a reputation for taste by commending in
company the passages so marked. Dorset suspected him
of the practice and turned down many pages in a very
dull book, with the result that the would-be man of taste
rushed to the coffee-houses and fell into raptures over a
piece of very dull writing. Finally convinced that he had
made a mistake, he gave himself away by crying out in
a passion, " That my L-d D-t had betrayed him out of
spite and dog's ear'd the book in the wrong places." [1]

Certain men like Dorset and Pope's friend Walsh seem
to have founded a real reputation as talkers, while even
the criticisms of Saint-Evremond were written only for his
private friends and afterwards pirated. The Coffee-house
or tavern was the central meeting place where these literary discussions ordinarily took place. The " Censure of
the Rota " and the " Academy of the Athenian Virtuosi "
present burlesque pictures of a critical cabal, and in dialogues such as " Wit for Money," " The Impartial Critic,"
and Gildon's " Comparison of the Two Stages " the dis-
putants usually retire to a tavern. The coffee-houses, we
learn from " The Reason of Mr. Bays's Changing his Religion " (1688), were commonly thought somewhat more
respectable.

The first of these Coffee-houses, each of which constituted a public club, was opened in London in 1652, and
by the beginning of the eighteenth century three thousand
were said to be open there. [2] The crowd was very miscellaneous, but the critic was a familiar figure, as may be
observed from an interesting pamphlet " The Character

[1] *A Vindication of the English Stage Exemplified in the Cato
of Mr. Addison.* 1716.
[2] Boulton. *The Amusements of Old London.*

of a Coffee-House " (1673). The company is described as consisting of " a silly fop and a worshipful justice, — a worthy lawyer and an errant pickpocket, a reverend non-conformist and a canting mountebank, all blended together to compose an oglio of impertinence." All met to read the gazette, to listen to the opinions of others, and to air their own. Along with the town wit, an arrant Hobbesite, who values himself chiefly on his knowledge of that part of the town that is not worth knowing, may be found " a cabal of kittling critics that have only learned to spit and mew." A poet slips in to hear his beloved work damned, and is glad he came incognito.

So much for the satirist's view. But at Will's the great Dryden himself was easy of access and a little later Steele and Addison frequented Button's. At the coffee-house where a man might idle away several hours at the cost of a few pence, the impecunious could secure that feeling of Olympian idleness from which the impulse to criticism is most likely to spring. How important this familiar interchange of ideas was in the development of critical literature is evinced by the frequency with which critical pamphlets are cast into the form of familiar dialogues.

Though the critic made a great figure in the literary world, greater than he had ever done before, he was far from having his own way, and whether formal classicist or mere pamphleteer, was subject to many attacks. Though the classics were revered, the classical critic was fortunately not always followed by the dramatist, and his dogmas were frequently repudiated. In his " Upon Poetry," [1] Sir William Temple made a dignified plea for the freedom of inspiration as opposed to submission to

[1] In *Miscellanea. Second Part.* 1690.

the rules; and as for the dramatists, they cared too much
for popular success to wish to jeopardize it by following
too closely the doctrines of orthodox criticism.   They
bowed to the unities so far as to prune the Elizabethan
exuberance which liked to spread a play over a whole
lifetime and move the scenes over the whole face of the
earth, and they felt that it was better as a rule to confine
scenes to a relatively restricted area and the time to a
few days; but they refused to cramp themselves as Hédelin,
for instance, demanded, within the twenty-four hours of
a natural day, or to follow Rymer's precepts which would
have converted the drama into something wholly removed
from life.   Like Molière, the dramatists were inclined to
laugh without asking if Aristotle forbade it, and like Lope
de Vega to say that while classicism might be all very
well, the audience would not stand for it, and that it was
" St. James' beaux and Covent Garden rakes " rather than
the learned whom they had to please.   And it was well
that they did so, for in France, as Saint-Evremond complains, " on n'a jamais vu tant de règles pour faire des belles
tragédies; et on en fait si peu, qu'on est obligé de re-
presenter les vielles."   M. d'Aubignac had boasted that his
unsuccessful play followed everywhere the rules of Aristotle, but " Je sais bon gré a M. d'Aubignac, dit M. le
Prince, d'avoir si bien suivi les règles d'Aristote; mais je
ne pardonne point aux règles d'Aristote d'avoir fait faire une
si méchante tragédie a M. d'Aubignac." [1]   Or, as the same
idea was expressed in English: [2]   " I would no more excuse
a dull rogue that should entertain me ill by the rules of
Aristotle and Horace, than a physician who should in-

[1] Quoted by Ker in preface to *Essays of John Dryden*.
[2] *Chit-Chat — A Comedy*.   Quoted in *Critical Remarks on the
Four Taking Plays of the Season*.   (1719).

crease my disease, by the rules of Hippocrates and Galen."
Samuel Butler expresses his opinion thus:

> " Whoever will regard poetic fury,
> When it is once found idiot by a jury;
> And every pert and arbitrary fool
> Can all poetic license overrule;
> Assume a barbarous tyranny to handle
> The muses worse than Ostro-goth or Vandal;
> Make 'em submit to verdict and report,
> And stand or fall to th' order of a court?
>
> * * * * * * * * *
>
> Reduce all tragedy by rules of art
> Back to its antique theater, a cart,
> And make 'em henceforth keep the beaten roads
> Of reverend choruses and episodes;
> Reform and regulate a puppet-play,
> According to the true and ancient way,
> That not an actor shall presume to squeak
> Unless he have a license for't in Greek.
>
> * * * * * * * * *
>
> These are the reformations of the stage,
> Like other reformations of the age,
> On purpose to destroy all wit and sense,
> As th' other did all laws and conscience;
>
> * * * * * * * * *
>
> An English poet should be try'd b' his Peers
> And not by pedants and philosophers,
> Incompetent to judge poetic fury,
> As witches are forbid to b' of a jury." [1]

Ever since the critic has existed, he has been the mark
of the author's scorn. His trade seems to consist in a

---

[1] From Butler's posthumous works. Pub. 1759 in "Genuine
Remains of Samuel Butler," and by Spingarn in his *Critical Essays
of the Seventeenth Century*. I have modernized the spelling.
Butler expressed his unfavorable opinion of the critics in other
works as well.

double impertinence — that of telling his betters what they
should write, and his equals what they should like — and
all the hard things that could be said about him were said
in the latter seventeenth and early eighteenth centuries.
He was generally regarded (and in the case of Rymer and
Dennis there was some basis for the opinion) as an unsuccessful writer who out of malice took to abusing the works
of others. Another charge often made was that the critic
wrote only to make money, and that criticism existed only
for the purpose of being sold. Thus Swift:

> " Read all the prefaces of Dryden,
> For these our critics much confide in;
> Though merely write at first for filling,
> To raise the volume's price a shilling." [1]

Pope expresed the same idea. [2]

> " Yet then did Dennis rave in furious fret;
> I never answered — I was not in debt.
> If want provoked, or madness made them print,
> I waged no war with Bedlam or the Mint."

Dullness and ill nature were held to be the critic's distinguishing characteristics. Swift in the " Battle of the
Books " makes criticism the child of Ignorance and Pride
and describes her as having claws like a cat but a head,
ears, and voice like an ass. Garth thought the only use
of critics was to display authors by contrast:

> " So diamonds take a lustre from their foil
> And to a Bentley 'tis, we owe a Boyle."

But perhaps Gay [3] gave the crowning insult:

> " Here sauntring 'prentices o'er Otway weep,
> O'er Congreve smile, or over D(ennis) sleep." [4]

---

[1] *Poetry. A Rhapsody.*
[2] *Epistle to Dr. Arbuthnot.*
[3] *Trivia.* II.
[4] It is possible however that the " D—— " refers to D'Urfey.

Yet in spite of the stiff-necked dogmatism of many of its professors, and in spite of the contemptuous opposition of some of the wits, criticism was winning its battle for recognition as a living force, and in the years from 1660, when comedy was achieving a brilliant success without troubling itself much about some of the fundamental doctrines of the pseudo-classicists, criticism was gradually, by continual repetition, impressing on the public mind certain ideas which the reformers were to seize upon and turn against the prevailing style of comedy. Those of its dogmas which concern us chiefly, and which will be treated in the next chapter, are as follows:

1. The fundamental purpose of literature is to teach morality.

2. It is the duty of the tragic, and perhaps the comic poet, to distribute poetic justice.

3. Decorum demands that types be presented in accordance with their typical rather than their occasional characteristics.

4. Obscenity is a fault of taste.

CHAPTER IV

SOME CRITICAL DOGMAS

VERY few imaginative writers in whose minds the desire to give moral instruction was always uppermost have ever produced great literature and very few people ever read great literature primarily because it gave them explicit moral instructions. Yet in spite of these facts, the commonest of all critical doctrines is that such instruction is the fundamental purpose of literature. The theory of art for art's sake has never been popular because it is a part of a doctrine that, however consistently acted upon, people have generally been loath to admit — namely, that pleasure is the highest good.

That literature pleases has usually not been enough to satisfy the philosopher, and when the problem has been consciously thought about, the tendency has been either, as in Plato's " Republic," to expel the poet, or, as with the pseudo-classicists, to give him a moral function. The justification of the poet is the beginning of literary criticism in the Renaissance. That the purpose of literature was the teaching of morality was the common belief of the ancients; it finds expression in Plutarch and in Horace, while Strabo mentions the existence of dissent on this point. Aristotle (Poetics, Chap. IV) in saying " the end of the fine arts is to give pleasure or rather enjoyment " is distinctly heterodox, for the commonly accepted idea was that the end was instruction.[1] With the coming of Christianity the task of defending literature became more and more

[1] Butcher. *Aristotle's Theory of Poetry and Fine Art.*

urgent, for literature was pagan. When, during the Renaissance, criticism received a new birth, the critics " set themselves to prove that poetry was not a sweet pleasant deceit or corrupting influence in the republic, but a stronghold and rampart of religion and philosophical truth." [1] To them poetry was simply philosophy in a more persuasive form, and the delight which it offered was only a sugar coating to the bitter pill of " doctrine."

When English criticism was born, it showed no tendency to be unorthodox. Ascham denounced the popular romances and tales on the ground of immorality, and with Sidney's " An Apologie for Poetrie " we have a systematic presentation of the conventional view. It had been written (about 1580–5) as a reply to Gosson's " The School of Abuse," which had spoken of " poets, pipers, players, jesters and such like caterpillars of a commonwealth." Poetry, by which Sidney means all imaginative literature, is, he says, a speaking picture made to teach and delight. The end of all knowledge is virtuous action, which philosophy undertakes to teach by precept, history by example, and law *formidine poenae* rather than *virtutis amore*. But the precepts of the philosopher are cold, and the historian is handicapped by facts, while the poet may present a perfect and moving picture of what should be. If he fails to do so, he is perverting his art, but the abuse of his power is no argument against its legitimate use. Sidney himself lamented that the " Naughtie Play-Makers and Stage-Keepers " had justly made comic poetry odious. Poetry is in itself good, he says, but in these days its power is abused. This is the burden of the usual treatise on poetry, and here is the first systematic and permanent expression in English of this orthodox doctrine. As such, it must have had considerable influence in making the

[1] Saintsbury. *A History of Criticism.* Vol. II.

conventional view of critics familiar to Englishmen.
Rymer refers to Sidney (Preface to Rapin's Reflections),
and, in connection with the " Arcadia," the " Defense " was
published fourteen times between 1600 and 1700. Moreover it was used in the Collier controversy. Filmer quotes
it at length in his " Defense of Plays."

As was said in the preceding chapter, Flecknoe's " Discourse of the English Stage " (1664) was the first formal
critical treatise to be published after the Restoration, and
hence it was the first to present the conventional doctrine,
though Cowley (Preface to the " Cutter of Coleman
Street ") had already made a short defense of the stage.
Speaking of the drama, Flecknoe says: " Its chiefest end
is to render folly ridiculous, vice odious and virtue and
nobleness so amiable and lovely, as everyone should be
delighted and enamoured with it: From which if it deflects,
as corruptio optimi pessima, of the best it becomes the
worst of recreation and this his majesty well understood
when after his happy restoration he took such care to
purge it from all vice and obscenity; and would to God
he had found all bodies and humors as apt and easy to
be purg'd and reform'd as that." And we may quote
again: [1] " I deny not but aspersions (these latter times)
have been cast upon the stage by the ink of some who
have written obscenely and scurrilously, etc. but instead of
wiping them off, to break the glass, was too rigid and
severe. For my part I have endeavored here the clearing
of it, and restoring it to its former splendor, and first
institution; (of teaching virtue, reproving vice, and amendment of manners) so as if the rest but imitate my example,
those who shall be enemies of it hereafter, must declare
themselves enemies of virtue, as formerly they did of vice:
whence we may justly hope to see it restored again, with

[1] *Love's Dominion.* 1654.

the qualification of an honorable coadjutor of the pulpit, to teach morality, in order to the others divinity, and th' moulding and tempering of mens' minds for the better receiving the impressions of godliness." Flecknoe's statement in the same preface that Fletcher was the first to introduce into his plays " that witty obscenity " which " like poison infused in pleasant liquor, is almost the most dangerous the more delightful " is interesting as correctly tracing to Fletcher the germ of that later style of dialogue which was so brilliant in manner and so corrupt in matter.

I have ventured to quote these two long and clumsy passages merely because they happen to be the first expression after the opening of our period of the idea commonly held by people who were not practical playwrights. Neither Collier nor Steele was advancing novel ideas when he demanded a moralized stage. Each was engaged simply in stirring up the public to demand that the experiment (which turned out to be a disastrous one) should be made of consciously putting into practice the conventional theories. Thus the following, which is the opening sentence of Collier's " Short View," would have struck no one familiar with the formal criticism of the times as in any way novel: " The business of plays is to recommend virtue, and discountenance vice; to show the uncertainty of human greatness, the sudden turns of Fate, and the unhappy conclusions of violence and injustice: 'Tis to expose the singularities of pride and fancy, to make folly and falsehood contemptible, and to bring every thing that is ill under infamy, and neglect." Mr. John Palmer, in a book of excellent criticism of the Restoration comedy, maintains repeatedly that Jeremy Collier invented the moral test as applied to comedy. Nothing could be farther from the truth. One has but to read classical, Renaissance, and English critics to see that, far from being new, the demand that all literature must have a moral justification has been handed down from age to age and that to question it was to be heterodox.

Rymer is equally uncompromising in his attitude. According to him poetry's end is to teach, and it delights only in order that it may teach. One can delight only by following the rules, and one can teach only if he delights; and so, ultimately, the purpose of following the rules is to make instruction possible. In the days of Aristophanes, he says, it was universally agreed that the best poet was he who had done most to make men virtuous. Horace, too, agrees with the Greek and provides the oft-quoted phrase, " Simul et jucunda et idonea dicere vitae." As schools are for teaching children, so the stage, says Rymer, should be a school for men of riper years and judgment, and hence the poet must see that his doctrine is good and wholesome. So important, he says, is the drama and its influence, that it should not be permitted except under the eye of a virtuous government, for otherwise it may degenerate until it deserves all that the clerics have said against it. Rymer was only following the French. " The end of any discourse," said Dacier, in the " Essay on Satire " (trans. 1692), " is the action for which the discourse is compos'd; when it produces no action, 'tis only a vain amusement, which idly tickles the ear, without ever reaching the heart." Similarly Dennis assumes these principles as self-evident, and it would be but repetition to quote him.

From the formal critics no dissent was to be expected, but the playwrights who made their living by amusing an actual audience were likely to dissent or to give only a formal assent, for the audience was more eager for amusement than instruction, and if it got the one, it was not over particular about the other. Dryden, never very consistent in his critical dogmas, and true now to his rôle as dramatist and now as critic, vacillates on this point as has already been pointed out. When speaking generally he agrees with the orthodox view, but when he comes to defend his own practice, he switches about and doubts if instruction be after all a part of comedy. What Mrs. Behn said on the subject has already been pointed out. Shadwell, however, was insistent in his championship of the orthodox view; though it may be doubted whether or not his comedies tended much to the raising of the moral standard. Generally speaking, the Restoration writers of belles lettres, whether dramatic or otherwise, were not much concerned with instruction. They gave formal assent to orthodox critical doctrine in much the same spirit that they accepted the teachings of the Church of England. A gentleman would hardly think of denying or practising either.

Assuming, as the orthodox critics did, that the business of the poet was to teach virtue, the next step was to decide how this could best be accomplished. Aristotle's doctrine of Catharsis did not seem quite definite. The renaissance critic either expected frank didacticism or fell back upon allegorical interpretation. In England was developed especially the theory to which Rymer first gave the name Poetic Justice. Tragedy, it was maintained, should instruct by showing the virtuous rewarded and the vicious punished according to a system more perfect than was observable in actual life. Whether or not this should be extended to comedy was doubtful. Rymer and Dennis thought not. They maintained that ridicule was the proper method of comedy. But Steele demanded that, in comedy as in tragedy, virtue must be rewarded and vice punished, so that the extension of poetic justice to comedy

was one of the cardinal doctrines of his creed, and in fact
a distinguishing characteristic of sentimental comedy. Accordingly we shall examine the roots of this doctrine.

Though Rymer seems to have been the first to use the
phrase " Poetic Justice," the idea was extremely old.
Essentially it is the idea that things are to be presented
not as they are, but as they ought to be, and this idea
is found in classical thought, and influenced even the writing of history. Tacitus himself, though condemning the
historian of the empire who lied for the purpose of flattery,
" does not forbid the shaping of a story according to
artistic probability and moral end." [1] Similarly, the world
as it ought to be is the essence of Plato, and a kindred
idea, as applied to literature, finds expression in Aristotle
who, though he does not exactly recommend poetic justice,
maintains that tragedy presents things not as they are
but as they ought to be.

In England the doctrine grows more explicit from Sidney
to Jonson, and receives final expression with Rymer.
In Sidney it is fully implied. Some poets, he says, borrow
nothing of what is, but rise into divine consideration of
what might be. While the historian is tied down to what
actually is, the freedom of the poet gives him greater
liberty to teach, and hence there is more doctrine to be
learned from the latter's method. The historian, being
limited to facts, must often give a bad example by con-
fessing that vice triumphs; but " If evil men come to
the stage, they ever go out (as the tragedy writer answered
to one that misliked the shew of such persons) so manacled,
as they little animate folks to follow them. But the historian, being captived to the truth of a foolish world, is
many times a terror from well doing, and an encouragement

[1] See Boissier, *Tacite*. Cited by H. Osborn Taylor. *The Mediae-
val Mind*. I.

to unbridled wickedness." Jonson (dedication of "Volpone") comes very close to the actual words "Poetic Justice" when in defending the punishment of the villainous character in this comedy he employs the phrase "it being the office of a comic poet to imitate justice and instruct to life." This very phrase was quoted by Collier [1] in his attack on the contemporary stage.

It is in "The Tragedies of the Last Age" (1678) that Rymer gives final expression to the theory. The ancients, he says, rejected history for the fable of a tragedy because they found that in history the same end happens to the just and the unjust, and saw often wickedness triumphant and virtue oppressed. They realized that such monstrous occurrences represented only particular incidents and not the universal and eternal truths which it is the business of the poet to present, and, accordingly, they neglected history and chose stories in which they were not tied to facts, but were able to distribute "Poetic Justice" according to eternal truth. The theater, he says, was wont to be called the school of virtues, but no longer deserves this title because poetic justice is neglected. To say that a play is natural he considers no excuse for it, since it is the business of the poet to represent typical or eternal nature; and individual instances where the great laws of poetic justice are violated represent only a partial view of nature and not its eternal truth.

The extreme to which this theory was carried is well illustrated by Dennis in his "Remarks upon Cato" (1713). He writes: " 'Tis certainly the duty of every tragic poet, by an exact distribution of poetical justice, to imitate the divine dispensation, and to inculcate a particular providence. 'Tis true indeed upon the stage of the world that the wicked sometimes prosper, and the guiltless suffer.

[1] *Defense of the Short View*, etc. 1699.

But that is permitted by the governor of the world, to show from the attribute of his infinite justice that there is a compensation in futurity, to prove the immortality of the human soul, and the certainty of future rewards and punishment. But the poetical persons in tragedy exist no longer than the reading or the representation; the whole extent of their entity is circumscribed by those; and therefore during that reading or representation, according to their merits or demerits, they must be punish'd or rewarded." Applying this principle to "Cato," he says: "That Cato's being writ with a design to support liberty, is an objection of no manner of force; that let the design be what it will, the effect is sure to be contrary; that the shewing a man of consummate virtue unfortunate only for supporting liberty, must of necessity in a free nation be a pernicious consequence, and must justly raise the highest indignation in all true lovers of liberty."

The dogmatist, enamoured with the specious logic of this theory, seemed blind to its essential childishness. That virtue should be emulated only because it is thought profitable, and that no one could be expected to admire the dignity of right triumphant even in defeat, is a characteristic eighteenth century opinion; but to suppose that an audience thus minded would be encouraged by a picture of virtue triumphant to seek virtue in hope of reward when the picture was admittedly at variance with the facts of life, is simply infantile. If a man in actual life is supposed to be influenced by the reflection that his misfortunes are merely a device employed by God for the purpose of proving that there must exist a compensative future, it is not at all clear why this same man cannot apply similar reasoning to an imaginary representation of distressed virtue unless, indeed, belief in God is considered impossible in the theater. If one insists on drawing a moral from history or literature it had better be, not that justice is triumphant and virtue rewarded, but that no righteousness can assure success, and that one had best prepare himself for endurance. Addison, indeed (Spectator 40), attacks the absurdity of poetic justice, observing truly that " We find that good and evil happen alike to all men on this side of the grave "; but in spite of its artificiality, poetic justice became one of the cardinal doctrines of orthodox poetic theory. Thus in 1699 Drake [1] speaks of " Poetic Justice, which has now become the principal article of the drama," though he remarks that Aristotle is so far from teaching it that he recommends as most suitable for tragedy the story of the misfortunes of a person unhappy through his mistakes not his fault, which is quite contrary to the principle that a man must be given an end nicely adjusted to the merit of his character. Aristotle does say that tragedy should not represent the downfall of a perfectly good man, but his approval of " Oedipus " shows that he allowed considerable latitude. Nevertheless, as will be seen later, poetic justice continued to receive ardent support from theorists.

Though the doctrine of poetic justice seems palpably absurd, it must be admitted in fairness that the whole question is bound up with, and receives support from, Plato; for to the Platonist the contrast between things as they are and things as they ought to be is not a contradiction, as the rationalists would have it, between truth and falsehood, but merely between higher and lower truth, the things as they ought to be being ideally more general and true than the incidental and temporary things as they are.

At first poetic justice was thought to be chiefly the concern of tragedy. Jonson, though it is in the preface to " Volpone " that he develops the idea, thinks a certain

[1] *The Ancient and Modern Stages Survey'd.*

amount of apology necessary to defend its use in comedy, and Dennis himself is inclined to believe that laughter is a sufficient punishment for the wicked in comedy. Steele, however, demanded the extension of the principle to comedy, and in the sentimental plays the pleasure arising from the spectacle of virtue finally triumphant was, in a large measure, to supplant the pleasure of laughter. The influence of Molière in establishing the tradition that the evil doer in comedy should be punished may be suggested. Miles [1] points out that he sometimes, though not consistently, employs poetic justice, and attention is called to the similarity between the situation in " L'Ecole des Femmes," where Arnolphe reaps but little reward for his unenlightened attempt to secure the fidelity of his wife, and that in " The Country Wife," where Pinchwife marries an innocent country girl so as to be sure to have her all to himself, but is destined to suffer from the intimacy between her and the suggestively named Horner. It will be seen that the doctrine of Poetic Justice plays an important part in the Collier controversy.

The relevance to our subject of the third of the critical dogmas enumerated at the end of the last chapter — namely the duty of the poet to present characters according to their typical rather than occasional characteristics — is not immediately evident. But in his attack on contemporary plays Collier devotes considerable space to a consideration of the abuse of the nobility and clergy, and execrates the poets because they sometimes represent a lord as an ass. His opponents replied that sometimes lords were asses, and to understand why this reply seemed irrelevant, it is necessary to go back to Horace and his commentators.

In the Art of Poetry, Horace had said:

[1] *The Influence of Molière on Restoration Comedy.*

" . . . If you bring great Achilles on the stage,
Let him be fierce and brave, all ire and rage,
Inflexible, and headstrong to all laws,
But those, which arms and his own will impose.
Ixion must be treacherous, Ino grieved,
Io must wonder, and Orestes rave.
But if you dare to tread in paths unknown,
And boldly start new persons of your own;
Be sure to make them in one strain agree,
And let the end like the beginning be." [1]

With their usual over-literalness and their passion for
definition, the commentators made this general principle
into a set system, and the general features of every character were analyzed and described, so that the poet was
presented with formulae from which he must not vary, for
the composition of all stock characters. " In Minturno
and Scaliger we find every detail of character minutely
analyzed. The poet is told how young men and old men
should act, should talk, and should dress; and no devia-
tions from these fixed formulae were allowed under any
circumstances." [2]

Rymer brings this idea into England and turns it against
Shakespeare in an astounding manner. In his attack on
" Othello," he falls upon Iago with particular vehemence,
calling him the most intolerable thing in the whole play,
because he is not like a soldier. Shakespeare has been
guilty of representing him as crafty and under-handed,
when every one from Horace on has known that a soldier
should be " impiger, iracundus, inexorabilis, acer." Shakespeare, fully conscious that he was inconsistent, was determined to do something surprising " against common sense,
and nature " by presenting a soldier who deviated from

[1] Oldham's translation.
[2] Spingarn. *A History of Literary Criticism in the Renaissance.*
Chap. III.

the type. It must be remembered, of course, that by
" nature " Rymer did not mean particular, but general or
typical nature. He recognized that a crafty soldier might
exist, but would insist that such a one was the exception
rather than the rule, and hence that he should not be
represented on the stage, where only general truths should
be presented.

Here, then, is the key to Collier's position in regard
to the indignities offered to the nobility and clergy. While
it is perfectly true that you may here and there find a lord
who is an ass, asininity is not commonly regarded as the
typical and distinguishing characteristic of the nobility,
and to represent a lord so, instead of showing him as
noble in accordance with the typical characteristic of a
lord, is, he thinks, but another illustration of the general
perversity of the dramatist. The same argument applies
a fortiori to the clergy. In this connection it should be
noticed that Horace had not said that all soldiers should
be represented as he described Achilles, but this sublime
leap from the particular to the general is in accordance
with the general method of the pseudo-classicists in deal-
ing with ancient authors.

The fourth and last of the dogmas which were developed
during the latter part of the century, and which formed
a weapon to be used in the determined attack on contemporary dramatic practices, is that which declares obscenity a fault of taste. It may as well be admitted
frankly that in the practice of the Restoration dramatists
nothing was more characteristic than habitual lewdness
of language. Whatever the matter in hand, and whatever
differences may have existed in the shades of their motives,
whether they were frankly appealing to the lasciviousness
of their audience or whether, as at times was the case, they
seemed animated by genuine if transitory disgust with men

or manners, the language in which they expressed themselves was always the plainest and most particular that could be found, for they were inspired with a passion for revealing all that convention ordinarily veiled. Moreover, even when the subject under discussion was as far removed as possible from the sexual, they habitually chose metaphors and turns of expression that would bring in a comparison from the subject which seems to have been usually uppermost in their minds. A single instance from Dryden will illustrate this familiar phenomenon. It is the prologue to "An Evening's Love," as clever as any piece of writing Dryden ever did, but unprintable. The technique of expression which he uses there was conventional.

The critics, however, frowned upon obscenity not only because it was definitely antagonistic to the purpose of literature (which was moral instruction), but also because it was a fault of taste. This idea, though a common one, was given epigrammatic expression in Mulgrave's "An Essay upon Poetry," where, referring to Rochester, he wrote:

> "Here, as in all things else, is most unfit
> Bare ribaldry, that poor pretence to wit;
> Such nauseous songs by a late author made
> Call an unwilling censure on his shade.
> Not that one thought of the transporting joy,
> Can shock the chastest, or the nicest cloy;
> But obscene words, too gross to move desire,
> Like heaps of fuel do but choke the fire.
> On other scenes he well deserves our praise,
> But cloys that appetite it meant to raise."

It is especially worthy of note that the quotations which have been given to illustrate the orthodox view regarding literature and morals came without exception from men who were not successful dramatists, and who were in nearly every case out of sympathy with the drama of their time. Sidney not only did not write plays but condemned the popular drama of his time, while Flecknoe, Rymer and Dennis were unsuccessful dramatists. As to the playwrights themselves, they were usually interested only in providing plays which would be successful and which would satisfy their own artistic consciences. If one looks at Congreve's letter "Of Humor in Comedy"[1] he will see that Congreve is interested in discussing what a cultured man considers funny, but that he has not one word to say about morality. Among critics, perhaps St. Evremond was closest to the literary group to which his gay, polished and epicurean spirit made him closely akin. His criticisms were written for private circulation only, but were so much admired that they were printed in pirated editions, and forged writings were sold under the attraction of his name. But like Congreve, when he writes an essay on English comedies[2] he tries them upon purely aesthetic grounds. That the Restoration dramatists cared nothing for the moral aspect of their work is a commonplace, but it is a commonplace which takes on a significance when we observe, first that in so doing they were in a way heterodox, and second that Steele and Cibber, the leaders in the sentimental movement, proclaimed their allegiance to orthodox criticism. In other words, sentimental comedy when strggling for supremacy could call upon orthodox criticism for support.

It has already been shown that the Restoration dramatist was sometimes, when pressed, forced to admit the validity of the theory which regarded literature as a form of moral instruction; but such an admission was made usually as a defense, and abandoned both in practice and, often,

---

[1] *Letters upon several occasions; written by and between Mr. Dryden, Mr. Wycherley, Mr. Congreve, and Mr. Dennis,* etc. 1696.
[2] In *Mixt Essays,* etc. 1685.

in more frank expressions of theory. He believed that the value of a piece of literature should be judged rather by the effectiveness and polish of its expression than by the value of its subject matter. This attitude was expounded in an extreme form by Robert Wolseley in his preface to Rochester's tragedy " Valentinian " (1685), which had been attacked by Mulgrave in his " Essay on Poetry " on the ground that it was obscene. Wolseley maintains that the manner of treatment, not the subject matter, must be the basis for any judgment passed upon a work of literature. No one, he says, except Mulgrave, ever thought of judging a poet by the worth of his subject matter, inasmuch as an ill poet will disgrace the highest subject just as a good poet will dignify the lowest. Growing enthusiastic over his own theory, he exclaims: " Nay, the baser, the emptier, the obscurer, the fouler, and less susceptible of ornaments the subject appears to be, the more the poet's praise, who can hide all the natural deformities in the fashion of his dress, supply all the wants with his own plenty, and by a poetical daemoniasm possess it with the spirit of good sense and gracefulness." He then draws support for his theory from the kindred art of painting, and quotes Dryden's preface to " Tyrannic Love " where the latter says that there is as much art in the representation of a lazar as in a Venus. Wolseley defines wit as " a true and lively expression of nature " and then proceeds ingeniously to reduce Mulgrave's censure to nonsense. Mulgrave characterized Rochester's work as " bawdry bare-face'd, that poor pretense to wit," and Wolseley, working like a mathematician with his equations, substitutes for " wit " his definition of it, and reads, " bawdry bare-face'd, that poor pretense to a true and lively expression of nature," which is, as he says, manifestly nonsense. Again he takes Dryden's definition of wit as " a propriety of thought and words" and again reduces Mulgrave's phrase to an absurdity.

This is all very interesting and probably represents very well the attitude of the typical Restoration dramatist or poet, but it was not the conventional critical view adopted by Collier when he wrote "Smuttiness is a fault in behaviour as well as in religion. 'Tis a very coarse diversion, the entertainment of those who are generally least both in sense, and station,"[1] or by Cibber when he spoke in "The Careless Husband" of former plays as "unfit entertainments for people of quality." The Sentimental comedy was more orthodox critically than that of the Restoration.

[1] *Short View.*

CHAPTER V

THE ONSLAUGHT ON THE STAGE

THE deep-seated distrust of the theater, which at different times finds more or less passionate expression, is in itself perpetual. It is more deep-rooted than Christianity, and arises as a logical application of the much more ancient doctrine of asceticism. As the seventeenth century controversialist was fond of pointing out, not only did the early church Fathers thunder against the theater, but the sterner sort of Pagans, from whom surely less was to be expected than from Christians, were at best doubtful concerning it. True, Aristotle wrote a treatise on the drama, but Plato banished the players from the Republic, and even in the actual government of the ancients there were many statutes which implied that the theater was regarded at best with suspicion.

With the coming of Christianity, asceticism received a support of incalculable strength. The ancient philosophers had urged the contempt of pleasure because pleasure was undignified, and because in the end it was found to be really not pleasure — a doctrine which the vulgar found it difficult to understand. Christianity, however, appealed to less rarefied sentiment. The man who found the pleasures of earth sweet was not asked to give them up for nothing, but was persuaded that for a little self-denial in the present he would be rewarded with incalculable blisses in the future, whereas, if he persisted in the short-sighted policy of choosing the unimportant present, his folly would be rewarded with torture more terrible and enduring than any which Caligula had been ingenious enough to invent. Though the latter had given instructions that his victims were to be made to "feel themselves die," he was incapable of inflicting a perpetuity of pain, for to him man was mortal, a fact which imposed a limitation that God was able to transcend. Thus many a man unable to follow the Stoic in the contempt of pleasure was appealed to on prudential grounds and resolved, like a sensible man, to take some thought of the future. In this manner asceticism became a religion not only for the philosopher but also for the rabble.

With such a condition established, opposition to the theater was inevitable. Fundamentally the objection was not to bad plays — to indecency and profaneness — though of course these aggravated the evil; but to plays as such, and, indeed, to all art; for the beautiful is the pleasant, and the pleasant is damnable. This life is, *a priori*, a vale of tears, and any attempt to make it otherwise is sinful. Moreover any interest in the affairs of the world is dangerous. The more one can withdraw from life the safer he is. The wise man will, therefore, live in seclusion, and only a madman will, after all the temptations which living in the world necessitates, seek to increase them by allowing imagination to strengthen his interest in the world. Even with the utmost care it is hard to conquer the passions, and art, instead of teaching men to despise the world, is likely to lead them to love it.[1]

The bearing of these general ideas upon seventeenth-century controversies will be seen later on, when it will be evident that the movement for the reform of indecency was confused and even hindered by the introduction of a purely ascetic element, and that those who wished to

[1] Tolstoi's *What is Art* might be cited as a modern example of somewhat similar reasoning.

purify the stage were joined in a somewhat unstable union with those who wished to destroy it. Two chapters have been devoted to giving the critical background of the reformers. These brief paragraphs will have to suffice to suggest the ascetic tendency which was constantly arising to confuse the issue.

This moral and ascetic objection to the theater, though it constantly exists, is not always very strongly felt. Today, no doubt, the question engages the attention of many provincial pulpits, but, as at most times, it hardly reaches the theater-going public. At various times, however, some circumstance or other has aroused it to greater vigor. It has then ceased to be an undercurrent and become a matter of universal attention. Two such periods occur in English literary history. The first began even before the Elizabethan drama entered upon its period of glory, and ended in a complete triumph for the enemies of the stage, when the theaters were closed in 1642. But this particular movement against the theater was so closely associated with the political and religious fortunes of the Puritans that when that class suffered defeat the theaters were reopened as a matter of course. In 1662, long after the author's death, was published " Theatrum Redivivum," written by Sir Richard Baker in answer to Prynne. The ordinary arguments — namely, that the Bible nowhere forbids plays, that the Pagans and early Christians who opposed the theater opposed only its corruption, and that vices exhibited on the stage are only to teach virtue — were advanced, but were hardly necessary. Opposition to the theater was so closely associated with Puritanism that its wrongness was assumed. For some time after the Restoration one would scarcely have dared raise again the old arguments, for they would have smacked too much of disloyalty. Even some forty years later, when the controversy was revived, it was remarked that the last time a party had torn down the stage in the city it had set up a scaffold in the court, and though the stage has seldom been so licentious as it was during the Restoration, opposition was but tentative and sporadic between 1660 and 1698.

Opposition was neither dead nor completely inactive, though it found no one with sufficient energy to make it a leading issue until Jeremy Collier, a non-juring divine, already famous, gathered together all the weapons, religious, moral, and ascetic, that could be turned against the stage, and flung himself upon it with a fury·and an exultation that seems to have left the wits momentarily stunned. But he called forth a great and very miscellaneous company of wits, critics, philosophers, and fanatics who fell upon one another in a most undignified battle-royal through which no one really distinguished himself except Collier. He alone is much remembered, but he achieved a fame that has lasted faintly, though genuinely, until today, when his other writings and his political exploits have not even the semblance of that popular fame which in some manner does attach to his work as an opponent of the stage. Before discussing this battle, it will be well to devote a few pages to the opinions concerning the stage which found expression between 1660 and 1698.

There has been perhaps too great a tendency to regard the Collier controversy as something wholly unexpected and unprepared for, and to think that his attack was an isolated phenomenon in the history of late seventeenth-century literature. Such was not the case. Neither satire, sermon, nor essay had failed to touch upon the subject, and what distinguished Collier was determination and vigor rather than originality of idea. The political odium attached to Puritanism, and popular knowledge that the court was at least as bad as the stage, naturally tended to

make comment less severe, but it was nevertheless made.
Pepys, a constant play-goer, was often shocked at the immorality of the court, but he does not seem to have been
much disturbed by the reflection of contemporary immorality on the stage, and Evelyn finds " Love in a Tub "
merely a facetious comedy.[1]   The latter, however, enters
a protest that many must have felt when he writes to
Viscount Cornbery in February 1664–5.[2]

Part of the letter is worth quoting. " It [playing] is
not allow'd in any city of christendom so much as in this
one town of London, where there are more wretched and
obscene plays permitted than in all the world beside.
At Paris three days, at Rome two weekly, and at the other
cities of Florence, Venice, etc., but at certain jolly periods
of the year, and that not without some considerable emolu-
ment to the public; whiles our enterludes here are every
day alike; so as the ladies and the gallants come reeking
from the play late on Saturday night, to their Sunday
devotions; the ideas of the farce possesses their fancies to
the infinite prejudice of devotion, besides the advantages
it gives to our reproachful blasphemers. . . . You know,
my Lord, that I (who have written a play and am a
scurvy poet too sometimes) am far from Puritanism; but
I would have no reproach left our adversaries in a thing
which may so conveniently be reform'd. Plays are now
with us become a licentious excess, and a vice, and need
severe censors that should look as well to their morality,
as to their lines and numbers."

Burnet too, whose history though not published until
after his death was written many years before, expresses
disapproval. He speaks of the stage as the great corrupter

[1] Diary, April 27, 1664.
[2] *Memoirs of John Evelyn, Esq., F.R.S.* Edited by Bray, 1827.
Vol. IV.

of the town, and the bad people of the town as the chief
corrupters of the stage. "It is a shame," he writes, "to
our nation and religion, to see the stage so reformed in
France, and so polluted in England; Molière for comedy,
and Racine for tragedy, are patterns; few can, and few
will study to copy after them. But, 'till another scene
appears, certainly our plays are the greatest debauchers of
the nation."[1]

The anonymous author of "A Defense of Dramatic
Poetry" (1698) remarks that if the drama is as bad as
Collier says it is, then one must conclude from the "universal silence of the whole clergy" on the matter that they
have been negligent in their Christian duty. But as the
author of "The Stage Condemn'd" (1698) pointed out,
this, also, is hardly accurate. He cites the case of Samuel
Wesley, who recently at St. James's Church, Westminster,
and also at St. Brides, had anticipated Collier and declared
that "our infamous theaters seem to have done more mischief than Hobbs himself, or our new Atheistical Clubs to
the faith and morals of the nation." Moreover, Baxter in
his "Christian Directory" (1673) had written: "I think
I never knew or heard of a lawful stage play, comedy or
tragedy in the age that I have liv'd, and that those now
commonly used are not only sins, but heinous aggravated
sins." The popular Dr. Anthony Horneck had also condemned contemporary plays in the second edition of his
"Sirenes" (2nd ed. 1690) by including them under the
general heading of revellings which are condemned by the
Scriptures, while Dr. Bray, in his sermon on the baptismal
covenant, had specifically mentioned the stage as one of
the things renounced in the baptismal vows.[2] Attention
should also be called to Archbishop Tillotson's famous ser-

[1] *History of His Own Times.* 1724–34. Vol. II.
[2] Preached in 1697.

mon " On the Evil of Corrupt Communication," which the controversialists quoted from; for, though he refuses to condemn plays *in toto*, he declares that they are in their present form intolerable and not fit to be permitted in a civilized, much less a Christian, community. Moreover, as will be seen from a succeeding chapter, the Societies for the Reformation of Manners had, as early as 1694, advocated the suppression of the theater.

Nor were there wanting lay writers who criticised the immorality of the stage and who may be regarded as forerunners of Collier, since the ground which they took was much the same as that in the earlier portions of his book. Consequently they will serve to show that his importance depends rather upon his vigor and freshness of application than on his originality. Johanes Ballein in his book " Jeremy Colliers Angriff auf die Englische Buhne " takes the preface to Sir Richard Blackmore's " Prince Arthur " (1695) as the first of these preliminary skirmishes, but this is hardly correct. " The Country Conversations " of James Wright (1694) has also been mentioned by other writers, and I should like to add two others which I believe have never been mentioned in this connection before: namely " The Playhouse. A Satire " (1689), by Robert Gould, and the anonymous " A Reflection on our Modern Poesie " (1695), which is, in a way, more interesting than any of the other four works. All are distinguished, though perhaps somewhat indistinctly, from the critical works mentioned in the previous chapters by being not general treatises but specific protests against prevailing conditions, or, as in the case of Gould's poem, a direct and rather vicious satire upon them. I shall discuss briefly the four works mentioned above.

Of Robert Gould the satirist very little is known and two of his works, afterwards acknowledged, are attributed in the British Museum catalog to Tom Brown. "The Play House " appeared in a volume of 1689, and was afterwards printed, much enlarged, in a volume of 1709, shortly after his death.[1] Gould published two plays and miscellaneous poems, but his best work is Juvenalian satire — as violent as Oldham, but better rhymed. In the preface to the later edition of "The Play House " he confesses that this poem brought great odium upon him, and that no apologies availed to make the actors forgive him or to accept one of his plays — the latter statement arousing some suspicion. The opening lines of his poem are not without truth:

> "Of all the things which at this guilty time
> Have felt the honest satyr's wholesome rhyme
> The play house has scap't best, been most foreborne,
> Though it, of all things, most deserves our scorn."

Jonson, Shakespeare, Fletcher, Wycherley, and Southern are praised, but many are damned:

> "In short, our plays are now so loosely writ,
> They've neither manners, modesty, or wit.
> How can these things to our instruction lead
> Which are unchaste to see, a crime to read?"

Some lines from his lurid picture of conditions in the play houses have already been given.

"A Reflection on our Modern Poesie " (Anon., 1695) is less Juvenalian than Gould's satire, and more in the style of the usual Restoration verse essay. It has never, I believe, been referred to in this connection before, but it anticipates most of Collier's points and shows again how little was original with him, so far as the main heads of his discourse were concerned. As with Collier, this essay starts with the assumption that the stage was invented for

---

[1] My quotations are from the poem in its earlier form.

a moral purpose, and laments the degradation of the modern drama as compared with that of ancient times, which he represents as existing solely for its philosophy. He speaks of Sophocles:

> " Who ere he did pretend to poetry
> Search'd the grave precepts of philosophy; "

whereas, he says, modern dramatists forget the end for which they write and are negligent of precept if only they can delight. What especially suggests Collier is the part objecting to the ridicule of the clergy and the protest that the heathens never committed that impiety.

> " See, now the poet's bold in mischief grown,
> And turns to ridicule the sacred gown!
> The grace Divine a laughing stock he makes
> And the firm basis of religion shakes:
>
> * * * * * * * *
>
> Happy the heathen! Whose impiety
> Ne'er mounted yet to such a high degree."

Juvenalian satire is of doubtful value, either for the correction of contemporaries or for the enlightenment of the historian seeking information concerning the actual conditions of the satirist's time. The lurid tone which characterizes it gives rise to the suspicion that the satirist realized too well the literary effectiveness of total depravity to fail to see it everywhere. Hence neither the doubtful testimony of such satire nor the denunciation of preachers to be expected more or less at any time, indicates so well the existence of some dissatisfaction with the theater and contemporary drama in the minds of the moderate class as does the little essay " Of Modern Comedies " in the " Country Conversations " published anonymously in 1694 by James Wright.[1] Wright was a

---

[1] Attribution by Halkett and Lang.

pleasant and unpedantic writer, and, moreover, a lover of old plays, of which he had an extensive collection; so his criticisms are significant as showing that within the body of play-goers itself was to be found a spirit of protest such as was much more likely to produce a change in the drama than any denunciation from the satirists or the pulpiteers. The " Country Conversations " are in the form of dialogues between groups of gentlemen who visit a friend in the country.

" The Plain Dealer " and " Sir Fopling Flutter " are commended, but many of the new comedies are denounced as immoral. It is admitted that by satire comedy may achieve its true end of instruction, but objected that in many comedies vice is protected rather than satirized, and the rakish heroes held up not to scorn but to admiration. " I must observe," says one of the speakers, " that the common parts and characters of our modern comedy are two young debauchés whom the author calls men of wit and pleasure, and sometimes men of wit and sense — The bottle and the Miss (as they phrase it) twisted together make their Summum Bonum; all their songs and discourse is on that subject. But at last, partly for variety of faces, and partly in consideration of improving their estate (shatter'd with keeping) they marry two young ladies, one of which is as wild as possibly can be, so as to 'scape the main chance, the other, more reserved, but really as forward to be marry'd as her sister."

Wright's well-bred protest, and the more or less literary indignation of the satirist, indicate that even in the lay mind the freedom of the theater was not always complacently regarded. But none of these protests was likely to arouse a controversy. All were obviously of minor importance, and the author of no one of them seemed animated by any great determination to force a reform.

The preface to "Prince Arthur" (1695) was written by a somewhat more determined reformer. Sir Richard Blackmore, its author, was an indefatigable writer on ethics and was the scorn of the wits who, according to Dr. Johnson, hated him more for his virtue than for his dullness. Posterity, however, has been inclined to agree with the judgment of the wits, and perhaps it would not be unfair to say that Dr. Johnson loved him more for his piety than his poetry.

Blackmore held firmly that the poet should, first of all, instruct, and hence, perhaps, he should not feel too much disappointed that his epics do not seem to delight moderns. At any rate, the preface referred to contained a more or less impassioned protest against the stage. Like Collier, he begins his attack under the support of critical principles. From universal confession, he says, the purpose of poetry is recognized to be " instruction of our minds, and regulation of our manners " ; and, as to dramatic poetry, tragedy is designed to frighten, and comedy to laugh men out of their vices. He grants that drama should also delight, but insists that this is only a subordinate end, and really only a means, and that only men of little genius will employ their wit for no purpose higher than that of merely pleasing the imagination. In all ages, he says, there have been men who have perverted the end of poetry, but never so many as in his own day. As to Collier, so to him, it seems that the poets are engaged in a general confederacy to ruin virtue and religion, and, along with them, their own art. The stage, which was first, he says, raised for the protection of religion, has been betrayed and given over to enemies who have turned its artillery against the place they should defend. If anyone doubts this, let him read the plays. " A man of sense, and the fine gentleman in comedy, who as the chief person propos'd to the esteem and imita-

tion of the audience is enrich'd with all the sense and wit
the poet can bestow; this extraordinary person you will
find to be a derider of religion, a great admirer of Lucre-
tius, not so much for his learning as for his irreligion, a
person wholly idle, dissolv'd in luxury, abandon'd to his
pleasures, a great debaucher of women, profuse and extravagant in his expenses; and in short, this finished
gentleman will appear a finished libertine." He wishes that
the poets were completely in the pay and under the control of the State and might be suffered to write nothing
prejudicial to religion or government.

"Prince Arthur" was reprinted twice (1695 and 1696)
before 1698, and Blackmore, in his earnestness, is Collier's
most significant predecessor in the attack on the stage. As
Dr. Johnson[1] remarks, Blackmore anticipated all that
was afterwards said by Collier. There is, however, one
thing to be noted. As we shall see, Collier's affected
modesty did not set well upon him, and was indeed cast
off; whereas there is in Blackmore's preface no indication
that he would have gone to the same lengths of fanaticism
as his better known successor.

It is certainly not true then that in 1698 there was
anything novel in the idea of attacking the theater, that
Collier's general principles were in any way unfamiliar
to the public, or that no one had ever pointed out the discrepancy which existed between orthodox critical theory
and contemporary dramatic practice. On the contrary,
Puritanism had made the attacks on the side of religious
authority familiar, and several minor writers had called
attention to the discrepancy between dramatic theory and
practice. It is true, however, and it is this which gives to
Collier his importance, that no one had made much of all
this. The dramatic tradition was long established, and
though many moderate people might be shocked, especially

[1] *Lives of the Poets.*

if their attention was directed to the fact that they ought
to be shocked, they were familiar with the tradition
which had been firmly established at a time when most
men then living were at least only youths and they did not
tend of their own accord to question it. None of the men
whose works have just been discussed had shown much
determination, and not since the civil war had anyone
flung himself against the stage with the fanatical enthusiasm which makes for change. But a general movement for
reform was beginning to spread, the debauchery at court
which generated the comic tradition was reformed, and
people were more or less familiar with the arguments which
could be used against the stage.

By 1696 affairs were approaching a climax. The audience was obviously dissatisfied with the old tradition.
Cibber's obtrusively moral play, " Love's Last Shift," was
a tremendous success, and three plays of that season [1] refer
in their prefaces to the fact that they were objected to on
moral grounds. Moreover, a controversy concerning the
stage was already raging in France, and the English public
knew of it, for we read in the " Gentleman's Journal": [2]
" The controversy is now as hot for and against the lawfulness of the French stage, as it was of late about the
ancients and moderns," and several French books for and
against the theater are mentioned. Both the prologue and
text of " The Provok'd Wife " (1697) show that an uneasy
feeling of imminent disturbance was in the air, and the
line in the prologue

" Kind heav'n! Inspire some venom'd priest to write,"

was positively prophetic.

The " venom'd priest " received his inspiration, and appeared in the form of Jeremy Collier, non-juring divine

---

[1] *The Country-Wake, The Cornish Comedy,* and *The She Gallants.* [2] November, 1694.

and born controversialist; master of all weapons fair and
unfair, sure of himself as only a hopeless fanatic can be
sure of himself, and possessing an unholy joy in combat,
where he lays about him with all the exultation of Samson
slaying Philistines with (to make the metaphor complete)
a jawbone. There is no doubt as to Collier's ultimate purpose. The end of his discourse, as the seventeenth-century
rhetoricians would have said, was action. He was not
writing literary satire or aesthetic criticism. His enemies
succeeded in alleging a variety of indirect motives. Some
said that he was merely striking at the government, which
had always supported the theaters; others that he sought
fame and money, and still others that he had an extraordinary nose for bad odors, and that his corrupt nature
took pleasure in providing innocent passages with an obscene gloss, or, as a satirist put it, in making a " chymical
extraction " from the poets and then " subliming 'em after
to blasphemy." [1] But these charges are unfair. His was
the genuine and irritating zeal of the reformer. From this
fact arose his greatest merit and greatest defects. Nothing is so likely as this same zeal to inspire confidence and
enthusiasm, and on the other hand, nothing is so sure to
spoil the temper and banish urbanity.

Collier had already achieved a certain amount of prominence. He was known as a man of learning, but also as
a fanatic. The blessings of the revolution were too obvious
not to make the sensible part of mankind regard with aversion those stiff-necked clergymen who refused to take the
oath to William and maintained an ineffectual but trouble-
breeding loyalty to that James who had done all in his
power to ruin them and their church. The doctrine that
complete submission to any ruler, even a Nero, was a
religious duty did not appeal to English common sense.

[1] *Visits from the Shades.* 1704.

Moreover, Collier had just drawn attention to himself by giving absolution on the scaffold to two traitors executed for complicity in the Jacobite plot in 1698, and was even then living under censure by the government. Yet in spite of this initial unpopularity, his personal triumph was complete. Even his opponents testify to the éclat which attended his performance. " The tide of prejudice runs high for my adversary," says one,[1] and another complains that " The Short View " " has been receiv'd by the world with a generous applause, and stood the shock of some of the greatest wits of the age." [2]

Prynne, for his book against the stage, was sentenced to be deprived of his university degrees, to be expelled from Lincoln's Inn, to pay a five-thousand-pound fine, to have his ears cut off, and to be imprisoned for life. Collier won an everlasting fame and was granted by William an order of " Nolle prosequi," which released him from all further fear of prosecution as a political offender in the case of the Jacobite plot.[3]

More than two score separate books, pamphlets, prefaces, etc., may be counted as part of the storm which he raised. To discuss each of them separately would be obviously impossible and undesirable. Many may be grouped and treated only as they represent general tendencies which arose during the controversy. But the importance of the " Short View " is so much greater than that of any other book in the literature of the controversy, that it must be

[1] Drake.
[2] Filmer.
[3] It is true that the severity of Prynne's sentence was due to the fact that his attack upon the theater was regarded as an attack upon royalty. The fine was never collected but his ears were cut off and, for a subsequent offense, the remaining stumps were also amputated. He was released from prison after the opening of the Long Parliament.

discussed at some length. "Mr. Collier has said" is a phrase that meets one everywhere. No one, either friend or enemy of the stage, ever doubted that he was the head of the affair.

Since Collier's purpose was primarily a practical one — to get something done — he wisely assumed at the beginning an apparently moderate position. He realized that to make his appeal wholly on the grounds of ascetic Christian piety, while it might appeal to his brother divines and the strictly religious class, would not appeal to the worldly, and consequently he determined to meet the wits on their own ground — namely, the commonly accepted critical dicta. Accordingly he begins with a well-known formula.

A brief summary of his argument will be given before any attempt is made to censure or praise him. Poetry, he says, is a noble institution. Its purpose is to recommend virtue. The poets have in their hands a powerful weapon for the battle against vice. But in his age it has fallen into bad hands, and been turned against those whom it should serve, so that nothing has gone so far to debauch the age as the playwrights. These wicked men are not even indifferent to virtue. They are its declared enemies, and in order to advocate vice most effectually, they have craftily attacked religion and priests, which they know to be virtue's chief supports.

His first charge — and one that certainly had some foundation — is immodesty. He finds that the lewdness of the playwrights' language not only raises evil passions, but is unworthy of a gentleman, is a fault of behavior, and degrades men to the level of beasts. "Goats and monkeys, if they could speak, would express their brutality in such language as this." Especially reprehensible is the habit of putting obscenity in the mouths of ladies of quality. In the "Double Dealer" there are but four ladies, and three of them are debauched. There can be no plea of satire. Even if such things do exist they had best be concealed, and moreover the language of the prologue, where the author himself speaks in person, is just as bad. Plautus and Terence are much less open to objection. Their language is comparatively pure and they never make ladies of quality or married women strumpets. Jonson, too, is comparatively refined, and " The Faithful Shepherdess " is a sort of exaltation of chastity. But Shakespeare is " too guilty to make evidence."

Here Collier reveals one of his characteristic weaknesses. There was enough undeniably objectionable in Restoration drama to make it unnecessary to allege any doubtful cases. The case of Shakespeare is sufficiently doubtful to cause many people to question his judgment. So, too, there were enough cases where the intent of the author was definitely to satirize religion and the commonly accepted standards of morality, and it was unwise to cite such a case as he does from the " Relapse," where Lord Fopington makes the following remark: " Why faith madam, — Sunday is a vile day, I must confess. A man must have very little to do at church that can give an account of the sermon." This, in the mouth of a ridiculous fop, is evidently not meant to be approved. In citing it, Collier gave color to the defence of his opponents who maintained that all such speeches could be justified on the ground of satire.

Collier's next chapter deals with the profaneness of the stage, including the use of oaths which are plainly forbidden by the statute Third Jac. I cap. 21. But the blasphemy, he says, is still worse. Wildblood in the " Mock Astrologer " expresses a preference for the Turkish idea of Paradise, and (*horribile dictu*) in another of Dryden's plays where a devil appears his sneezing is explained on the ground that he has been too long from the fire. Dry-

den's preface to Juvenal apologizes for some pious lines,
and in his "Love Triumphant" occurs the following
passage:

> "May heaven and your brave son, and above all,
>   Your own prevailing Genius guard your age."

"What, says Collier, " is meant by his genius, in this place,
is not easy to discover, only that 'tis something which is
a better guard than heaven. But 'tis no matter for the
sense, as long as the profaneness is clear."

Chapter III is devoted to a discussion of the abuse of
the clergy, a point on which Collier was especially and
vulnerably earnest. The cases of "The Spanish Friar,"
"The Old Bachelor," and "The Relapse" are cited.
"These poets I observe, when they grow lazy, and are inclined to nonsense, they commonly get a clergyman to
speak it. Thus they pass their own dullness for humor,
and gratify their ease and their malice at once." He will
not allow that clergymen may be satirized under any
conditions; and demands not only that they be shown to
be pious, but that they be given worldly respect and position. They have a right to such respect, he says, because
of their close relation to God, so that " To expose a priest,
much more to burlesque his function, is an affront to the
Deity "; because of their importance to society; and because of tradition, for they have always been honored
among Jews, Egyptians, Greeks, Latins, and the English.

How the wits made merry with Collier's rather intemperate zeal for the dignity of his own profession will appear
later. So great was his respect for the priesthood as such
that he was quite as tender of the reputation of heathen
members of the order as he was of Christian ones. Dryden's line in " Absalom and Achitophel," " For priests of all

religions are the same," must have stuck in his mind.
Molière, Virgil, and Sophocles, he says, all treat priests
better than do the English poets. Priests seldom appear
in classical plays (never in Molière or Corneille), and when
they do " 'tis business of credit that brings them there."

In Chapter IV Collier is on safer ground in making the
charge that the stage poets create their principal persons
vicious and then reward them at the end of the play.
Some few like Dryden might plead the facts of life in
excuse, or might maintain that delight and not instruction
is the chief end of comedy, but the contrary was generally
believed. The idea of poetic justice was becoming more
and more generally accepted. And the idea profoundly
influenced comedy. That reward should be given to virtue
and punishment to vice became almost axiomatic. Collier
cites Horace, Aristotle, Jonson, and Rapin to prove this
point. Moreover, all this he regards as an impropriety of
manners as well as a violation of critical doctrine.

So far, Collier had eschewed more or less strictly theo-
logical arguments, and leaving the methods of Prynne
alone had had almost always a background of critical
support. In this first part of the book it is not so much
the Bible or the Church Fathers or the theologians that
he cites, as it is Aristotle, Rapin, Boileau, and Dryden,
and, as Professor Spingarn points out, the very title
" Short View " suggests Rymer's " Short View of Tragedy,"
as does the hectoring language and the main thought. We
might add that there is nothing in the following sentence
from Rymer's translation of Rapin's " Reflections " which
might not have come from Collier. Possibly, indeed, it
was the inspiration for his work. " Comedy has become,
by the licentiousness of these late times, a school of debauchery; 'tis only to re-establish it in its natural estate,

as it ought to be, according to Aristotle, that I pretend to speak. The rest I leave to the zeal of the preachers, who are a little slack on this subject."

Collier's ultimate purpose is, of course, only moral, but in pursuit of that purpose he wishes to destroy contemporary comedy, and to do so he attacks it wherever he considers it vulnerable, whether it be for the moment from the point of view of morality or of literature. Thus in his remarks on " The Relapse " he devotes a considerable portion of his space to pointing out the improbability of the plot, not, of course, because he cares whether or not plays are improbable, but because he sees here an opportunity to weaken the position of the enemy by attacking a matter indifferent to himself yet important to the writer. Hence his connection with criticism. It was a tool or weapon. Since he hoped to persuade the literary world to accept the validity of current literary dogmas, he expected thus to win to his side many who cared more about art, formally considered, than about ethics. Among the plays which he picked out for detailed censure are Dryden's " Amphytrion," D'Urfey's " Don Quixote," and " The Relapse." He censures the latter because while all good plays should have the action confined within twenty-four hours, the story of this must cover at least a week, and because, also, it has two plots and so violates the unity of action. Of course Collier cared nothing about the unity of action, and the English dramatists had no notion of submitting themselves to it; Congreve protested that all this was mere pedantry. But Collier answered stoutly: " Mr. Congreve is so kind as to inform me that I talk pedantical cant of Fable, Intrigue, Discovery, of Unity of Time etc. He means the pedantical cant of Aristotle and Horace, and Bossu and Corneille, Rapin, and Mr. Dryden." As long as the formal critics opposed the methods of con-

temporary comedy, Collier was willing to swear by them
for the sake of damning the drama.

That his main contention — *i.e.*, the end of art is morality — was in accord with contemporary theory has already
been made evident. Dryden questioned " whether instruction has anything to do with comedy," but Collier falls
upon him with Horace's praise of poets for reforming
manners, with Aristotle, with Jonson's " it being the office
of a comic poet to imitate justice, and instruct to life,"
with a quotation from Rapin, and with the following from
Boileau, adapted to English conditions:

> " I like an author that reforms the age;
> And keeps the right decorum of the stage:
> That always pleases by just reason's rule:
> But for a tedious droll, a quibbling fool,
> Who with low nauseous baudry fills his plays;
> Let him be gone and on two trestles raise,
> Some Smithfield stage, where he may act his pranks,
> And make Jack-puddings speak to mountebanks."

He sums the matter up thus in his own vigorous style:
" Indeed to make delight the main business of comedy is
an unreasonable and dangerous principle: It opens the
way to all licentiousness, and confounds the distinction
between mirth and madness." As to the method which the
dramatists should employ, he falls in with the recently
emphasized principle of poetic justice, for which he had
critical authority, and in accordance with which he attacks
the dramatists for allowing their debauched persons not
only to go unpunished but actually to be rewarded. Thus
because the rake of " The Relapse " gets the bride, he says
of the moral: " It points the wrong way, and puts the
prize into the wrong hand. It seems to make lewdness the
reason of desert, and gives Young Fashion a second fortune,
only for debauching away his first."

How Collier followed the critics in pointing out that obscenity is a fault of taste has already been mentioned, and some of his less obvious absurdities can be explained on the same ground. He blames the playwrights with great severity for representing a lord as a fool, and praises Molière because he makes no one higher than a Marquis ridiculous. It was vain to answer that a lord might as well as anyone else be a fool, for Rymer had taught that one must represent character by types, and the type of a lord was not a fool, but a truly noble man. So with the women. Speaking of " The Relapse " he says that " The fine Berinthia, one of the top characters," is impudent and profane, whereas the " character " of a woman is modesty, and she must be so represented, just as a soldier must be represented as harsh and tumultuous. In attacking the theatrically effective but hardly proper scene in which the relapsing husband bears Berinthia, resisting but feebly, from the darkened stage to an adjoining closet, Collier bases his censure not primarily on the moral tendency of the characters and scenes, but on the fact that it is not in accordance with the rules. He quotes not the Scriptures but Rapin and Rymer. The former, he says, blames Ariosto and Tasso for representing two of their women as " too free and airy," and Rymer in the " Tragedies of the Last Age " says that Nature (of course the general nature of the critics, not actuality) knows nothing in manners which so properly distinguishes a woman as modesty, and that an impudent woman is fit only to be exposed and kicked in comedy. So, too, in his plea for immunity for the priesthood, Collier points out that Homer and Virgil treated it with respect, for " They were govern'd by the reason of things, and the common usage of the world. They knew the priesthood a very reputable employment, and always esteem'd as such. To have used the priest ill, they must have call'd their own discretion in question: They must have run into impropriety, and fallen foul upon custom, manners and religion." Be it said again that Collier chose this method not because he esteemed the authority of Horace above that of St. Paul or Tertullian, but because he knew that he was addressing not the theologians but the wits.

In choosing his method Collier was extremely skillful, but in choosing plays for elaborate analysis and condemnation he showed a certain lack of discretion which is notable throughout his work. He selected Dryden's " King Arthur " and " Amphytrion," D'Urfey's " Don Quixote " and Vanbrugh's " The Relapse," and was led to do so, no doubt, by the fact that they were all comparatively recent. But, although not one was absolutely unimpeachable, still none was by any means the worst of its class. A good deal could be said in extenuation of the morals of each of them. " Don Quixote," especially, though occasionally coarse, would pass as a very innocent play in comparison with almost any one of Mrs. Behn's; and although not particularly delicate, it is certainly not vicious. It lacks the literary art of Congreve, and also lacks his cynical perversity. By wasting his eloquence on the peccadillos of this play, Collier has nothing left which is really effective when excitement might be less uncalled for. " Amphytrion " is probably the happiest choice which he made, and the least defensible of the plays, so that it justifies pretty well all that Collier said about. its lusciousness. But as always he over-steps bounds. Instead of criticising it merely as an extremely loose tale, he alleges roundly that Dryden, by making Jupiter a somewhat unexalted character, secretly intends to satirize Jehovah. And who but Collier, seeking for a typical example of Restoration depravity, would have lit upon the same poet's " King

Arthur " to present *in extenso* as a horrible example? It
is a feeble and silly performance, but because it intro-
duces the devil and magic, Collier exclaims: "Those that
bring devils upon the stage, can hardly believe them anywhere else. To mix Christian and heathen story, is to
imply that one is no more worthy of belief than the other."
Collier was constitutionally incapable of distinguishing a
mote from a beam.

Students of Restoration Comedy have long been engaged
with the question as to how far Vanbrugh represents a
turn toward a more healthy tone in drama. Though more
or less engaged with this question himself, the present
writer believes firmly in the impossibility of success in
any attempt to determine the exact amount of instruction
to be derived from a play. Still he is inclined to believe
that Vanbrugh does indeed move with the reform stream,
and that here again Collier made a mistake in choosing
" The Relapse," rather than some less equivocal comedy,
as the object of a special attack. In it Vanbrugh himself
alludes to the need of a reform, represents some virtuous
characters in an extremely favorable light, does not distribute epigrams of perverse morality to all his witty characters, and actually has one man pay a tribute of respect
to chastity. Yet Collier attacks the play so violently that
one cannot refrain from quotation and comment. His
summary of the plot is reasonably fair. "Fashion, a lewd,
prodigal, younger brother, is reduced to extremity: upon
his arrival from his travels, he meets with Coupler, an
old sharping match-maker; this man puts him upon a
project of cheating his elder brother, Lord Foppington, of
a rich fortune. Young Fashion being refused a sum of
money by his brother, goes into Coupler's plot, bubbles Sir
Tunbelly of his daughter, and makes himself master of a
fair estate." The play, he says, had more properly been

called "The Younger Brother, or the Fortunate Cheat."
The moral, he says, "puts the prize in the wrong hand,"
and he sums it up as follows: "First, that all younger
brothers should be careful to run out their fortunes as
fast and as ill as they can — Secondly, that when a man
is press'd, his business is not to be governed by scruples,
or formalize upon conscience and honesty."

Now, as has already been confessed, the general charge
that Restoration plays represent heroes as debauched and
also represent them as attractive is true; but one cannot
deduce neatly formulated morals from them without being
ridiculous. "The Relapse" is a comparatively moral play,
and Collier's method could deduce as bad a moral from
an even more innocent performance. The fact that Vanbrugh wrote a play in which a younger brother loses his
money and afterwards marries a rich girl does not necessarily prove that he meant to teach that "All younger
brothers should be careful to run out their fortunes as
fast and as ill as they can." And as for putting the prize
in the wrong hand, Sir Foppington is a heartless and brain-
less ass, and certainly deserves a prize as little as does his
brother. Besides, it is doubtful if the girl is much of a
prize after all. Her speech indicates that the behavior
which she plans for life in town with her husband is such
that his fortune will not be easily earned. Might one not
with as much show of truth as Collier can boast, formulate
the moral thus: "He who seeks a wife for her fortune will
get a bad bargain"? What I mean is, that from a play no
more than from life can one deduce hard and fast
"Morals," and that Collier made a mistake in choosing
"The Relapse," since its general tone is more healthy than
that of dozens of other Restoration plays. Whoever reads
the "Short View" must see that while Collier had much
evil to attack, and knew how to express himself forcibly,

he was too easily shocked, and weakened his case by being
unable to differentiate between what was of doubtful
propriety and what was undoubtedly abominable.

After finishing his detailed examination of a few contemporary plays, Collier turns aside from criticism and
bases his attack on what must have been more congenial
to his temperament — namely, authority. He summons
the testimony of the ancients and that of the church,
and it soon becomes evident that he shares to the fullest
extent the ascetic Christian hatred of all art, and that the
authority of Ben Jonson, or Dryden, was appealed to only
because it happened to suit his purpose, and not because
he could possibly have had any sympathy with either of
them. It has been said in criticism of Collier that
the argument from the ancients was irrelevant. Actually
it was, but it could not seem so to his contemporaries.
It must be remembered that the Renaissance worship of
antiquity still lingered very markedly, that education was
based upon the study of Latin and Greek, and that there
was still a strong tendency to regard the sterner side of
the ancient character as a model of excellence, and to
speak of " Roman virtue " as something that even a mil-
lennium and a half of Christian civilization had hardly
been able to equal. Just as Horace was the model of taste,
so Cato the Censor was a model of virtue.

Collier begins the new phase of his subject thus: " Having in the foregoing chapters discover'd some part of the
disorders of the English stage: I shall, in this last, present
the reader with a short view of the sense of antiquity. To
which I shall add some modern authorities; from all which
it will appear that plays have generally been look'd on as
the nurseries of vice, the corrupters of youth, and the
grievance of the country where they are suffer'd." Here is
a notable transition from what he had previously said.

From the first portion of his book one would get the impression that plays had been invented to recommend virtue, that such was their normal function, and that the English dramas, particularly those of his own time, had formed an exception and had been unaccountably perverted. But here, be it noted, he says that plays have usually been looked upon as " nurseries of vice." From now on he throws aside the disguise and appears frankly as an enemy of the stage as such.

Plato, he says, " tells us that plays raise the passions, and pervert the use of them, and by consequence are dangerous to morality. For this reason he banishes these diversions from his commonwealth." Here we get at the root of the matter discussed at the beginning of the present chapter. Plays, like other forms of literature, raise the passions of love, ambition, and honor. These are the things that to the worldly mind make the world worth while. But they are fundamentally opposed to asceticism, which does not want to make the world worth while and looks upon all the passions which attach one to it as necessarily evil. Hence, though Collier believed the contemporary stage worse than most stages, he believed that all were evil. His opponents accused him of posing as a reformer of the stage, whereas he really wished to destroy it, and in his defenses he never denied this allegation. He praises Terence only comparatively, he says, and means only that he was not so bad as the English authors. Following the line of argument taken up, he shows that Aristotle had objected that the young should not see plays, that Cicero, Livy, Tacitus, and Valerius Maximus had protested against immoral plays; and then, passing to the legal aspect, shows that the Spartans banished the theater completely, that the Athenians, the Romans, the Elizabethan English, the French, and the Flemish had all at one time or another put some stigma or restriction upon the theater, and that the early church had excommunicated players. Lactantius, Augustine, and Ambrose are ransacked for all references weighty or trivial against the stage or shows. Authorities are piled one upon another in an effort to damn the whole institution on the strength of traditional opposition.

After all deductions are made for the facts that Collier wrote at an extremely opportune moment, that the English stage was in many ways so objectionable that almost any attack, however violent, must seem more or less justified, and that a very definite reform movement both in regard to the theater and to society in general was in progress, it still is impossible to deny to Collier's own ability a considerable part of the credit for the enormous stir which his book made. That he was essentially narrow-minded, and that he was in no sense merely a stern, frank friend of the stage, I think is already evident; yet he presented his case with such force that people very different from himself expressed approval of his work, and men like Cibber and Steele, who fundamentally were on the other side, were driven partly by the depraved condition of contemporary drama on the strictly moral side, and partly by the effectiveness of his book, to profess themselves in agreement with him.

His earnestness was one great asset, his style another. To the modern ear the latter is sometimes offensive, but it was admirably in the tradition of seventeenth-century controversy. His contemporaries liked learning and liked raillery. Collier appealed to both of these traits by mixing a bewildering number of citations, pertinent and impertinent, with sneers, taunts and irony, together with exuberant raillery and abuse. He is constantly hovering somewhere between eloquence and bombast, and his genuine earnestness often goes a long way toward convincing the reader that the latter is the former.

Dryden's line suggesting an explanation of the superior endowments of Absalom,

> "Whether inspired with a diviner lust,
> His father got him . . . "

though expressing only an idea familiar in popular literature, lashed Collier to a fury. "This is downright defiance of the living God! Have you the very essence and spirit of blasphemy, and the Holy Ghost brought in upon the most hideous occasion. I question whether the torments and despair of the damn'd, dare venture at such flights as these. They are beyond description, I pray God they may not be beyond pardon too." The light use of a Scriptural phrase brings this comment: "This is an eruption of hell with a witness. I almost wonder the smoke of it has not darken'd the sun, and turn'd the air to plague and poison!" And "They conclude he [God] wants power to punish, because he has patience to forbear. Because there is a space between blasphemy and vengeance; and they don't perish in the act of defiance; because they are not blasted with lightning, transfixt with thunder, and guarded off with devils, they think there's no such matter as a day of reckoning. But let no man be deceiv'd, God is not mock'd; not without danger they may be assured. Let them retreat in time, before the floods run over them." Speaking in general, he says: "On what unhappy times are we fallen! The oracles of truth, the laws of omnipotence, and the fate of eternity are laughed at and despis'd! That the poets should be suffer'd to play upon the Bible, and Christianity be hooted off the stage! Christianity that from such feeble beginnings made so stupendous a progress! That over-bore all the opposi-

tions of power and learning; and with twelve poor men,
outstretch'd the Roman Empire. But that this glorious
religion so reasonable in its doctrine, so well attested by
miracles, by martyrs, by all the evidence that fact is
capable of, should become the diversion of the town, and
the scorn of buffoons: And where, and by whom is all
this out-rage committed? Why not by Julian, or Porphyry,
not among Turks or heathens, but in a Christian country,
in a reform'd church, and in the face of authority." No
wonder that Collier was read. Whether such writing be
justified by the facts or not, and whether it be eloquence
or bombast, it is certainly not dull.

One gets, perhaps, the highest idea of Collier's ability by
regarding such passages apart from the things which call
them forth. He has a very keen eye for blasphemy, and
often an innocent or trivial thing brings down a ludicrously
disproportionate tirade. How he saw blasphemy in the
fact that one of Dryden's imps sneezed from having been
too long away from the fire has already been referred to.
Many other examples of an exaggerated sensibility might
be mentioned, but one will suffice. He quotes the following song from D'Urfey's " Don Quixote ":

> " Providence that formed the Fair
>   In such a charming skin
> Their outside made his only care,
>   And never look'd within."

This seems a harmless bit of wit, yet Collier calls it " a
bold song against Providence " and says it is a " direct blas-
pheming the creation, and a satire upon God Almighty."
D'Urfey [1] spoke not untruly of Collier as " foaming at the
mouth." One would like to ask with Prior, " Odds life!
must one swear to the truth of a song? "

[1] Preface to *The Campaigners*. 1698.

The choice of such feeble examples when many better offered themselves cast doubt on his power of discernment, and offered weak points for the attacks of his enemies. Moreover, these examples show that no possible stage could really have pleased him, for he was able to find blasphemy and obscenity in the most innocent phrases. His own language was sometimes coarse. Criticising a passage in Congreve's " The Mourning Bride," he says: " This litter of epithets makes the poem look like a bitch overstock'd with puppies, and sucks the sense almost to skin and bone "; and when he says of Shakespeare and Ophelia, " Since he was resolv'd to drown the lady like a kitten, he should have set her a swimming a little sooner," he proved nothing but his own insensibility.

The things that he praises are often as unaccountable as those that he abuses. Euripides is praised because, when Orestes is about to kill his mother, he mentions the murder of her husband but not her adultery — surely, no very material point in comparison with matricide. Only a lack of humor can account for Collier's tactical error in making so important an issue out of the necessity of giving a priest of any sort, Pagan or Christian, not only almost divine reverence, but also great worldly station. This position only gave point to remarks like the following by Vanbrugh, who maintained that " 'twas the quarrel of his gown and not of his God, that made him take arms against me — in all probability, had the poets never discover'd a rent in the gown, he had done by religion, as I do by my brethren, left it to shift for itself." The fact of the matter is that Collier was not really quite enough a man of the world for his task. The fairness and moderation which he tried to assume did not fit his character, and it took such a man as Steele, who could congenially put himself on the side of poetry, to effect the reform of English

comedy. That Steele did more harm than good I shall
maintain later on, but he brought to his task a power of
persuasion that Collier lacked.

The evils of the Restoration stage, and the fact that
Collier called forcible attention to them, have blinded many
later critics to the essential narrowness of his views. The
" Spectator " confessed himself a great admirer of Collier,
and public opinion has been, since that time, generally
on his side. In the eighteenth century we find Davies in
his " Dramatic Miscellaney " calling Collier " a severe,
but just corrector of their [the dramatists] indecencies and
blasphemy." Macaulay [1] also at least implies as much,
and such is the prevailing estimate of Collier's work.

But attention must again be called to the fact that so
to estimate him is to be over-impressed with the indecencies that actually existed, and to forget that while many
of his charges were substantiated, there is abundant proof
in the book that he was a narrow-minded fanatic apparently as much shocked by wit as he was by blasphemy,
and that no conceivable stage could have pleased him, since
he was fundamentally an enemy to imaginative literature
and belonged to that school of critics who, like Ascham,
found the " Morte D'Arthur " only a story of wilful murder
and bold adultery.

[1] *History of England.* Vol. III.

CHAPTER VI

THE ONSLAUGHT ON THE STAGE

(*Continued*)

COLLIER'S book, being both powerful and opportune, brought forth a flood of confutation and support, so that between the publication of the "Short View" and 1725 one may count more than forty separate books and pamphlets which are definitely part of the controversy which he raised. Nor were they confined to London alone; they came from as far west as Bath and as far north as Edinburgh.[1]

To mention in chronological order all the contributions to the controversy or to balance reply and counter-reply would be tedious, and since there is endless repetition, uninstructive. I have attempted to make the bibliography as exhaustive as possible, and can say that it at least includes more items than will be found in any other list. I shall discuss in detail only some of the most important books.

The dramatists who were attacked may fairly be allowed to speak first. Dryden's few words are best known. He was probably too weary of controversy and of life to say much, and contented himself with a few remarks in the preface to the "Fables" and in the prologue to "The Pilgrim." In the former he pleads guilty in so far as any

---

[1] The single pamphlet which emanated from the latter city has never been noticed before, I think, and the copy in the Edinburgh library seems to be unique, but it is interesting only as showing how far the noise of the discussion had proceeded, since it contains nothing beyond the capacity of a provincial parson.

of his expressions or thoughts can be fairly accused of
obscenity or profaneness. He says truly that Collier has
often put a worse interpretation on some passages than
they require, and that he has been hardly fair in calling
his age worse than any which had gone before. But on
the whole Dryden's tone is one of submission. He kisses
the rod, and in the prologue to "The Pilgrim" contents
himself with protesting merely that the parson has
stretched the point too far.

Dryden has usually been praised for his moderation and
for his candor, but one may wish that he had answered
more at length. No one was so fit as he to expose by
moderate censure of his time the unfair ferocity of Collier.
But perhaps he was too weary to enter into any new controversy. We can never know how sincere was his cry of
mea culpa, for he died too soon to prove repentance by
his works. The cleanness of the "Fables" is a point in
his favor, but one can never be sure. Some ten years
before he had written in the magnificent fourth stanza of
the "Ode to Mistress Anne Killegrew" a more moving la-
ment for the faults of his age and for his own too active
participation in them than any which appears in the
preface to the "Fables." Yet he had not hesitated, a
few years later, to lard "Amphytrion" plentifully. He was
a master of the art of saying what he wanted to say with
an air of conviction, whether he believed it or not; and had
he lived he might not have demonstrated in his works
the sincerity of the submission which he seemed so can-
didly to proclaim.

Congreve replied with "Amendments to Mr. Collier's
false and imperfect citations, etc., from the Old Bachelor,
Double Dealer, Love for Love, Mourning Bride," and
Vanbrugh with "A Short Vindication of the Relapse and
the Provok'd Wife." Both disclaimed any intention of

defending what was actually objectionable in the contemporary comedy, but neither was wholly wise in his method. For while each could show that Collier was over-anxious to find offense where none could reasonably be found, and while some support could be given to Congreve's statement that the reformer had " blackened the thoughts with his own smut," each made the mistake of himself stretching the point too far and of pretending that Collier was only reading into plays things which any candid reader must admit the authors had put there themselves. Thus Congreve is quite right when he refuses to admit that a speech of Osmin in the " Mourning Bride " is, as Collier called it, " a rant of smut and profaneness." The speech is as follows:

> Osmin: Oh my Elmira
> What do the damn'd endure but to despair,
> But knowing heaven to know it lost forever.

Osmin is referring to the loss of his mistress and is perhaps a bit extravagant, but certainly not profane. Congreve is, however, not always so sincere. For instance, Collier had objected also to a scene in the " Old Bachelor " where one of the characters asks Bellmour if he would be content to go to heaven, and gets the response: " Hum, not immediately, in my conscience, not heartily." Now this is an innocent enough joke, and Congreve would have done well simply to say so, but instead he accuses Collier of distorting his meaning, for, he says, Bellmour continues: " I would do a little more good in my generation first, in order to deserve it." Of course this is facetious, and does not change the meaning, but " 'Tis one thing," says Congreve, " for a man to say positively, he will not go to heaven; and another to say, that he does not think himself worthy, till he is better prepared." Bellmour's little speech

is not, as Collier would have us believe, horribly profane,
but neither is it, as Congreve tries to make it out, a pious
reflection, and it does not have, as he says, " a moral meaning contain'd in it." Similarly, Congreve is right as long
as he maintains that there is no reason why he should not
ridicule a foolish clergyman, but he is insincere and unwise when he maintains that he did not intend ridicule
when he christened one " Mr. Prig." So, too, Vanbrugh
gets some telling blows at Collier, but weakens his own
cause by obvious hypocrisy when, for instance, he refuses
to see any *double entendre* in the remark of Rasor in " The
Provok'd Wife "; "And if my prayers were to be heard
her punishment for so doing shou'd be like the serpent's
of old, she shou'd lye upon her face all the days of her
life."

On the whole, Congreve's reply is hastily written and
not very successful. He showed that Collier sometimes
exaggerated, but he made no very satisfactroy reply to
the principal charge, i.e., that he represented vice in an
attractive light and made vicious characters successful;
for he hardly attempted to show either that this was permissible or that it had not been done. Vanbrugh was more
successful. He protested that if his plays did not expose
vice and folly to ridicule, such had at least been his aim,
and he did succeed in proving that while he might be guilty
occasionally of considerable freedom in speech and in the
full length depiction of rather questionable scenes, he could
not fairly be charged with teaching immorality. His illustration of Collier's inability to recognize satire when he
sees it and of his unforunate habit of attributing to the
dramatists themselves the opinions of any character is
particularly telling. Collier had objected to the following
speech of Lord Foppington in " The Relapse ": " Why faith
madam, Sunday is a vile day, I must confess. A man
must have very little to do there that can give an account

of the sermon." Vanbrugh replies very tellingly to the objection by remarking, quite truly, that in the play Lord Foppington does nothing that is not intended to be laughed at and despised, and that " though my Lord Foppington is not suppos'd to speak what he does to a religious end, yet 'tis so ordered, that his manner of speaking it, together with the character he represents, plainly and obviously instructs the audience (even to the meanest capacity) that what he says of his church-behaviour, is design'd for their contempt, and not for their imitation." There was in Restoration Comedy much perversity spoken for the approval of the audience, but this was no example of it, and Collier was so intent on finding matter for objection that he could not recognize satire when he saw it.

The replies of Vanbrugh and Congreve were replied to by " A Letter to Mr. Congreve, etc." (1698), by " Animadversions upon Mr. Congreve's late answer to Mr. Collier, etc." (1698), and by Collier himself in " A Defense of the Short View, etc." (1699). Neither of the former two is very important. The first is merely raillery, but the second makes one or two points, including the suggestion that since Congreve is a dramatist it is not sufficient for him merely to disapprove of what is immoral on the stage; he has a duty to attempt to reform it. Collier's reply exposes Congreve's unsuccessful attempt to represent his comedies as endowed with a moral purpose, and truly enough finds the real moral of the " Old Bachelor " in Bellmour's speech at the end of the fourth act:

> " No husband by his wife can be deceiv'd,
> She still is virtuous, if she's so believ'd."

On the whole he does succeed in showing up the weakness of Congreve's defense. Congreve had, indeed, shown that many of Collier's attacks were on frivolous grounds; but

Collier succeeded very well in maintaining his principal contention that Congreve's comedies were such as they were: that is, cynical pictures of contemporary society, not for the most part vicious in intent, but simply unconcerned with any moral consideration.

Collier's reply to Vanbrugh is less successful, for he returns to the attack and again shows his unreasonableness. Thus, the speech of Amanda (" The Relapse "): " What slippery stuff are men composed of? Sure, the account of their creation's false, and 'twas the woman's rib that they were form'd of," Collier cites as proof that the play " not only questions the truth of the Scriptures, but denies it." As to Vanbrugh's assertion that the various speeches to which Collier had objected were intended to be condemned by the audience and must not be taken as expressing the opinion of the dramatists, Collier falls back upon the assumption that evil is not to be spoken upon the stage under any circumstances, and argues: " One man injures his neighbor, and another blames him for't; does this cancel the guilt, and make the fact nothing? One man speaks blasphemy, and another reproves him; does this justify the boldness, or make the words unspoken? " Moreover, Collier says that whether what the characters say is intended to be reproved or ridiculed, yet the people who speak these blasphemies are fine gentlemen " and when vice has credit as well as pleasure annexed, the temptation is dangerously fortified." In other words, Collier would have no drama, only sermons; for drama may be misunderstood.

Neither side profited much from the anonymous " A Letter to A. H. Esq." (1698) and " A Letter to Mr. Congreve on His Pretended Amendment, etc." (1698), which were intended to support Collier (who was much better able to support himself), nor from " Some Remarks upon

Mr. Collier's Defense of his Short View " (1698), which, as became quite common, charged Collier with vanity, uncharitableness, and ill nature.

There was, in the replies to Collier, little that was conclusive. Whatever opinions the more worldly part of society might ultimately reach concerning the stage, he had scored a great triumph. Though his extreme view could not be accepted, it achieved its main purpose of arousing active interest in the condition of the English stage, and from his time on the question of how the stage might be held within the bounds of morality was in every one's mouth and on the tip of everyone's pen. Books on the stage became almost a recognized department of literature, and varied all the way from ponderous and unreadable volumes like that by Arthur Bedford, who boasts that he gives reference to almost two thousand instances of corruption in the plays of the two preceding years, to modest pamphlets for distribution among the masses by the religious.

Interest in the subject became so widespread as to be shared by every class of society. Steele could discourse in a spirit of sweet reasonableness for the benefit of the polished; men of a serious and ponderous nature like the lawyer Edward Filmer and the critic John Dennis could seek a philosophical basis for defending the stage; and learned but naïve clergymen could search the classics and the ponderous works of the fathers for light; while popular preachers could seize the occasion for denouncing the world's corruption. From the heights of literature in the " Spectator " the subject descends to the depths in the works of men like Tom Brown and D'Urfey. In a " Visit from the Shades " (1704) Collier was introduced holding a colloquy with Joe Haynes, the actor, and in " The Stage-Beau toss'd in a blanket: or hypocrisy a la mode " (attributed to Tom Brown) a Collierite is exposed by an easy formula, furnished by Tartuffe, wherein the hypocrisy of the over-virtuous is unmasked when the pious fraud makes love too recklessly. Settle, too, borrows an idea from the " Knight of the Burning Pestle " to ridicule the citizens' prejudice against the theater. Leaping from these extremes of frivolity to the opposite extreme of seriousness, we find that the terrible storm in November, 1703 (best remembered because of the reference to it in Addison's famous metaphor), which killed many and destroyed, among other buildings, the theater in Dorset Garden, was looked upon as " a dreadful judgment against the nation for the impieties of the play houses," [1] and that a special pamphlet called " Mr. Collier's dissuasive from the play house, in a letter to a person of quality, occasion'd by the late calamity of the tempest " (1703) was printed for the occasion.

Dennis made the Voltairian comment that the storm covered a very large area, so " that the Divine vengeance which they [i.e. the theaters] brought down upon us has involv'd the very innocent. Not only the poor inhabitants of Cologne, but the very Hamburgers and Dantzichers, and all the people of the Baltak, have suffer'd for the enormities of our English theaters; tho' I believe in my conscience they have never so much as heard of a play." But such irony was lost on a Bedford, who seriously replied to a complaint that it was hardly fair that innocent sailors should share the vengeance intended for London by saying that they were one of the foundations of England's greatness and hence a likely object to be visited with God's wrath against England.

Much of the mass of controversy which we are considering is anonymous, and even among the names which have

[1] Bedford. *Serious Reflections*, etc.

survived none is that of a man with half of Collier's arresting power. Probably John Dennis and Arthur Bedford deserve best to be remembered, though Dennis is certainly heavy, and Bedford is interesting only as a curious example of fanaticism. The latter was an industrious pedant who, after taking his M.A. at Brasenose in 1691, became chaplain to the Duke of Bedford and later in life to Frederick, Prince of Wales. He was so unworldly as to be completely out of touch with the world, and seems to have divided his time between various studies and puritanical fulmination. His mind was of a type which found congenial the most unprofitable parts of Collier's book — the narrow asceticism and the most super-ingenious twisting of innocent phrases into blasphemous ones — and the actual appearance of actors in Bristol, where he lived, spurred him to a furious denunciation. If to his opinion concerning the great storm (already cited) we add that he believed that God had given great success to certain medical baths in order to reduce the prosperity of the people of Bath who had permitted acting, we shall get some idea of the fanaticism, but not of the awful tedium, of his books.

The worst is called "The Evil and Danger of Stage-Plays: Shewing their natural tendency to destroy religion, and introduce a general corruption of manners; in almost two thousand instances, taken from the plays of the two last years, against all the methods lately used for their reformation" (1706). The title gives a sufficient hint as to its contents. Collier and most of the other controversialists are at least readable. Bedford certainly is not. This volume of 227 pages is hardly a book, but a catalog. The margins are not wide enough to hold all the page references for the 2000 cases of profaneness and immorality together with the notations of chapters and verses of the

Scriptural texts which condemn them, so that these lists
usurp the place of the text. Had Lamb known "The Evil
and Danger etc.," he would certainly have included it
among his list of "things in book's clothing!" The volume
may be called scholarly. About 30 biblical texts are given
to prove that swearing is a sin before we are informed
that conversation which contains such phrases as "Death
and Furies" is so bad that "the bare repetition of such
unparalleled blasphemy, will make the flesh tremble, and
the blood grow cold." Abundant references to page and
line in printed play-books are given, so that anyone may
see for himself how in different plays characters "Wish
that they may be damn'd, die, or rot, chang'd, confounded,
stricken blind, or stupid, that the devil may take them,"
and how on page 58, line 309, of "An Act at Oxford"
appears this crowning horror: "May the devil choke me
upon a red herring." Thus Bedford collects his 2000 instances by means of an unequal eye for blasphemy and
profaneness, so that an innocent song like the following:

> "To Fortune give immortal praise,
> Fortune depresses and can raise.
> All is as Fortune shall bestow
> 'Tis Fortune governs all below."

becomes terrible blasphemy, because it attributes to a
heathen God what belongs only to Providence.

Similar extravagances may be found in Bedford's other
books. "A Serious Remonstrance, etc." goes even further
than "The Evil and Danger, etc.," and includes almost
"7000 instances, taken out of the plays of the present
century," which show the "plain tendency" of the stage
"to overthrow all piety, and advance the interest and
honor of the devil in the world." It begins with "the
catalogue of about 1400 texts of Scripture, which are men-

tioned in the treatise, either as ridicul'd and expos'd by the
stage, or as opposite to their present practices." The list
is long because Bedford found evil everywhere. The lines
from "The 'Squire of Alsatia ":

> "But never solid joy could find,
>   Where I my charming Sylvia miss'd."

are proclaimed doubly sinful: first, because they use
"charming" in a favorable sense, when it is a plain teaching of the Bible that all magic and charms are from the
devil: and second, because they are a defiance of Psalm
IV, "Lord, lift thou up the light of Thy countenance
upon us. Thou hast put gladness in my heart." The idea
apparently is that the lover in the play, by declaring the
impossibility of finding joy where his mistress is not, is
considered as denying God's power to gladden the heart.
Bedford had simply pushed other-worldliness to a point
where any phrase not saturated with an immediate sense
of the presence of the Hebraic God must be ranked as
blasphemous.

Appalling as such works are, they cannot be neglected
by a student either of the present subject or the intellectual life of the time, for Bedford was not recognized as a
fool by his contemporaries. Defoe read him with approval,
and Defoe represents the prevailing mental attitude of a
large class of people of narrow but genuine piety. Bedford
represented merely the extreme of the spirit generally widespread — the spirit of the once dominant Puritan. The
bulk of even the middle class would not go to the extreme
of Bedford's unworldliness, but it understood nothing and
cared nothing for the purely literary excellence of the
Restoration drama. It was interested by literature and
might perhaps be amused at the theater, but it demanded
that no amusement, literary or otherwise, should outrage

its fundamental notions. The general attitude of this moderate middle class was well expressed in the anonymous " A Letter to A. H. Esq.," [1] which appeared shortly after the " Short View." The author favors a reformed stage and remarks that, as to Collier, " He has his faults, but they are such as I wou'd not have lost his book for." Among all the books which form the controversy there is scarcely one, even among those written by the dramatists themselves, which does not admit that there have been abuses, and there are practically no defenses of the *status quo.* To this extent Collier had won an undoubted triumph.

Some of the other books listed in the bibliography are almost as foolish as the " Evil and Danger," but not all. It represents simply an extreme, and in many others there are attempts to settle, on the basis of a less fanatical idea of the permissible, the questions which Collier had raised. The man moderately inclined to conventional morality had been awakened to the fact that he should be flagrantly outraged by a Restoration comedy. He was convinced that it could not be justified, and was now moved to wonder whether or not all drama was indefensible. Criticism was again face to face with the old question of the justification of literature, and it attempted to lay down rules and define methods by means of which a comedy to which reasonable men could not object could be produced. Of course such an attempt, in so far as it tried to be rigidly logical and definite, failed, since comedy is a wild jade that refuses to be bound; but certain ideas which were developed, and above all the general admission made by practically all the controversialists that comedy should be morally instructive, succeeded in producing the profound

[1] Probably Anthony Horneck of the Societies for the Reformation of Manners.

modification which dramatic writing underwent. We shall turn, then, to an examination not of the individual books but of the drift of argument which they represented.

It has already been pointed out in the chapter on Collier that at the base of many attacks on the stage lay the fundamental ascetic objection to all art that appealed to worldly interest and a love of life, since it is a part of the wise man and the Christian to hate all such things. Asceticism in bare and philosophical form is not particularly congenial to the English mind, but Calvinistic asceticism is plainly the background of the rather barbarous pedantry of men like the journalist George Ridpath and some of the authors of the amazing pamphlets in the literature of this controversy. Moreover it had found full philosophical expression in the French controversy concerning the stage, with which Collier was certainly familiar, since he made a translation from Bossuet under the title of " Maxims and Reflections upon Plays." The best expression in English of this fundamental objection to the stage is found in a translation from the works of Armand de Bourbon, Prince de Conti (a brother of " the grand Condé "), who in the latter part of a tumultuous life fell into an excess of devotion and wrote among other things a " Traité de la Comédie " which was published shortly after his death in 1666. It was answered by the Abbé d'Aubignac, and was published in English in 1711.

To the Prince de Conti the stage became simply one of the expressions of the lust of the flesh which it was necessary to suppress. " A Christian having renounc'd the world, its pomp and pleasure, cannot seek pleasure for itself, nor diversion for the sake of diversion. It must (that he may use it without sin) be in some manner necessary for him," and the stage is not necessary. Moreover, the whole subject matter of dramatic literature is nec-

essarily un-Christian, for the Christian virtues are not
dramatic. Corneille writes plays which are clean, but
ambition, revenge, and above all love are his subjects. All
of these are essentially un-Christian, but to treat of love
is especially so, for the Christian is the enemy of all sexual
passion, and sexual love is the subject of most plays.
Love, though lawfully exercised, " is nevertheless always
evil and irregular in itself, and it is not allowable to excite
it in one's self or others. We ought always to look on it
as the shameful effect of sin, as a source of poison capable
to infect us every minute." To make plays clean is to
make them more rather than less dangerous, for when they
are not fair-seeming the world more readily avoids them.

No English writer expressed this ascetic idea in its logical purity so well, though William Law came nearest to
it; and Law was, like the Prince de Conti, a mystic, and his
mind worked in the same way. To him also it is not a
question of good plays or bad plays, because to him all
imaginative representations of this sinful world are necessarily sinful. He has nothing to say of the reform of
the stage, for he does not believe that it is possible to reform it. To him the stage is sinful " not as things that
may only be the occasion of sin, but such as are in their
own nature grossly sinful." Theater-going is " contrary to
the whole nature of religion," and " to talk of the lawfulness and unlawfulness of the stage is fully as absurd, as
contrary to the plain nature of things, as to talk of the
unlawfulness and mischief of the service of the church."
His logic is unanswerable. The theater represents the
world and is necessarily worldly. Worldliness is anti-
Christian, therefore the theater is anti-Christian. He describes a mask of Apollo and Venus then playing. The
opening scene, he says, shows Venus and the pleasures
and, as Law asks, " Now how is it possible, that such a

scene as this should be fit for the entertainment of Christians? Can Venus and her Graces and Pleasures talk any language that is like themselves, but what must be unlike the spirit of Christianity? "

A similar spirit is expressed in a few other pamphlets. A play, no matter how moral in intention and instructive in fable, is represented in a spirit of frivolity, and the gaiety of the stage is considered inconsistent with the spirit of that religion which commands us to crucify the flesh and to turn away the eyes from vanity.[1]

Such a spirit offered, of course, no basis for a compromise, and had it animated the bulk of the people, not even a Steele could have been effectual, for it would have been logically necessary not only that the theaters be closed but that the "Spectator" itself be suppressed. In reply to ascetic objections, one could only translate a play like Racine's "Esther" and call attention to its innocence, or summon the authority of some devotee as Motteux did that of the Rev. Father Caffaro, whose opinions concerning the usefulness of a theoretically perfect stage Motteux printed as a preface to "Beauty in Distress" (1698).[2] Caffaro thought that the actual stage was for the most part lewd and immoral, but that there was no fundamental objection to the institution. Holy Writ, he says, is silent on the subject, and hence one may fall back upon reason. He cites the authority of Thomas Aquinas, who ranks play-going among lawful diversions. To this it was replied [3] that if the Bible does not specifically condemn

---

[1] *Conduct of the Stage. Some Considerations on the Danger of Going to Plays.*

[2] Caffaro was an Italian Monk and a Professor of the University of Paris. He had retracted his opinions in favor of the theater in 1694.

[3] *The Stage Condemn'd.*

plays it does so implicitly, for if plays teach immorality, then no one can defend them, and if they teach morality, they are nevertheless bad, for God has appointed other means for the teaching of morality, and " that which God hath appointed sufficient means to accomplish it is unlawful for men to appoint other means to accomplish."

It does considerable credit to the perspicacity of John Dennis that he saw more clearly than anyone else that such ideas lay at the back of even Collier's mind; that quibbles such as Congreve and Vanbrugh indulged in got nowhere; and that had they proved their plays as innocent as they wished, Collier and Bedford would have still found abundant cause for disapproval. Dennis saw that there was involved a fundamental question of the value of pleasure, and he set himself to formulate a moral but anti-ascetic philosophy. He maintains that pleasure is not in itself an evil, but that mankind lives for happiness. And happiness, he says, is concerned with the passions and comes only through such exercise of them as does not result in a conflict with the will. Since, then, happiness comes only through the rational exercise of the passions, to destroy them as the ascetics demand is to make happiness impossible. Drama arouses the rational passions, and is therefore useful to the happiness of mankind. A man who is familiar with the theater is less easily moved than one who is not, and therefore to say that the drama unduly stimulates the passions is false, for the theater-goer is less likely than another to be swept away by irrational emotion. It is true that plays may stimulate pride, but a good play will stimulate only a good sort of pride, for pride is not always sinful, but may, as in the case of patriotism, constitute a virtue. The question of love he also meets squarely. Only a bad play will encourage lawless love, but to encourage virtuous love is to perform a service rather than, as some would have it, to stimulate a vice.[1]

Aside from the general consideration of the antipathy between the stage and the spirit of Christianity, the reformer made much of the specific objections which had been offered at different times by the pagan philosophers and the church. Collier had emphasized the fact that in the early church players had been excommunicated, and that Lactantius, Augustine, Ambrose, and others had shown hostility, while Tertullian had devoted a whole treatise, " De Spectaculis," to the subject. The latter is, in fact, Tertullian's most famous work, for it contains the passage, made famous by Gibbon, in which is described the joy which the saved experience in watching the tortures of the damned. To the modern mind some of the Father's arguments seem somewhat far-fetched, as when he mentions the depreciation of God involved when we lift up to him hands which have applauded a player, or finds that to wear the tragic buskins is to defy that text which denies the possibility of adding a cubit to one's stature. Still Tertullian was not one whit more fantastic than Bedford, and Congreve and Wycherley were solemnly brought up before Tertullian for judgment.

This argument from authority was a favorite one and was taken up by many. The writings of the pagan philosophers as well as the Church Fathers, and the records of all the church councils, were ransacked for statements unfavorable to the stage, and an impressive collection was gathered by huddling together everything from blanket condemnations of the dramatist and all his works down to statements as mild as that of Aristotle, who, though he had written the most famous treatise on the drama, did

[1] *The Usefulness of the Stage,* etc. and *The Stage Acquitt'd* advance similar arguments.

remark that the young should not be allowed to see comedies.   One writer [1] cites sixteen church councils which occurred between 305 and 1617, all of which disapproved in some way of the stage.   The violence of the decrees ranges all the way from that of a council in Africa in 409 which proclaimed that "Stage plays are against the commandments of God" (which is certainly strong enough) to that pronounced at Cologne in 1549, which went no further than to forbid comedies in nunneries. Attention is also called to the fact that in England Bradwardine "wrote against the stage in 1345," that Wycliff in his "De Causa Dei" records his disapproval of plays, and that Archbishop Parker in "De Antiquitate Ecclesiae" says "that stage plays are not to be suffer'd in any Christian or well govern'd commonwealth."   Among more recent English ecclesiastics, Baxter, Wesley and Dr. Horneck had spoken against the stage.

To most of these arguments from authority there was some sort of answer.   The theater was pagan in its origin, and the Fathers opposed it only for this reason, since they feared the fostering of pagan influence through the continuation of a pagan institution, but they could have had no possible objection to a properly managed Christian drama.[2]   Dennis attacks the authority of the Fathers, and asks Collier roundly whether he is Catholic or Protestant, and how, if he is the latter, he can presume to cite the authority of the Fathers as inspired.   If they were not inspired, then their opinions were subject to revision in the light of reason.   To this Collier could only reply that they were not inspired, but that their purity of character made them the next thing to it.

[1] George Ridpath (?). *The Stage Condemn'd*, etc.
[2] Dennis. *Usefulness of the Stage*, etc.

The arguments taken from the pagan philosophers were likely to turn out double edged. One writer had called attention to the fact that Ovid recommended the theater as a favorable place in which to seek for a mistress, whereupon another pointed out that if this was to be considered conclusive, then it ought to be remembered that it involved the church also, for Ovid had mentioned the temple as the next best place. If Plato's republic was to be taken as a model, then it must be remembered that he advocated a community of women as well as the expulsion of actors.[1]

More significant than such quibblings was the argument of the defenders of plays that, since the pagan stage was not at all the same thing as the modern one, no opinions concerning the former had any weight. The old shows were admittedly immoral and scandalous, and Collier and others, in citing the opinions of the ancients concerning them, had confused pantomime and the spectacles of the arena with the drama, though there was no similarity between them. Much learned quibbling followed as to what might and what might not be fairly translated as "theater" or "play." Most of all this was irrelevant. .The many pages of quotations from ancient writers might have made a good history of the opinions of antiquity concerning the classical stage, but they had little to do with what English people should think of their theater. Its condition offered a good problem to a critic, and Collier showed at first some disposition to consider it, but he and his enemies and friends continually wandered off into the, for them, easier field of pedantry, and were constantly harking back to Greece and Rome, and leaving Wycherley and Congreve in order to argue over Plautus and Terence.

Next in importance to the attitude of the church was the

---

[1] Edward Filmer. *A Defense of Plays.*

attitude of the state. Historical citations showed that
from ancient times to the present, the stage had been frequently subject to regulation and at times to suppression.
Constantine, the first of the Christian emperors, is said
to have abolished it.[1] Other writers pointed out that this
did not outweigh the fact that it had been usually at least
tolerated.[2]

Collier and Bedford were of course members of the
Church of England,[3] and it cannot but have been a thorn in
their side that opposition to the stage in England had been
most closely connected with the Puritans. Collier had been
already accused of disloyalty, and this gave point to Cibber's remark: " I think the last time they pull'd down the
stage in the city, they set up a scaffold at court."[4] Accordingly, probably neither Collier nor Bedford was much
pleased by the elaborate book " The Stage Condemn'd "
(probably by George Ridpath) in which the whole controversy is moved to the political plane, and that corrupt
institution, the theater, traced directly to popery and the
Church of England. Ridpath was a violent Whig. He
assumes that the stage is damnable, but lays the blame
for its existence on the clergy, and declares that Collier's
abuse of the stage is inconsistent with his allegiance to
the Stuarts who encouraged it. He points out that though
Tertullian, Jerome, Ambrose, and other lesser known
Fathers attacked the stage, Laud and his associates left
it to the Puritan Prynne to speak against this great evil,
while they promulgated the Book of Sports, and that

[1] *Stage Condemn'd.*

[2] Filmer.

[3] Collier was a non-juror. Hence it would be more accurate to
say that he had been a member of the Church of England. At
least, his sympathies would not be with the dissenters.

[4] Preface to *Love Makes a Man.*

Charles I, whom Collier must regard as a saint, held a mask on Sunday in which Imposture appeared in the guise of a Puritan. Ridpath holds the school system equally blamable with the court. Origen declares that those of an amorous turn should avoid reading the Canticles, yet these are read in schools, where the heathen poets, who were inspired by Satan to advocate wickedness, are also read. His implied remedy, is of course, a return to Puritanism. Ridpath's is the spirit that smashed organs and knocked the heads off the statues in Gothic cathedrals. Prynne is his ideal, and the latter's appalling book, in which few modern readers have been able to get beyond the portentous title page, he praises as being " perhaps the largest, learned, and most elaborate " that has ever been written on the subject.

Ridpath was replied to in " The Stage Acquitted," where the author neatly reverses his argument. Ridpath had said, in effect, that plays were bad, that the English Government and Church had continuously encouraged them, and that therefore the English Government and Church were bad. His opponent says that the Church and Government have encouraged plays, that the Church and Government are good, and that therefore plays are good. St. Charles is as good, he maintains, as St. Chrysostom. As to Wesley, Horneck, and the others, they have spoken only of the abuses of the stage. Properly regulated drama, he maintains, teaches morality; and consequently a friend of virtue must defend it. Its value, he says, depends entirely on the manner in which you take it. St. Paul read plays to get morality, for he takes his famous phrase " Evil communication corrupts good manners " from a Greek play. Collier would do well to follow his example instead of reading them in order to collect smut. As to Prynne, he was an enemy of the church and the state as well as of the theater. Ridpath, he maintains in conclusion, has only succeeded in proving that various vicious men have attacked the stage.

Dennis (to whom Ridpath replies) had already attempted to settle the question of the relation of the state and the theater by reference to general principles which are laid down in his " The Usefulness of the Stage, etc." The abuses, he admits, are so great that there is a necessity for reforming them; and he declares that he would have praised Collier for his attack had Collier not in his last chapter showed himself the enemy of the stage itself, whereas it is, Dennis maintains, useful not only to religion and morality but also directly to the state. Public diversions are necessary for the contentment of the people, and, consequently, for the safety of the state. The theater is the best possible public diversion. In Greece, Rome, France, and England the period of the best national drama coincides with the period of the greatest national glory. Plays chastise the passions, show the disastrous effects of bad government and public tumult, and inspire patriotism and a noble union in the face of public enemies. The English people are by nature more inclined to tumult than any other, and consequently more particularly in need of the stage. Collier perhaps wished to suppress the stage in order more easily to foment the rebellion.

Such discussion of the expediency or inexpediency of permitting a theoretically perfect stage left untouched Collier's indictment of the vices of contemporary plays, an indictment which his followers had made more and more sweeping. The defenders, practically without exception, admitted there was much to be amended, but they had to concern themselves first of all with a defense of the stage from the condemnation *in toto*, and usually admitted with Dennis " there is no defending the immoral-

ity, or immodesty, or unnecessary profaneness of some
of our plays." They merely wished to prove that plays
might be innocent for, as Cibber said,[1] the lawyers and
clergymen of the Restoration had not been above reproach,
and if they were to be allowed to reform, why should not
the players be given an equal opportunity? Perhaps the
opinion of the largest number of pamphleteers could be
summarized thus: " There may be an innocent representation of persons and actions in a dramatic way; yet play-
houses as they have been, and generally are managed,
ought not to be frequented by Christians."[2]

Laying aside, then, the question as to whether or not
the stage was, in itself, essentially evil, we find the pamphleteers engaged in discussing just where the actual
contemporary comedies were evil, and attempting to lay
down the laws which should embody the characteristics of
innocent or instructive drama. Practically nothing new is
added to Collier's general charges against prevailing conditions, but while many of those who wished to defend the
stage were inclined to admit that there were grounds
for these charges in many cases, they saw, nevertheless,
that the method of procedure used by Bedford and others
led simply to finding blasphemy and irreligion in every
representation of life, and saw the necessity of drawing
the line so as to admit of the representation of evil on
the stage. Clearly, if you were to have bad men in your
plays, you could not represent them talking like saints,
yet if swearing and blasphemy are put into plays, it must
be to show the ridiculousness of evil men. Smut, said
Filmer, is not dangerous in itself, nor is swearing a contempt of God if it is shown in a vicious character. If the
stage is to castigate faults, it must show them. But Collier

[1] Preface to *Love Makes a Man.*
[2] *Conduct of the Stage.*

would have none of this. Profaneness, he said, is pernicious even if it is punished. It is a crime in itself, "the
bare pronouncing makes the crime; the guilt sticks upon
the syllables, and 'tis a sin in the sound." The poets protested that they did not speak for themselves, but this he
called no defense.[1] You would not swear before a lady,
he said; to which Filmer replied that if nothing happened
on the stage but what might happen in a drawing room,
you could have no drama. Nor could you have had any
drama which would please Collier.

Similar reply and counter-reply occupied themselves
with Collier's objection that the playwrights made vicious
characters triumphant heroes. Vanbrugh and Congreve
urged that it was unfair to attach to themselves the senti-
ments of their heroes, or to suppose that an author necessarily approved of all that his characters said. Realism
demanded that playwrights show persons as they were,
and vices must be depicted if they were to be satirized.
Of course their characters are vicious, for Aristotle says
that comedy is the imitation of the worst sort of people,
and that it is the purpose of comedy to laugh them out of
their vices. The examples are put there not for imitation
but for caution.[2] But Collier was not content, for, he said[3]
that the dramatist "treats loose characters with sense and
respect, provokes to imitation, and makes infection
catching."

Collier's insistence that the nobility and clergy should
be exempt from satire also aroused much discussion. If
there were evil clergymen, why, it was asked, should they
not be ridiculed? After all, the wicked parson is the

[1] *Further Vindication of the Short View*, etc.
[2] Drake. *Ancient and Modern Stages Surveyed.*
[3] *A Second Defense of the Short View*, etc.

most dangerous villain on earth, it was argued;[1] and until virtue comes to be conferred along with the title, there is no reason why one should not present a foolish or evil nobleman on the stage.[2]

In fact, says Drake, only evil or ridiculous noblemen have any right in comedy. Filmer makes the curious point that no Anglican priest should be ridiculed upon the stage, but that this exemption does not apply to dissenters. To Collier's statement that the clergy should be shown in plays only when surrounded by worldly power and respect, Vanbrugh answered scornfully that it must then be concluded "that Christ and his Apostles took the thing by the wrong handle, and that the Pope and his Cardinals have much refin'd upon 'em in the policy of instruction."

Some writers fell back on the pure argument of realism. There was nothing, they maintained, in plays that could not be matched in life,[3] and the corruption of the times was not due to plays, which only reflected what already existed.[4] " Plays were ever counted the genuine history of the age; and if their opposers wou'd have innocent entertainment, and leave poetry honorable example for imitation and instruction, 'tis but each amending himself; then not the little but the great stage of life, will be so reform'd, and in a state more suitable to wish, than possible to life."[5] Vanbrugh put the argument for instruction through realism very neatly as follows: " The stage is a glass for the world to view itself in; people ought therefore to see themselves as they are; if it makes their faces too fair,

---

[1] *Immorality of the English Pulpit,* etc.
[2] Drake. *Ancient and Modern Stages Surveyed,* etc.
[3] Thomas Baker. *An Act at Oxford.*
[4] Dennis. *Usefulness of the Stage,* etc.
[5] *An Act at Oxford.*

they won't know they are dirty, and by consequence will neglect to wash 'em."

The difficulty of the simple argument that whatever is in life may be in literature was that, unless it could be proved that such realism tended to make people virtuous, it went directly contrary to the cardinal doctrine of pseudo-classical criticism, that the purpose of literature is to teach virtue, and that it does this by showing life not as it is but as it ought to be. The old dramatists defended themselves sometimes by refusing to admit the validity of this principle, but the practical playwrights of the early eighteenth century assumed, on the other hand, the conventional critical attitude. I have already pointed out in an earlier chapter how under the Restoration the ideal of the dramatist was that of realism, wit, and polish, but as a result of the conflict which I have been describing the dramatists themselves took up a completely new attitude, so that not only the moralists but the dramatic critic and the playwright himself assumed as fundamental the moral purpose of the drama. That idea, which had, as it were, lain dormant and confined to pseudo-classical theory, became the leading principle not only of popular critics like Dennis and Addison but also of the most successful dramatists like Steele and Cibber. Dennis falls back on pure-pseudo-classical theory. "A Dramatic Fable," he says, "is a discourse invented to form the manners by instruction disguised under the allegory of an action;"[1] and from Dacier he borrows the idea that tragedy is but a sugar-coated pill for those who cannot swallow pure philosophy.

With this principle universally admitted, there remains still the question how plays were to be constructed to fulfill their purpose. In the case of tragedy it was compara-

[1] *Stage Defended*, etc.

tively easy. The downfall of the evil characters and the traditional speeches full of philosophy and morality might be fairly considered as constituting moral instruction. But with comedy it was different. It had to represent, as Aristotle said, the worst sort of people, and its theory demanded that it should provoke laughter. How was this to be made instructive? The Restoration Comedy writers had, when pushed, declared that they wrote for instruction, but the reformers failed to consider their works edifying and practically all the defenders of the stage admitted that the old comedy was full of abuses and that if the stage was to be defended it must be reformed. The enemies of the stage said that the vicious characters which had been represented uttered smut and blasphemy, that they seemed frequently to be marked out not for contempt but for admiration and imitation, and that certainly they did not make for virtue. Dennis, it is true, maintained that such plays as " Sir Fopling Flutter " were satirically instructive, but not many theorists agreed with him. Some new method must be found.

The easiest solution seemed to lie in the old doctrine of poetic justice, which all agreed might be applied to tragedy. Might it not be extended to comedy? Filmer, in one of the most elaborate discussions of the stage, maintained the doctrine unconditionally. The stage should be reformed, he said, not as Collier would have it, by the abolition of vicious characters, but by rendering the example of such characters instructive by " a constant proportionate reward of virtue, and punishment of vice;" and this, as we shall see later, was exactly what Steele advocated and practiced. Dennis, though he was an advocate of poetic justice in tragedy, would not admit that it was applicable to comedy. The method of comedy, he said, falling back again upon a doctrine taken from pseudo-classicism, was to punish vices only by means of the laughter which the audience directed against them. Just what position was arrived at and put into practice will be seen in the two concluding chapters, which deal with the new drama and the theory behind it. At present we are more directly concerned with the controversy which voiced the protest against the old comedy.

I have had occasion to mention by name by no means all of the forty-odd items listed in the bibliography of the literature of this controversy. I have, however, found and read all except those marked with an asterisk,[1] and, as the various books and pamphlets involve endless repetition, I think that they contain no point of view not alluded to. Their interest lies chiefly in their bulk, which shows how enduring was the interest in the questions involved, and in the variety of their methods of presentation, which shows that every class was appealed to. Collier's book contains something of interest to nearly every class. Others were more special. Only readers fond of rather heavy speculation could have been interested by the treatises of Filmer or Dennis; and only the pedantically pious would have understood much of Bedford's book, so overladen with the imposing pedantry of endless citation. But on the other hand there were a large number of unpretentious pamphlets, such as " Mr. Collier's Dissuasive from the Play House, etc.," or " Some Consideration about the Dangers of Going to Plays," in which journalists and popular preachers presented in brief and simple form the charges against the stage. If we add to them Steele's papers, to be discussed later, it is evident that every class was addressed, and that no class failed to take some interest in the question of the stage. If we remember, also, that hardly a writer fails to admit that something might be

[1] See Bibliography.

said against plays as they were constituted, it is easy to see that there existed a spirit of dissatisfaction that was bound to react on the theater. The general public was familiar with three questions: Is the theater a permissible institution? Is it its duty to teach morality? Can comedies best teach morality by administering Poetic Justice?

CHAPTER VII

THE REFORMATION OF MANNERS AND THE STAGE

THAT the attack on the stage came at an opportune moment when a movement toward a reform in life and a change of tone in literature had already begun has been stated, though not yet illustrated. In 1698 the reformation of manners was already an old story, but the reformation of literature was newer, and obviously the two movements were closely connected. But as Collier's attack came early in the literary movement, one is faced with the problem of determining to what extent he is responsible for it, and how far he may be said to be responsible for the change which took place in the drama. Most historians of the stage have been inclined to attribute to him a large share of whatever credit may be due for transforming a brilliant but immoral tradition into a dull and moral one. It was the orthodox view of the eighteenth and nineteenth centuries that he was largely responsible. In the early eighteenth century any mention of the reform of the stage (as in the " Comparison of the Two Stages ") was likely to be linked with his name. Cibber says that his work had a very wholesome effect; Davies says that the dramatists, " though unwilling to reform themselves, at last found, in Collier, a severe but just corrector of their indecencies and blasphemy." " The physic he administered," Davies continues, " was so powerful, that a sudden and almost effectual reformation took place." [1] Nichols [2] remarks that " it

[1] Dramatic Miscellanies. Vol. III.
[2] Literary Anecdotes. Vol. I, p. 342 n.

is allowed on all hands, that the decorum which has been for the most part observed by the later writers of dramatic poetry is entirely owing to the animadversions of Collier "; and Macaulay (as usual) goes the whole way, both in the " Comic Dramatists of the Restoration " and in the " History of England." In the former he remarks that " A great and rapid reform in all the departments of our lighter literature was the effect of his labors," and in the latter that " he is well entitled to grateful and respectful mention; for to his eloquence and courage is to be chiefly ascribed the purification of our lighter literature from that foul taint which had been contracted during the Antipuritan reaction."

But a startling difference of opinion now exists. The average seeker after light on this subject would turn naturally to Ward's " History of English Dramatic Poetry " and to " The Cambridge History of English Literature," but if he did so he would be much puzzled, for in the former he would read: " In truth, the position in which he (Collier) stood . . . . had been proved impregnable. From this time forward a marked change becomes visible both in the attitude of the Court, Government, and of a section at least of the ruling classes, towards the stage, and in its own consciousness of the purposes and restrictions proper to the exercise of its art; "[1] and in Mr. Whibley's chapter in the Cambridge History[2] he would read: " The poets bowed their knee not an inch in obedience to Collier. They replied to him, they abused him, and they went their way. Congreve's true answer was not his Amendments but The Way of the World. . . . The pages of Genest . . . make evident the complete failure of Collier's attack." To add still further to the confusion of the authorities, it may be

[1] Vol. III.
[2] Vol. VIII.

added that Beljame also regards " The Way of the World "
and " The Provok'd Husband " as in a way answers to
Collier, but that, unlike Whibley, he thinks that in them
the authors " se montrèrent plus retenus qu'ils ne l'avaient
été jusque-là."

From what has been said of Collier's position, it is obvious that Ward's statement that it was impregnable cannot be true unless we admit that the position that the stage
is inherently damnable is impregnable, and, on the other
hand, if as Mr. Whibley maintains, the attack failed completely, we must find some other explanation for the change
which certainly did take place about this time, and which
at least produced a new species of comedy if it did not
immediately annihilate the old. Ward certainly has tradition on his side, but before we can come to a conclusion,
three questions will have to be considered. First, we
must determine to what extent a general reform movement
existed, aside from the Collier controversy. Second, we
must inquire how much conviction Collier and his party
carried, and how much action they aroused. Third, we
must analyze just what happened to the dramatic tradition
and discover just when it happened. The present chapter
will be concerned with the first two of these questions, and
the next with the third.

The orgy of dissipation into which the ruling class
plunged after the Restoration could not possibly last.
England was not, like the Roman Empire, decadent and
hence destined to wear itself out and die. The mass of
the people was still probably even narrowly pious, pru-
dent, and sane, and the condition at the court itself was the
result rather of a triumph over a party which had made
virtue hateful than of a radical decay. As the effects of
the reaction passed, English moderation naturally reas-
serted itself. As long as the Merry Monarch lived, the

tradition of debauchery would have a strong support; but when he had died and James had run his brief and contemptible career as libertine and bigot, William brought a new age. No adjective could be less applicable to him than " merry." Saturnine and able, he cared nothing for literature or for the stage, which had occupied so much of Charles' thought. He was not to be seen with Tom D'Urfey on his shoulder, he did not forgive incompetence and corruption because of an able wit. Mary was fond of plays, and had at least sufficient leniency to admire Congreve, but she was also interested in reform, and wanton indecency could no longer look for support and example at court. Libertinism was naturally becoming less fashionable. As time passed, the social tradition probably changed more rapidly than the dramatic, and the plays of 1685 mirrored more truly court ideals than did those of 1695, which followed preceding drama rather than actual life.

Besides its influence on the social life of the upper class, the revolution had another effect. It tended to give the middle class a new importance in government and hence helped it to a voice in literary matters. Books and the theater became less and less the affair only of the aristocracy; and the middle class, which was not only more regular in life but also less capable of regarding literature with moral detachment, made its influence felt. Early in the eighteenth century, at least, it found voice in the newspapers of Defoe and of Tutchin.

The middle class is inclined to care more for what is said than for the manner of saying it, and with the passing of the seventeenth century passed also the age of pure wit. The Restoration prided itself especially on polish and sophistication, and no quality was prized above that of saying a sharp thing. It was willing to forgive the im-

morality of a play if it could be sure of its brilliance.
Even Mary, so Cibber tells us, though she disapproved
strongly of "The Rover" witnessed it because of her
admiration for the brilliant acting of the man who played
the hero.

The age of Anne also admired the power of expression,
but it wanted morality in addition. Pope is very different
from Congreve and Rochester, and Steele's success in his
plan to moralize wit was too complete not to show that
people were no longer satisfied with mere brillance if it
outraged their sense of propriety. The merits of the Restoration Comedy had been purely intellectual ones. The
merit of polish had become a sufficient excuse for all
things. As Wolseley had said, wit might be just as good
in treating a filthy subject as in treating a clean one.
Moderation, however, began to assert itself, and there arose
a controversy on the subject of wit which throws considerable light on the intellectual movement of the times.
"Solid men" were exasperated by the supreme tribute
paid to brilliance, and the serious-minded tended to depre-
ciate paradox. As early as 1695 the satire "A Reflection
on our Modern Poetry" entered a protest. The dedication points out that "Poetry is no longer a fit trainer up
of youth, a bridler of the passions, and exorbitant desires:
But on the contrary, he is reckoned to be the ablest poet,
that is most dexterous, at crying up these evil spirits, to
disturb the calm and quiet of the soul." Sir Richard
Blackmore rose as a representative of that class in which
moderation was somewhat closely related to dullness, and
became the arch enemy of wit. Wit had, indeed, become
almost a disease with which everyone was infected. No
character in comedy is more frequent than that of the
empty-headed beau who sets up for a wit, and the more
moderate part of society was not wholly wrong in feeling

that truth was being neglected in the worship of epigram
and paradox.   The distemper, we learn from a play,[1]
spread in the town like the itch, so that even the tradesman
had caught it, and would rather offend his customers than
stifle a jest.

Sir Richard Blackmore was a physician, and so he
undertook to cure the general disease, beginning with " A
Satyr against Wit " (1700) in which he writes:

> " Who can forbear and tamely silent sit;
> And see his native land undone by wit.
>
> *   *   *   *   *   *   *
>
> " How happy were the old unpolished times
> As free from wit as other modern crimes?
>
> *   *   *   *   *   *   *
>
> They justly wit and fool believ'd the same,
> And jester was for both the common name.
> The mob of wit is up to storm the town,
> And pull all virtue and right reason down.
> Quite to subvert religion's sacred fence
> To set up wit, and pull down common sense."

He received a satiric reply from the wits, but found others
willing to share his views.   Dennis, who was emphatically
not a wit, and is said to have hated a pun above everything
else, is driven to exclaim: " That it is not wit, but reason
which distinguishes a man of sense from a fool." [2]   The
" True Born Englishman " is not a wit and so one is not
surprised to find Defoe writing in " The Pacificator ":

> " The men of sense against the men of wit,
> Eternal fighting must determine it,"

or to see that in his extraordinary " The History of the
Devil " he refers, in a chapter heading, to the wits as the
devil's " particular modern privy counsellors."

[1] *Epistle Dedicatory* to *The Comical Gallant.*   1702.
[2] Baker.   *The Humor of the Age.*   1701.

There is a real significance in this controversy over wit versus sense. The age of Anne was an age of reason, not only in its opposition to mysticism, but also in its reaction against the physically and politically destructive moral anarchy of the Restoration. In a criticism of Fletcher's " The Scornful Lady " Steele attacks hotly the " corruption of mind, that makes men resent offenses against their virtue, less than those against their understanding. An author shall write as if he thought that there was not one man of honor or woman of chastity in the house, and come off with applause; for an insult upon all the ten commandments with the little critic is not so bad as the breach of unity of time and place." Again: " A thing which is blamable in itself, grows still more so by the success in the execution of it." This is, of course, a direct denial of Wolseley's doctrine. Blackmore returned to the attack in a prose essay [1] where he attempted to consider the subject philosophically. Wit he treats as a dangerous indulgence which is often the enemy of truth and encourages a distaste for intellectual pursuits. The men most characterized by its possession, he says, are often lacking in prudence, and more likely than others to fall into debauchery. Parents are warned to encourage their children in intellectual pursuits instead of refining their conversation. All this would have seemed the most barbaric heresy to a Restoration gallant proud of England's new-found urbanity. But it represented the spirit of the new age, and mere wit disappears rapidly from the drama as the eighteenth century advances. Addison in " The Freeholder " [2] replies to Blackmore, but goes only so far as to maintain the value of properly directed raillery.

The final flower of middle-class protests against all

[1] Published in *Essays upon Several Subjects*. 1716.
[2] No. 45. May 25, 1716.

glitter not strictly sensible is found in the so-called Bourgeois Tragedy.   This is usually supposed to begin with
Lillo's "George Barnwell" (1731), but it had its fore-
runner in earlier comedy, which expressed the ideals of
the middle class.   In the early days when the theater had
been only an amusement of the upper class, the bourgeois
was not particularly concerned, but in the literature of the
Collier controversy there is much stress on the ill effect of
plays upon the middle class, and the theater is attacked
not only on strictly moral grounds but also on the charge
that it tends to undermine the industry and application
necessary for success in trade.   In this connection especial
interest attaches to a few sentences which occur in the
essay "Of Plays and Masquerades."[1]   "They [plays]
give a wrong notion of things, they undermine industry by
representing life in a more romantic aspect than is actually
true and thus give the mind a distaste of all that is common — how odd a turn is this for a man who must keep
plodding on, with a mind intent upon his business, and be
contented to drive as it will go?"   Collier might speak
for the learnedly religious, but here is the authentic voice
of a nation of shop keepers.   Eighteenth-century comedy
tries to meet this objection by stressing the more ordinary
virtues, and "George Barnwell" makes a definite appeal
to the middle class by insisting on the virtue of the mer-
chant and the nobility of his trade.

During the Collier controversy, the middle class, because of its predisposition, lent support to the reformers
of the stage.   It found voice in Defoe and Tutchin, both
of whom conducted political newspapers.   The latter was
particularly violent, declaring that the play house was the

[1] Published in *A Collection of the Occasional Papers for the year
1708*, an anonymous collection of moralizing essays by various authors.

devil's chapel,[1] and Defoe in his writings makes many references to the theater. He advocates the suppression of acting and the purchase of the theater by funds raised among the pious,[2] but he is not always, however, so violent. He devoted a whole number of " A Review, etc." [3] to a discussion of the opening of the new theater in the Haymarket, and while entirely unsatisfied with the performance which he saw there, rightly enough undertook to lay the blame rather on the public than upon the actors or playwrights. More sensibly than most of the reformers he writes as follows: " But, gentlemen and ladies, if you would have a reformation in the play house, you must reform your taste of wit, and let the poet see, you can relish a play, tho' there be neither baudry nor blasphemy in it." He urges the audience to show its disapproval of any improprieties no matter how wittily expressed, and continues: " I cannot be without so much charity for our players, as to believe this of them: They cannot be men of action, without being men of sense, and as they are the latter, they could not but be as well pleased with what was clean, handsome and well perform'd, when it came from the pure channel of honor and virtue, as from the black Stygian lake of nastiness and corruption, — in short, the errors of the stage lie all in the auditory; the actors, and the poets, are their honorable servants, and being good judges of what will please, are forced to write and

[1] See *The Observator,* March, 1703. Also Vol. I, 95 and Vol. II, 40, 57, 59, 78, 90, 91.

[2] Wilson's " Life of Defoe," Vol. III, p. 69. In *An Account of some remarkable passages in the life of a private gentleman* etc. (1708) sometimes incorrectly attributed to Defoe, the hero complains of his wicked companion who " seduced me to see a play " and then proceeds to a sort of summary of Collier's charges against the theater.

[3] Vol. II, No. 26.

act with all the aggravation and excesses possible, that they may not be undone and ruin'd, lose both their reputation and their employment." [1]

From what has been said in a previous chapter it will be evident that the beginning of the general protest against the completely unethical attitude towards literature antedated Collier's attack on the stage, but that it was intensified by that attack and was hardly prominent before it. The movement for the reformation of actual manners is traceable considerably further back. It found its most tangible expression in the " Societies for the Reformation of Manners," organizations of enthusiasts which existed for many years, and about which there gathers a truly impressive bulk of printed matter, though their history has never been written in modern times. Burnet mentions them, and Lecky takes his short account mainly from secondary sources. The best contemporary history is " An Account of the Rise and Progress of the Religious Societies in the City of London and of their endeavors for reformation of manners," by the Rev. Josiah Woodward, which reached what was called the sixth edition in 1744.

The beginning of the Societies for the Reformation of Manners is obscure, but it is bound up with that of certain " Religious Societies " which had a less definitely practical purpose. Burnet traces the origin of the latter societies to the reign of James II, when a fear of popery led to gatherings of religious persons similar to those which had been held formerly only among the dissenters. After the Revolution, Burnet continues, these societies deter-

---

[1] Swift cared nothing for the theater, but in *A Project for the Advancement of Religion and the Reformation of Manners* (1709) devotes a paragraph to the stage. His tone would indicate that he had read Collier with approval although the name is not mentioned.

mined to inform magistrates of the names of swearers, drunkards, profaners of the Sabbath, keepers of lewd houses, etc., and hence they came to be called "Societies of Reformation." In the beginning, he says, they were conducted chiefly by Dr. Beveridge and Dr. Horneck, and he adds that as soon as Queen Mary heard of them she encouraged the good work by letter and proclamation.

The information given in "An Account of the Rise and Progress of the Religious Societies, etc." (1744) [1] does not differ materially from that of Burnet except that it places the origin of the societies as far back as 1678 and mentions the aid of Bishop Stillingfleet in enlisting the sympathy of Queen Mary. One hears most about the societies in the early years of the eighteenth century, but the "Proposal for a National Reformation of Manners, — also the Black Roll, containing the names and crimes of several hundred persons who have been prosecuted by the Society, for whoring, drunkenness, Sabbath-breaking, etc., published by the Society for the Reformation, etc.," published in 1694, shows that they were very active in the nineties. In another account of the Society published in 1701 its members are described as consisting of four different groups: One of parliament members, justices of the peace and the like; a second which occupies itself chiefly against lewd houses of which 500 are said to have been suppressed; a third consisting of constables; and a fourth consisting of young men banded together for the purpose of giving information. As its beginning, so the end of the Society was obscure. It flourished mightily for a number of years, and seems

[1] I do not know when the first account of the Societies was published, but the second edition of "An Account of the Rise and Progress of Religious Societies in the City of London etc.," is entered in the Stationer's Register for 1698, and there is a so-called 14th edition in 1706.

to have become more and more closely associated with the Methodist movement, for it is said that in 1763 nearly half of its members were of that sect.[1]

At any rate it lived and flourished until the close of the period we are considering, and, whatever its origin and conclusion, created a tremendous stir in the life of the period. To give even a bibliography of the large number of publications which it called forth, such as sermons preached before the societies, remonstrances and admonitions to magistrates, pleas for a general reformation, etc., would occupy more space than we have at our disposal. Further mention of the Society may be found in the various editions of Chamberlayne's " Angliae Notitia, or the Present Stage of England." The Societies were, apparently, not confined to London, but spread to various provincial cities also.

They depended as much on coercion as on persuasion, and were determined to " prove their doctrine orthodox, by apostolic blows and knocks." Their habit of acting as informers seems to have aroused some scruples against such methods, which find expression in a sermon preached 1709 by the famous Dr. Sacheverell,[2] who speaks of good nature and compassion and asks: " Do not these as strictly command us not to thrust ourselves pragmatically into his [our neighbor's] business, or meddle with those concerns that do not belong to us, or under the sanctify'd pretense of reformation of manners, to turn informer, assume an odious and factitious office, arrogantly entrench upon other's Christian liberty, and innocence and under show of more zeal than purity — turn the world upside

[1] See Tyerman's *Life and Times of Samuel Wesley.* Tyerman says that from 1730 to 1757 the Society was inactive, but the British Museum contains a 43rd Annual Report for the year 1738.

[2] *The Communication of Sin.*

down, and all mankind into quarrels and confusions? "
But the peppery Doctor no doubt smelled dissent under
the more-pious-than-thou attitude. He was replied to in
more than one pamphlet,[1] and the work of reformation
went merrily on. The story [2] of a holy war in Lincolnshire
is amusing. It seems that even in Cromwell's days it had
been impossible to break up the custom of spending the
three Sundays after Lammas in horse racing and other
diversions, but that certain serious minded persons gathered
together an army of parsons, constables, and others, so
strong " that the whole multitude were over-awed and
put to flight, — so that on such Lord's days, when there
used to be many hundreds of this lewd mob, you could
only have beheld several decent ministers with their constables walking around; or, if any vain person looked that
way, their care was, to flee with such speed as might secure
themselves from apprehension."

The Society acted in a vigorous and wholesale fashion,
and had a passion for statistics. Tract distribution was
one of its activities, and by 1720 upward of 400,000 tracts
are said to have been distributed. Prosecution of the profane and scandalous became a sort of popular sport, and
we find little hand-books of instructions for informers and
magistrates, in which the laws against profaneness and
blank forms for informing are published, along with cau-
tionary rules for the safe practice of the diversion. A
folio sheet which was published is also interesting. It is
called: " A sixth black list of the names and reputed

[1] " Remarks upon a sermon preached by Dr. Henry Sachaverell at
the assizes held at Derby . . . containing a just and moderate
defense of the Society for the Reformation of Manners, etc." (1711);
" The Judgment of H. Sachaverell concerning Societies for Reformation of Manners, compared with the judgment of many of
the Lords, etc." (1711).

[2] Published-in the 1744 Edition of *An Account* etc.

names of 843 lewd and scandalous persons, who, by the
endeavors of a society, for promoting a reformation of
manners in the City of London and suburbs thereof, have
been legally prosecuted and convicted — all of which (besides the prosecution of many notorious cursers, swearers,
Sabbath-breakers, and drunkards, not here included) have
been effected by the Society aforesaid, since the printing
of the former list, which consisted of 3,859 persons."
Similar lists were apparently published annually for a
number of years, and we learn from the one for the year
ending Christmas, 1708, that 626 people had been proceeded against during that year for cursing and swearing.
When one reads [1] that in the forty years just passed about
98,970 people had been prosecuted, one wonders that the
Justices of the Peace were not over-tasked.

Naturally the play houses were not overlooked. As
early as 1694 [2] it is proposed " To supplicate their majesties, that the public play-houses may be suppressed," and
argued that while such diversions may be lawful for the
recreation of princes, public dramatic entertainments are
unadvisable for all people making even a pretense to Godliness, since all agree that " in these houses, piety is strongly
ridiculed, the holy reverend and dreadful name of God
profaned, and his glory and interest rendered contemptible
or vile." The account of the Society published in 1701,
and already referred to more than once, remarks that
" Blasphemy, was too often the wit and entertainment of
our scandalous play-houses, and sincere religion became
the jest and scorn of our courts in the late reign," and

[1] *The Nine and Thirtieth Account of the Progress made in the
Cities of London and Westminster and places adjacent, by the
Societies,* etc. Published at the end of A. Bedford's sermon before
the society in 1734.

[2] *Proposal for a National Reformation of Manners,* etc.

among the rules for the members of the Society was that they were "wholly to avoid lewd play-houses." [1]   The arrest of the actors, to be mentioned later, was also no doubt due to their influence.

Creating such a stir as they did, it is not surprising that these Societies came to be very well known, and helped to give general currency to the idea, very strong with the people of this time, that they were living in a reforming age. Some indication of the prominence of the Societies may be found in the fact that both the "Tatler" [2] and the "Spectator" [3] mentioned them. The Tatler was himself a member, and in the "Spectator" was published a letter, a bit satiric, purporting to be from a very active participant in the work of the Society. He writes: "I am one of the directors of the Society for the Reformation of Manners, and therefore think myself a proper person for your correspondence — I can tell you the progress that virtue has made in all our cities, burroughs, and corporations, and know as well the evil practices that are committed in Berwick or Exeter as what is done in my own family — I can describe every parish by its impieties, and can tell you in which of our streets lewdness prevails; which gaming has taken the possession of, and where drunkenness has got the better of them both."

Cynics like Tom Brown might jibe:

> "'Tis now some years since drowsy reformation
> Rous'd its dull head, and saw its restoration;
> What influence has this upon the nation?
> Ye Rakehells of the Rose, let Rouse confess
> If at his house he draws one hogshead less.

----

[1] *A Brief Account of the Nature, Rise and Progress, of the Societies for the Reformation,* etc. Edinburgh. 1700.

[2] See No. 3, April 16, 1709.

[3] See No. 8, March 9, 1711.

And you intriguing sparks inquire of *Jenny*
If it has baulk'd her of one baudy guinea.
Is gaming grown a less destructive vice
Or fewer families undone by dice?
*　　*　　*　　*　　*　　*　　*　　*　　*
" Now let us cast our eyes upon the City,
These (there?) are no vices — no — none that are witty.
But frugal, gainful vices are for cits.
They never swear, because for that they pay
But they will lie — yes, — in a trading way." [1]

But the success of the reform movement was another triumph for the middle class in its struggle for recognition. The mention of it in the " Tatler " and " Spectator " is sufficient to show that men of fashion and influence had been drawn into a participation in the middle class movement, but still stronger proofs are found in the account of the Societies published in 1701, which contains a declaration of approval signed by thirty-four Lords Temporal, nine Lords Spiritual, and seven Judges of England. In pursuance, too, of a special request by her Majesty, the poet laureate, Nahum Tate, combined with various other gentlemen to produce in 1713 twenty numbers of a poetical " Monitor " consisting of instructive verses " for the promoting of religion and virtue, and the suppressing of vice and immorality." While it may be doubted whether or not such verses as the following, which begins a piece called " The Swearer,"

" Of all the nauseous complicated crimes
　That both infect and stigmatize the times,
　There's none that can with impious oaths compare,
　Where vice and folly have an equal share,"

served any very useful purpose, either moral or aesthetic, still the " Monitor " is another indication of the *furor reformandi* which had seized the nation.

―――――
[1] Epilogue to *Stage Beau Toss'd in a Blanket.* 1704.

In this movement the government took a determined stand on the side of the Reformers. After the Revolution, the court no longer gave by example open encouragement to dissipation. It is true that Charles had, immediately upon his restoration, issued a proclamation against vicious and debauched persons which was published May 30, 1660,[1] and that James had done the same on the 29th day of June, 1688,[2] but neither of these was likely to be very effective as long as there was the example of extravagance at court. After the coming of William, however, all this was changed; and as for Anne, instead of encouraging her courtiers to disregard such proclamations (as Charles by his example had done), she mentioned particularly in her proclamation for the " Encouragement of Piety and Virtue " (26th March, 1702) that debauchery was to be discouraged " and particularly in such as are employed near our Royal Persons; " and added " That for the greater encouragement of religion and morality, We will, upon all occasions, distinguish persons of piety and virtue by marks of our royal favor." This proclamation was but one of a long series. William had considered the reformation of manners one of the duties of his new government. On January 21, 1691–2, was issued " By the King and Queen, a proclamation against vicious, debauched and profane persons," [3] in which it was noted that the laws had been neglected and that the King and Queen were moved by an address of the Bishop to command all Justices, Sheriffs, etc., " to execute the laws against blasphemy, profane swearing and cursing, drunkenness, lewdness, prophanation of the Lord's Day, etc." On February 9, 1697–8, the Commons desired William again to issue

[1] Sommers' *Tracts*, Ed. 1812, Vol. VII.
[2] Published Copy in British Museum.
[3] Copy preserved in British Museum.

a proclamation for the enforcement of existing laws and added, moreover, " since the examples of men in high and public station have a powerful influence upon the lives of others, we do most humbly beseech your Majesty, that all vice, profaneness and irreligion, may in a particular manner be discouraged, in those who have the honor to be employed near your Royal Persons."[1] The King replied with request for a more effective law, and as a result there was passed on February 26th " An Act for the more effective suppressing profaneness, immorality, and debauchery " ; and in 1699 the King issued another proclamation.

When Anne came to the throne she took up the fight. John Tutchin's newspaper " The Observator " (No. 91, March 3–6, 1702–3) speaks of " Her Majesty's new proclamation for the encouragement of piety and virtue, and for the preventing and punishing of vice, profaneness and immorality, wherein she has generously pleased to direct and command all her judges of the assize, and justices of the peace, to give strict charges at their respective assizes and sessions, for the due prevention and punishment of all persons that shall presume to offend in any of the kinds afore mentioned." And in the following number of the newspaper we are informed that the " wits " are offended by the proclamation. In the British Museum there is a published copy of a similar proclamation which is dated 26th June, 1702. Probably more than one was issued. From all this it is evident that the Societies for Reformation had the support of the Crown in their prosecutions.

Since the Societies for Reformation approved of legal coercion, it is not surprising to find that they tried this method in regard to the theater. The incident of the

[1] Cobbet's *Parliamentary History*, Vol. V.

arrest of the actors is a very curious one in theatrical history. Cibber mentions it and Gildon refers to the occurrence thus in his " Comparison of the Two Stages " (1702):

Sull (en):   But did you hear the news?

Ramb (le):   What news?

Sull (en):   The trial between the play-houses and informers, for profane, immoral, lewd, scandalous, and I don't know how many sad things, utter'd and spoken on the stage.

Crit (ick):   Who were the persons that spoke 'em, and what were the words?

Sull (en):   Betterton, Brace-girdle, Ben Jonson and others; but the words may not be repeated. . . .

Sull (en):   The two first were fined, but the latter escaped.

Crit (ick):   'Tis fit both poet and player shoul'd be corrected for their immorality; but I do not like the accusation that passes thro' such hands; 'tis often a question of truth, and at best there's an alloy of cant and hypocrisy in their zeal."

Nearly all subsequent historians of the stage have mentioned this matter of common tradition. But different authors give different dates, according to the source from which they derive their information, and no one seems to have taken the trouble to investigate. Owing to the incomplete and confused character of the legal records made at the time, and now preserved in the Public Records Office, it is impossible to give a full history of the affair, but I have collected some isolated fragments of information which are of interest.

There are many difficulties and pitfalls. Mr. Gosse quotes [1] Narcissus Luttrell (May 12, 1698): " The Justices

[1] English Men of Letters. *Congreve*.

of Middlesex did not only prosecute the play-houses, but also Mr. Congreve for writing the 'Double Dealer,' D'Urfey for 'Don Quixote' and Tonson and Brisco, book-sellers, for printing them." Now this is very interesting as an illustration of the feeling against the persons mentioned, but it is likely to be misunderstood. A legal action actually involving Congreve and D'Urfey would be very interesting and the records would probably be preserved, but it is extremely unlikely that any such legal action was taken. A note in Dawkes' "News-Letter" No. 297 (May 12, 1698) presents the matter in a clearer light. It reads simply: "Last day of the session, at the Old Baily, the grand jury of London delivered a presentment against all stage-plays and lotteries (which tend so much to the cor-ruption and debauchery of youth) and the Bench were pleased to say they would take the same into considera-tion." The exact identity of dates makes it certain that Luttrell and the news letter refer to the same event, but a presentment to the grand jury is not a legal prosecution. Congreve and D'Urfey were probably not prosecuted, for if they had been it would most likely have been noted in Dawkes' "News-Letter." The presentment of the grand jury means simply that certain citizens exhibited the popular prejudice against the stage and that they men-tioned it to the judge. He evidently let the mattter drop.

But there were cases of actual trial and arrest. One of the controversial pamphlets[1] makes mention of three al-leged trials. It states, first, that in 1699 several players were prosecuted in the Court of Common Pleas upon a statute of 3 Jac. I for profanely using the name of God on the stage, and that verdicts were obtained against them;

[1] *A Representation of the Impiety and Immorality of the English Stage*, etc. 1704.

second, that in the Easter Term of 1701 the players of
one house were indicted at the King's Bench Bar before the
Right Honorable the Lord Chief Justice Holt for certain
speeches contained in " The Provok'd Wife "; third, that
the players of the other house were indicted in the same
term for expressions in " The Humour of the Age " and
" Sir Courtly Nice," but that owing to a technical error
they were acquitted.

Of the first of these trials I have been able to find no
record. There is perhaps some error in the statement,
since it is hard to see how a criminal charge could be
considered by the Court of Common Pleas. The offense
was a statutory one and consequently would be considered,
as the other cases were considered, by the Court of the
King's Bench.

I have, however, discovered documentary evidence which
seems to concern the second instance mentioned above.
In the Coram Rege Roll No. 2147 Michaelmas Term 13
William III[1] one may read, if he has the patience to
decipher the obsolete handwriting and translate the barbarous Latin, that in October of the 12th year of the reign
of William III, Thomas Betterton, Thomas Doggett, John
Bowman, Cave Underhill, Elizabeth Barry, George Bright,
Elizabeth Bowman, and Abigail Lawson were charged in
the Court of the King's Bench with having set up a common play-house in Little Lincoln's Inn Fields in which the
said Thomas Doggett on the 25th day of December in
1700 " several times profanely and jestingly used the
sacred name of God upon the public stage in the said
theater — in the hearing of divers persons being then and
there present in these words viz: *'E God there isn't more
fear of his head aching than my heart. 'E God I wou'd be
hanged first before I wou'd be your husband. 'E God take*

[1] Preserved in Public Records Office, London.

care of your own helm. 'E God I shall stick like pitch, God! I'le tell you one thing." and that the said Cave Underhill did on the said 5 and 20th day of December in the year aforesaid jestingly and profanely use the sacred name of God upon the public stage in the said theater. Cave Underhill and Abigail Lawson are similarly charged, and the indictment sets forth, in addition, that daily, Sundays excepted, between the 24th day of June and the 12th day of February the players acted irreligious and immodest spectacles tending to excite to fornication and adultery, on account of which there resulted many evil deeds and the shedding of blood besides the corruption of youths and virgins to the great sorrow of their parents and friends. To all this the actors pleaded not guilty.

In another part of the same roll it is charged that Thomas Betterton, Thomas Doggett, Cave Underhill, Elizabeth Barry, Ann Bracegirdle, George Bright, George Pack, and John Hodgson, did between the 24th day of June and the 7th day of March in the 13th year of William's reign present a certain obscene, profane, and pernicious comedy entitled " The Anatomist or Sham Doctor " in which were contained the following obscene and profane words: "*I'me sure he left his breeches long ago the devil take him, a curse on his systol and dyastol with a pox to him, the devil fly away with him, the devil pick his bones.*" The actors are further charged with having presented " The Provok'd Wife," from which a number of quotations are given, including the following: " But more than all that, you must know I was afraid of being damn'd in those days for I kept sneaking cowardly company, fellows that went to church and said grace to their meat, and had not the least tincture of quality about 'em — woman tempted me lust weaken'd and so the devil overcame me, as fell Adam so fell I." To this as to the other indictments the actors pleaded, through their attorney Simon Harcourt, not guilty.

It appears that the policy adopted by the actors was that of delay; for further information concerning the course of the case we must refer to the Rule Book,[1] where we read under the heading of Friday next after Michaelmas, 13th William III, that in the case of the King *vs.* Betterton and others a decree of "nihil dicunt" (i.e., judgment by default) will be entered unless the several defendants separately answer sufficiently by the following Wednesday. Then on the Thursday after the Morrow of All Souls of the same year it is entered that unless sufficient answer be made by Monday next, the decree "nihil dicunt" shall be entered. On that Monday there is another entry stating that unless sufficient answer is made by the following day the decree shall be entered peremptorily against them. The next entry occurs on Saturday after Christmas in the first year of the reign of Anne, and orders that separate recognisances of the defendants be estreated into the Exchequer. On the following Monday it is ordered that upon the payment of such costs as shall be taxed, and upon the withdrawing of the indictment at the first session of the next term, the estreat of the recognisances of the defendants shall cease, and on Wednesday on the Morrow of the Purification of the Virgins it is ordered that the estreat of the recognisances of Thomas Betterton and Elizabeth Verbruggen shall cease until next term.[2]

[1] Public Records Office. King's Bench 21–26.

[2] In this case a recognisance is an agreement to appear in court at a certain time. An estreat of a recognisance is a process by which a recognisance, forfeited by a failure to appear, is made the basis of a plea for judgment by default. The stopping of an estreat of a recognisance is a blocking of this attempt to gain a judgment by default.

These records inform us merely that the case dragged on into the reign of Anne and that the actors had considerable success in securing delays. I have not been able to find any further records of the case in the legal documents themselves, but fortunately further information may be derived from two letters preserved among the records of the Lord Chamberlain's office.[1] Since these letters have never been published and are very interesting I give them in full.

The first is particularly interesting since it refers to Betterton. It was overlooked by Mr. Lowe in his interesting life of that actor.

> To the Queens most Excell[t]
> Maj[tle] The humble Petition
> of Thomas Betterton Eliza-
> beth Barry, Ann Bracegirdle
> & others Your Maj[tles] Come-
> dians Acting in the New
> Theatre in Little Lincoln's
> Inn-fields.

Sheweth

That ever since the happy Restauration of your Royal Uncle King Charles the second (of ever blessed memory) for prevention of any indecent expressions in any playes which might be Acted, The Lord Chamberlaine of the Household for the time being hath constantly restrained the acting of all new playes until they were first perused by the Ma:[e] of the Revells who used to expunge whatever he thought unfitt to be acted. And your Petition:[rs] ever since they have had the hono[r] to serve your Maj:[tle] and your Royal predecessors in that quality have constantly given all due obedience to the said order and have not been till very lately disturbed for acting any plays

[1] Public Records Office. L. C. 7-3.

that had passed such examination, and always thought
they might safely act any play so perused & approv'd by
the Ma^e of the Revells —

Notwithstanding which your Petition:^{ers} have been
lately prosecuted by Indictm^t for acting plays perused &
approved as aforesaid in which were (as is alleged) divers
expressions not lawful to be used and the petition:^{rs} have
been put to great expenses and are yet prosecuted on
such Indictment.

To the end therefore since the prosecutors of such Indictments are not satisfied with the method that hath soe
long been used to prevent the Imorality of the Stage that
your petition:^{rs} may be quiet for the future.

May it please your Maj^{tie} to give such orders and directions as in your princely wisdom you shall think fitt for
perusing & correcting plays prepared to be Acted, that
your petition:^{rs} may not be misled to act any plays wherein
may be contained any expressions that may give just occasion of offence and that the prosecution on such Indictment against your petition:^{rs} may be stayed.

> And yo:^r Pet:^{rs} (as in all
> Duty bound shall ever pray
> etc.

The second, which also has never been printed, follows.

> The Case of Geo: Bright.
> Comoe^d: at ye Theatre in
> Lincols Inn fields.

That some time since, ye saide Bright was playing his
part, in ye play called Sr Fopling Flutter, & in ye Conclusion of his part, these words are Exprest (Please you
Sir to Commission a young couple to go to bed to-
gether a' Gods name) wch being Lyconed & permited, y^e
said Bright did humbly conceive, y^t there was neither
imorality or prophainess therein, ye said Bright as well as

sev: [ll] others, having often Exprest ye said words publickly
on ye stage, & no notice ever before taken thereof; But
some maliciously buissy person or psons informing agst y^e
said Bright have taken hold of ye Law, prosecuted him un-
knowingly, & have surreptitiously obtained a verdict
against him for 10 £ besides Cost & Charges wch amounts to
as much more, so y^t the s. Bright is in Continual danger
of being taken up for ye s^d: 10 £: & Cost & committed to
gaol.

The said Bright therefore humbly Begs yo^e Honor to
consider the hardness of this his case, & hopes y^t since
the whole company are equally concerned in this matter,
That you will be Pleased to Order it so, That ye s^d Company may be Equall sharers in ye payment of ye s^d 10£
wth cost of suit, since by Law it is ordered to be paid or
y^t you would be pleased to protect him.   Otherwise the s^d
Bright & family must suffer.

This [i.e. the law against profanity on the stage] was
Enacted in ye 3d year of King Jeams 1st as appears by
Keebles Collections & Statuts.

These petitions are interesting in several respects. They
bring up the whole question of the licensing of plays, a
question which will be discussed presently; but they are
quoted here only to show that in at least one case a large
fine was actually assessed against an actor.

The statement concerning the unsuccessful prosecution
of the actors at the other theater, which was made by the
author of " A Representation of the Impiety and Profaneness of the English Stage " and quoted above, may also be
given documentary support, but is less interesting. Among
a collection of very much battered documents [1] may be
found an indictment charging John Powell, John Mills,
Robert Wilkes, Elizabeth Verbruggen, Mariah Oldfield,

[1] Public Records Office. King's Bench 10–11

Benjamin Jonson, William Pinkman, William Bullock, Philip Griffin, Colly Cibber, and Jane Rogers with having acted, and continued to act after public notice, obscene and profane comedies in the theater called Drury Lane between the 24th day of June in the 12th year of the reign of William III and the 24th day of February in the 13th year of the reign of William III. The specific passages on which the charge is based are taken from " Volpone, or the Fox," " The Humour of the Age," and " Sir Courtly Nice." They also pursued the method of delay and they were finally dismissed *sine die*.[1]

Strangely enough I have not been able to find in any contemporary source a definite statement concerning the conclusions of these attempts on the part of certain people to invoke the law against the actors. We do read, however, in " The Laureat: or, The Right Side of Colly Cibber " (Anon. 1740) that Anne stopped the prosecution by a *noli prosequi*. This seems extremely probable, for though Anne promised to take the state of the stage under consideration, and certainly made efforts to reform it, the arrest of the actors was obviously unfair, and those who resorted to such methods showed only the intemperate zeal of reformers who can see no wrong except that against which they are incensed. Poor Bright was but a subordinate, and to send him to jail for performing a play which his superiors, under the license of the Crown, had ordered him to act, was a manifest injustice. Moreover the Crown, as he pointed out, was morally bound to protect him since the speeches for which he was convicted had been licensed by the Master of the Revels. As will be seen later, Anne or her ministers made an effort to deal with the situation through the instrumentality of that officer

[1] Coram Rege Roll. 2–147.

and so, no doubt, in fairness, stopped the prosecution of
the actors.

As an illustration of the widespread interest among the
official class in the regulation of the stage may be cited a
manuscript to be found in the library at Lambeth Palace.[1]

It comes from Nahum Tate, Poet Laureate, and is as
follows:

A Proposal for Regulating the Stage & Stage-Players.

All endeavors for a National Reformation being likely
to prove Ineffectual without a Regulation of the Stage,
the following is humbly offered to Consideration.

First, that supervisors of Plays be appointed by the
Government.   Secondly, that all Plays (capable of being
reform'd) be rectify'd by their Authors if Living — and
proper Persons appointed to Alter and reform Those of
Deceased Authors and neither old or modern Plays permitted to be acted till reform'd to the satisfaction of the
S[d] supervisors.   Thirdly, that sufficient Encouragement be
for such Persons as make y[o] Aforesaid Alterations &c likewise for supervisors, and Penalties upon Default in Either.
And this Matter so adjusted as to have due Effect, as long
as any Stage shall be Permitted.   Fourthly, the Theatres
& Actors to be Under Strict Discipline & Orders, that no
gentlemen be suffered to come behind the Scenes, nor
Women in Vizard-Masques admitted to see a Play &c.
Such Regulation of Plays and Play-houses will not only

---

[1] Lambeth Misc. 933, Art. 57.   This is from the miscellaneous
collection belonging to Edmund Gibson, Bishop of London, to
whom it was perhaps sent, but in the opinion of the Reverend
Claude Jenkins, Librarian at Lambeth Palace, the endorsement is
in the handwriting of Archbishop Tenison.   There is another manuscript in Lambeth Palace (Misc. 953, Art. 131) which is a sort
of memorandum or petition addressed apparently to some eccle-
siastical authority and setting forth the evils of the stage.

be a publique Benefitt, but also Beneficial to the Stage itself — if Continued: for whether the present stages be Reform'd or Silenc'd is left to the Government, but the one or Other is Absolutely necessary.

[Endorsement.] Mr. Tate's Proposal for Regulating the stage. Rec'd. Feb. 6, 1699.

Particularly worthy of note is the fact that Tate speaks of his suggestion as valuable only in case it is decided not to suppress the theaters. So great indeed, was the outcry against them that this was evidently actually considered, for Dennis in his "Person of Quality's Answer etc." (1721) tells us that "there was a warm report about town, that it had been twice debated in council, whether the theater should be shut up or continued." Moderate councils, however, prevailed. The documents quoted earlier show how earnest Anne, at least, was in her desire to regulate the stage, but she was not averse to plays herself and had no intention of listening too seriously to the fanatics. The orders which were sent out by the Lord Chamberlain show the method which she intended to pursue.

Since the court was on the side of reformed plays, it may well be asked why such reform could not have been easily brought about through the control nominally exercised by the Master of the Revels. There were two difficulties. In the first place, the custom of actually censoring plays had fallen more or less into disuse, and in the second place, as the letter from Bright shows, plays which had been licensed in looser days no longer seemed excusable, though they had legal sanction. For some reason, the records of the Lord Chamberlain's office covering this period have never been published. An examination of them shows, however, that the Crown was extremely anxious to gain control over the drama on the ethical side, but that it found it extremely hard to do so. Since these records have not been published, and this phase of the subject not fully studied by historians of the stage, I shall print some of the most interesting documents.

There had never been such a thing as a technically free stage in London. In Elizabeth's time the drama came, of course, under the control of the Master of the Revels, and there are recorded instances of his prohibition of certain plays. Though he had considerable power, it is not likely that he influenced to any great extent the development of the Elizabethan drama.[1] When the theaters were reopened after the Restoration, Sir Henry Herbert, who had been Master of the Revels under Charles I, eagerly reassumed his supposed right to what he evidently looked upon as a profitable sinecure. The published records of his office show how assiduous he was in demanding tribute for the licensing of every sort of popular spectacle down to the exhibition of a " monster," but do not reveal any particular desire to regulate the stage, except in so far as it was financially profitable to do so.[2] When he died in 1673 and the office was handed over to Killegrew, the latter apparently continued Herbert's tradition, and so the office continued to be regarded chiefly as a source of revenue.[3]

From the order quoted below, it is evident that plays were sometimes performed without having been licensed. Probably the fee was paid and no more said on the subject. Cibber states that this was the censor's practice later. Now when the Crown had undertaken to reform society,

[1] Gildersleeve. *Government Regulation of the Elizabethan Drama.*

[2] *The Dramatic Records of Sir Henry Herbert,* edited by Joseph Quincy Adams. These extend to 1673 only.

[3] Chambers. *Apology for Believers in the Shakespeare Papers.*

and turned its attention to the stage, it discovered that it had lost the power of controlling the drama, and the records of the Lord Chamberlain's office show a long and unsuccessful effort to regain this authority. On the 24th of January 1695–6 the Earl of Dorset, Lord Chamberlain, sent out the following order:

Whereas several playes &c are Acted & prologues spoken wherein many things ought to be struck out and corrected, And ye plays approved and Licensed by ye Master of the Revells according to ye Antient Custome of His place and upon the Examination of the said Master I find that he complanes that of Late several new & Revived plays have been Acted at ye Theater of Drury Lane & Dorsett Gardens without any Licence And that of Late ye Managers of that Company have refused to send such play^{es} to be purused Corrected & allowed by ye Master of ye Revels We therefore Order and Command that for ye future noe playes shall be Acted but such as shall first be sent (and that in due time) to Charles Killegrew Esq. Master of ye Reveles by him to be purused and diligently Corrected & Licensed And I Order all Persons concerned in the Management of both Companys to take notis hereof on ye Penalty of being Silenced according to ye Antient Custom of His place for such default And I Order all ye said parties to pay to ye said Master His Antient Fees for such new & revived plays soe Licensed And Doe further Order & Command the said Master to be very carful in Correcting all Obsenitys & other Scandalous matters & such as any ways Offend against y^e Laws of God Good Manners or the Knowne Statutes of this Kingdome as hee will answer y^e same to me Given under my hand & seal this 24th day of Janu 169$\frac{5}{6}$ in the seventh yeer of His Maties Reigne.

Dorsett [i.e. Lord Chamberlain][1]

[1] Public Records Office. L. C. 7–1.

This order seems to indicate a desire for a general tightening up. It is directed not only against the negligence of the players, but also against the Master of the Revels himself, who is ordered to take his office seriously. The sentence " and that in due time " seems to indicate that copies of new plays had sometimes been submitted at the last moment under the assumption that only the payment of fees was required for licensing.

Evidently all this did not have the desired effect, for on the 4th of June, 1697, we find Sunderland, then Lord Chamberlain, sending out the following order:

Order to the Comedians in
Lincolns Inn fields.

Whereas I am informed that many of the new plays acted by both companys of his Maj⁸ Comedians are scandalously lewd and Prophane, and contain Reflections against his Maj⁸ Government. For Preventing therefore so notorious abuses for the time to Come I do hereby strictly order that you do not presume to Act any new Play till you shall have first brought it to my Secretary, and Receive my directions from him therein as you shall answer the Contrary att your Perill. Given under my hand and seal this 4th day of June, 1697. In the Ninth year of his Maj⁸ Reign.

Sunderland

To Mr. Thomas Betterton and the rest of his Majesties Comedians Acting in Lincolns Inn Fields.

The like order verbatim as above to the Pattentees for his Maj⁸ Company of Comedians acting in Dorsett Garden and Drury Lane.[1]

Two years later we have two more orders as follows:

[1] Lord Chamberlain's Warrant Books. Public Records Office. L. C. 5-152.

Whereas I am informed that not wth Standing an order lately made for the better regulating of the Stage: Severall new Plays have been since Acted containing expressions contrary to Religion and good manners. These are therefore to Signify his Maj^s Pleasure, that you take great care not to License any plays, wherein there are any such expressions, and if you shall find that at any time, either company of his Maj. Comedians do presume to Act any thing which you have though fitt to strike out, that you immediately give notice thereof. Given under my hand this 18th of Februry In th^e Eleventh year of his Maj^s Reign.

> Pere: Bertie [i.e. Peregrine Bertie,
> Vice-Chamberlain]

To Charles Killegrew Esq.,
  Master of the Revels;
Whereas I am informed that notwithstanding an Order made the 4th of June 1697 by the Earl of Sunderland then Lord Chamberlaine of his Maj. Household to prevent the Profaness of the stage Several new Plays have lately been Acted, containing expressions contrary to Religion and good manners. And whereas the Master of the Revells has Represented to me; that in contempt of the said order, the Actors do often neglect to leave out such prophane expressions, as he has struck out. These are therefore to Signify his Majesties Pleasure, that you do not hereafter presume to act any thing in any new play, which the Master of the Revells shall think fitt to be left out, as you shall answer it att your utmost perill. Given under my hand 10th of February. In the Eleventh year of his Maj^s Reign.

> Pere: Bertie.

To Mr. Thomas Betterton &
the rest of his Mat^s. Comedians
acting in Lincolns- Inn Fields.

The like order verbatim to the Patenties for his Majesties Company of Comedians acting in Dorsett Garden or Drury Lane. 18 Feb. 1698–9.[1]

Queen Anne inherited the difficulty from her predecessor, and her Lord Chamberlain made similar orders, as the following will show:

Whereas Complant has been made y^t notwithstanding ye severall orders lately made for ye regulation of ye Stage, many of ye Old as well as New Plays are still acted wth out due Care taken to leve out such Expressions as are contrary to Religion & Good Manners. And whereas I am informed that this Abuse is in great Measure owing to ye Neglect of both Companys, by not sending Plays to ye Master of ye Revels, to be Licens'd but all ye Parts are got up, & ye play ready to be acted, by which Means his Censure & License cannot be so well observed And also that Prologues, Epilogues, & Songs wch are often indecent are brought upon ye Stage wth out his License. These are therefore to Signify her Majesty's Special Command that you do not Presume to Act upon the Stage any Play New, or Old, containing Profane or Indecent Expressions which may give Offence. And that you hereafter bring ye Master of ye Revels fair Copys to be Licens'd of all Plays, Songs, Prologues, & Epilogues before they be given out in Parts to be study'd, & Acted, which copys so Licens'd shall be kept safe for you for your Justification — And you are hereby Requir'd not to fail in Observing these Orders upon pain of her Ma:^{ts}

[1] Lord Chamberlain's Warrant Books. Public Records Office. L. C. 5–152.

high displeasure and being silenc'd from further Acting.
Given under my hand, this 15th day of January in y^e
second year of her Majesty's Reign.

To ye Company of her Ma^ts Sworn Comedians Acting
in Little- Lincoln's Inn- Fields.

The like Warrant Verbatim was sent to the Company
of Comedians Acting in Drury Lane.[1]

Whereas I am informed that the orders hitherto made for
Reformation of the Stage are yet ineffectual thro' the
Neglect of both Companies of Comedians in not sending
Plays to you for your Inspection and License till they are
ready to be acted, by which means, what you strike out
as indecent, is often spoke upon the Stage and also that
of late Several Prologues, Epilogues and Songs have not
been brought to you for your License.

I do therefore hereby Order you to take special Care not
to License anything that is not Strictly agreeable to Re-
ligion and good Manners And to give Notice to both the
Companies of Comedians acting in Lincolns Inn Fields
and Drury Lane that they do not presume to give out any
New Play into parts before they have brought you a fair
Copy thereof to be Licens'd; nor do presume to bring upon
the Stage any Prologue, Epilogue or Song without your
License, and if you shall at any time know that either
Company do act any thing which you have thought fitt to
strik out that you immediately give me Notice there of
Given under my hand this 17th day of Jan^ry in the second
year of her Majesties Reign.

To Charles Killegrew Esq. Master of the Revels to her
Majesty.

Jersey.[1]

In these last orders two new features may be observed.
First, great stress is laid on songs and epilogues (especially
attacked in Collier's book, which had by this time made

[1] Warrants of Several Sorts. Public Records Office. L. C. 5–153.

its impression) and second, a play containing " profane and indecent expressions " is not to be permitted even though it has been formerly licensed. The phrase " which copies so Licens'd shall be kept safe by you for your justification " is evidently a reference to the arrest of the actors and no doubt a reply to Bright's appeal for some means of security. Perhaps it coincides with the suspension of prosecution against the actors.

Unfortunately no records of the censor's excisions seem to have been kept, but Cibber tells us that he became much more strict. The Censor's activity, however, was founded only on tradition, and since that tradition had been allowed to lapse, it could not be effectively revived. Finally Cibber [1] flatly defied him and there was an end of an effective authority, although he continued to exist. This defiance, however, did not take place until after George I had granted a patent to Steele. Meanwhile, in 1709, an elaborate set of rules was formulated for the Haymarket Theater which contains the following: " That you forthwith prepare and transmitt to me an exact list of all such Comedyes you propose to act the next year that were Licens'd before her Majestys accession to the Crown, in Order to their being more carefully revis'd and new Licens'd by the Master of the Revells and that from and after Lady Day next you shall not suffer or permit any such play to be acted until it has received new license."

Anne (or her Ministers) was evidently anxious, in some measure, to satisfy the reformers, but she did not desire, as they did, the complete suppression of the stage. Nor did she show any inclination to take its management out of the hands of those men to whom the Reformers especially objected. Bedford in the " Evil and Danger of Stage Plays " notes triumphantly that her Majesty has been graciously pleased by letters patent, dated 14th of December 1705, to

[1] *An Apology for His Life.* Chapter VIII.

authorize Sir John Vanbrugh and William Congreve to inspect plays for the better reforming of abuses and immoralities. At first sight this looks like the establishment of a new sort of censorship, which indeed Bedford took it to be. But such was not Anne's intention. Bedford himself probably did not know just what he was referring to, or he would not have been so pleased, for the patent to which he refers provided for the establishment of a new theatrical company that was established in the Haymarket. The warrant does, indeed, begin as follows:

Anne R

Whereas We have thought fitt for the reforming the abuses, and Immorality of the Stage That a New Company of Comedians should be Established for our Service, under stricter Government and Regulations than have been formerly.

We therefore reposing especial trust, and confidence in our trusty and welbeloved John Vanbrugh & Willm Congreve Esq. for the due Execution, and performance of this our Will and Pleasure, do Give and Grant unto them the s John Vanbrugh and Willm Congreve full power and authority to form, constitute and Establish for us, a Company of Comedians with full and free License to Act & Represent in any Convenient Place, during Our Pleasure all Comedys, Tragedies, Plays, Interludes, Operas, and to perform all other Theatricall and Musicall Entertainments Whatsoev^r and to Settle such Rules and Orders for the good Goverm^n of the said Company, as the Chamberlain of our Household shall from time to time direct and approve of. Given at our Court at St. James this 14th day of December in the third year of our Reign.

By her Majestys Command
Kent.[1]

[1] Warrant Books. Public Records Office L. C. 5–154. Congreve resigned his share in the management of the Company the same year. See Gosse's *Congreve* in the Great Writers series.

But if Anne thought that this new project would conciliate the Reformers, she must have been greatly disappointed. Vanbrugh was, no doubt, a very suitable person
to manage a new theater, but the choice of him was not
likely to please the party which had taken speeches from
his plays as a basis for securing the arrest of the actors.
Before the theater was opened, his appointment brought
a protest from the Societies for the Reformation of Manners in an impudent pamphlet called " A Letter — To the
Most Reverend Father in God, Thomas (Tenison) — Arch-
Bishop of Canterbury " (1704). In it Vanbrugh is denounced as having debauched the stage "to a degree beyond the looseness of all former times," and the Archbishop is called upon to use his influence to prevent
the confirmation of Vanbrugh's appointment. The Society
has, it says, been less active of late in attacking the theater
because of confidence in the Queen's statement that she
had given special orders to the Master of the Revels for
the correction of irregularities, but it has heard the general
report that the management of the new theater in the
Haymarket is to be intrusted to Vanbrugh, " the known
character of which gentleman has very much alarmed us,
and a full consideration of which, has given us so warm
a concern for Her Majesty's honor, as to inform Your
Grace, whose post and degree in the church and state
give you so happy an opportunity of giving Her Majesty
an account of these reports." " Tho' this be given out
both by him and his friends," the pamphlet continues,
" yet we must suspect the truth, because 'tis impossible
that Her Majesty, who has declared against immorality
and profaneness, and against these crimes on the stage,
should act so directly contrary to the end she proposed,
as to commit the management of the stage to that very
man, who debauch'd it to a degree beyond the looseness
of all former times. Both the present houses were in-

dicted and found guilty by the court of Queen's Bench,
for the several obscene and profane expressions in the
' Relapse,' ' Provok'd Wife,' 'False Friend,' and the rest of
his plays, in which he is not satisfied to reflect on the
teachers of the Christian religion, but carries his impious
fury as far as the church, morality, and religion itself."

The Reformers were certainly not won over by the opening of the new theater. Defoe, a good index of bourgeois
opinion, devoted a whole number of his " Review " (Vol.
II, No. 26, 1705) to the event. Speaking ironically of the
unfulfilled promise of reform, he falls into verse thus:

> " The fabrick's finish'd, and the builders' part,
> Has shown the reformation of his art,
> Bless'd with success, thus have their first essays,
> Reform'd their buildings, not reform'd their plays.
>
> *   *   *   *   *   *   *   *   *
>
> Never was charity so ill employ'd
> Vice so encourag'd, virtue so destroy'd."

The new theater had made a brave bid for popularity
with the moderate element by beginning with Shirley's
" The Gamester," which had some claims to be considered
a moral play. They were, however, indiscreet with their
prologue, which contains the lines:

> " The architect must on dull order wait,
> But 'tis the poet only can create.
>
> *   *   *   *   *   *   *
>
> In the good age of ghostly ignorance,
> How did cathedrals rise, and zeal advance!
>
> *   *   *   *   *   *   *
>
> " But, now that pious pageantry's no more,
> And the stages thrive, as churches did before." [1]

The sentiment expressed in the last four of these lines
was obviously not calculated to conciliate the clerical

[1] By Dr. Garth.

parties, and experience with the vagaries of the reformers should have warned the managers of the new theater that some one would find, as indeed Defoe did find, blasphemy even in the apparently innocent reference to the poet as the only creator. Bedford [1] finds this first performance at the Haymarket such "That the horrid blasphemy is so rash, as to raise the blood at the reading thereof."

The reformers were, indeed, determined not to be satisfied under any circumstances, and did not wish it to be thought that any progress had been made towards a reformation. Thus Bedford, in his "Evil and Danger of Stage Plays, etc.," is careful to note that the two thousand instances of corruption which he has gathered are taken from the plays of the last two years "against all the methods lately used for their reform," and to analyze "The Gamester" in orded to show how bad a supposedly moral play can be. He and his tribe wished the complete destruction of the stage and no reform would have satisfied them.

The study of plays to be made in the next chapter will show that the movement for reform was producing very definite results, but much of the change came from within, and at no time during our period did the Crown succeed in gaining quite the power which it wished over the theaters. George I inherited Anne's difficulty. But power seemed rather to slip from his hands than to accrue to him. Steele, in conjunction with Wilkes, Cibber, Doggett and Booth, received a theatrical patent signed 18th October 1704.[2] He replied with a petition [3] in which he showed

---

[1] "Evil and Danger of Stage Plays, etc." (1706).

[2] Public Records Office. L. C. 7-3.

[3] Public Records Office. L. C. 5-156. I do not print this and the remaining documents referred to as they have already been published in Aitken's *Life of Richard Steele*.

"That the use of the theater has for many years last past been much perverted to the great scandal of religion and good government" and protested that since the reformation would be an arduous task, he should be given power for the term of his natural life and for three years thereafter. This petition was referred to the attorney general, who replied with more words about the need for reforming the stage and with an expression of the opinion that such power might be given to Steele "subject to such regulations as have been usual in grants of the like nature." But on October 25th, 1718, we find a letter to the attorney general [1] in which it is stated that the managers of Drury Lane refused to obey orders and regulations from the Lord Chamberlain. And on the 23rd of January, 1719, Steele's license was revoked.

Throughout this attempt to establish the authority of the Lord Chamberlain, the government had been animated by a variety of motives, by no means all of which were connected with a desire to improve the moral state of the stage; but in the case of Anne at least, the wish to exercise a moral censorship was strong. The passage of the Licensing Act in 1737 ends the struggle but falls without our period, and has, besides, been treated fully by other writers.[2] It is sufficient here to point out that though it was partly political in purpose it was nevertheless passed under the guise of a moral measure, and that when Sir John Barnard brought in the bill he made a considerable point of the mischief which had been done in the City of London by the theaters, which had corrupted the youth and encouraged vice.[3] Accordingly the bill may be

[1] Public Records Office. L. C. 5–157.
[2] See Watson Nicholson. *The Struggle for a Free Stage in London* and Cross, *The History of Henry Fielding.*
[3] Cobbett. *The Parliamentary History of England.*

regarded as, to some extent, one of the results of the government's interest in the movement against the stage which we have been considering. It is also, in one sense, the end of the story. From that time on the morals of the theater were under the control of the government censor, a person whose decisions have so often aroused feelings of anger or amusement according to the temper of the observer.

The two preceding chapters demonstrated the widespread interest in the question of the theoretical relation between drama and morality, and the rather heterogeneous collection of facts in the present one illustrates how this interest translated itself into a number of attempts to regulate the stage practically or to suppress it entirely. These practical attempts, like the theoretical discussion, had their beginning before Collier's book, for the earliest order of the Lord Chamberlain and the earliest expression of hostility on the part of the Society for the Reformation of Manners came before 1698. But as in the case of the theoretical discussion, development proceeded much more rapidly after the appearance of the " Short View."

The following chapter will discuss the change which took place in the drama itself.

CHAPTER VIII

THE DEVELOPMENT OF SENTIMENTAL COMEDY

EIGHTEENTH-CENTURY comedy is by no means merely Restoration comedy purified. True, to the moralist it is much less objectionable, and his protest helped its development, but it is not merely the old comedy expurgated. It is a different species. It embodies the reforms that were demanded, for in its fully developed form the language is pure, the moral not only good but obvious, and the hero always intended to be ultimately admired. But in addition to this, it adds the element called Sentimentalism, which I take to be merely facile and, usually, shallow, illogical emotion.

The best of the old writers of comedy were largely intellectual. They observed a hard and unfeeling society and they pictured it with delight, taking a cynical and purely intellectual pleasure in contemplating its follies and its vices. To this cold picture, the inferior dramatist added a large amount and the better ones a small amount of the purely luscious to tickle the imagination of the groundlings. But the emotions, except sometimes the misanthropic, were usually absent. With the coming of the sentimental drama, comedy began to take on some of the functions of tragedy. The audience is expected now not only to laugh at the characters, but to share their joys and sorrows. It is no longer to look on with an Olympian detachment, but to suffer with distressed virtue and rejoice when the dark clouds reveal their silver lining. Moreover, all of this is to be connected with a sentimental (i.e., not necessarily genuine or deep rooted) admiration of virtue. The spectator is to be always on the side of the angels, and not only to believe that virtue always triumphs but also to feel a personal exultation when it does. Benevolence takes the place of *esprit* as the most admirable human characteristic, and the reform of some vicious person becomes a favorite theme.

The attitude toward love undergoes a change. In the Restoration plays there is no hint that it possesses a "seraphic part." At best, love is merely gallantry, a game rather than an experience. The mystical elements never appear, and in a word love is Ovidian rather than Dantesque. As sentimental comedy develops, the romantic elements enter and the lover begins to languish. Face to face with his mistress he ceases to banter and begins to exclaim. Rapture becomes *la mode*.

In the plays of Wycherley or Etherege sentiment as well as sentimentality is absent. People seldom sigh. Though they may, as a matter of convention, talk of flames and darts, it is merely a convention. When the hero is about to marry he does not tell his mistress that they are twin halves of the same soul, or that he cannot live without her. He merely admits that he is hard-up and a bit tired of many mistresses, and that, as he thinks her an attractive woman, he believes he would rather settle down with her than with anyone else whom he knows. The heroine accepts in the same spirit. He is a handsome and vigorous young fellow. All the world admires him, and if he will promise not to restrain her liberty, she will have him.

In the early years of the eighteenth century, however, the characters come more and more to speak of love with a capital " L," even though the old machinery of amorous intrigue is kept up. Not the amour, but married love, comes to be the ideal; and instead of constantly making fun of the matrimonial institution and all connected with it, the new dramatists vie with one another in lauding its delights. The typical plot runs somewhat after this fashion: A virtuous person comes in contact with a vicious one. The sympathy of the audience goes out to the virtuous one. Through some series of circumstances, the vicious person is convinced of his error and every one is made happy, the audience sharing in the joy of the characters and rejoicing that another member has been added to its party — i.e., the believers in virtue.

It is evident that a play of this type satisfies the more moderate requirements of the critics of the Restoration stage. It is, in the first place, purged to a very considerable extent of those things which might be objected to merely on the ground of delicacy and good taste. Moreover, it aims to present conventional virtue in an attractive light, to convey the impression that uprightness is rewarded, that repentance brings happiness and reconciliation, and that the ideal gentleman is not a selfish rake but a kind and even soft-hearted philanthropist. That it did not succeed very well in doing all these things will be clear; but it is equally clear that it had the ostensible aim of doing so, and that this aim is the one which critics had maintained comedy should pursue. Consequently we must assume, either that the criticism and denunciation had some effect on actual drama, or that both the criticism and the new drama were the result of the same general movement, though one did not influence the other.

To make the sweeping statement that the Collier controversy had no effect on the drama seems to me to be almost as wrong as to say that it actually produced sentimental comedy. There was a general movement toward reform, but the Collier controversy called attention directly to the stage as flagrantly out of key with such a movement, and the stage was modified.

To estimate how closely the attack of Collier and the general moral movement were connected with the development of the new comedy, it will be necessary not only to know what this comedy was like and when it was born, but also when it began to win for itself a recognized place on the stage and when, also, it came to dominate. To say that Steele in 1722 wrote a very moral play which was very successful tells a great deal, but it does not tell all. What we need to know also is, when and by what steps the audience began to expect that sort of thing and to consider Restoration comedy as a style which had been outgrown. This chapter will suggest a scheme which may enable us to watch the development of the new type and its gradual displacement of the old.

Misapprehension is likely to result from a partial survey of theatrical conditions at this time. If one reads only the plays of Farquhar, Gay, and Fielding, and, moreover, observes that the old plays continue to make up the bulk of the bills in the early years of the eighteenth century, he will be inclined to believe that theatrical conditions were not undergoing any very rapid change. On the other hand, if he will read all the new plays being produced at any given period in that time, and compare them with all the plays produced in an equal length of time during the eighties of the seventeenth century, he will perceive at once that they are characterized by different complexions.

It is obviously impracticable to mention and discuss all the plays from 1660 to 1725, but on the other hand to select certain plays or certain authors is likely to be misleading. Nor will it do to select only the most successful plays, for undoubtedly the Restoration dramatists and those of their school were the abler playwrights, while many failures or partial successes show definitely the drift of dramatic experiment. The ideal method would be to examine all the comedies (with the exception of mere revisions and pure farces) of, say, the years 1685, 1696, 1700, 1705, 1710, 1715, 1720, 1725, and thus secure a practicable means of comparing the dramatic complexion of the English stage at different times over this critical period. The only deviation from this perfect symmetry which conditions will necessitate is caused by the fact that the bulk of dramatic writing was never very great, and varied considerably. Consequently we shall have to stretch the year a little. Thus 1685–1689 will represent the typical product of the earlier period, 1696 that of about the time when the appearance of sentimentalism began to be recognized, while the years 1704–5 and 1705–6 will represent conditions about the year 1705, etc. However, since we take all the new comedies in each period the comparison will be fair. Genest will furnish the canon.

The years 1685–6–7–8–9 will yield us nine comedies which show how little variation there was in general tone. None is by a dramatist of the first rank, but four, Crown's " Sir Courtly Nice," Sedley's " Bellamira," and Shadwell's " The Squire of Alsatia " and " Bury Fair," are capital comedies. Two, Mrs. Behn's wretched farce, " The Emperor of the Moon," and a low comedy, " The Devil of a Wife," are not worth mentioning except to say that they offer nothing to contradict what will be said of the others. Shadwell may be passed with no other comment than that given in an earlier chapter.

" Sir Courtly Nice " is a very light-hearted, very loose, very " smutty " (to use Collier's favorite word), and very amusing comedy. As often happens, the character who

gives his name to the piece is not the hero.   Leonora is in
love with Farewel, whom her father refuses because of
an old family feud.   He wishes to marry her to the fop,
and when she asks why he has chosen a fool, he replies
" Because none but fools will marry."   Farewel employs
a go-between, remarking:

> " Pimps manage the great business o' the nation.
> That is, the heavenly work o' propagation."

Of course the lovers are successful in outwitting the
parents, but they are hardly the sort of lovers whom all
the world loves, for as always in Restoration plays, the
love has very little of the seraphic part.   There is no
reason to suppose that the hero differs very much in his
ideas from the other speaker in the following dialogue:

" Fa(rewel) :   Have you no love for women?

Sur(ly) :   I ha' lust.

Fa: No love?

Sur: That's the same thing. The word love is a figleaf
to cover the naked sense, a fashion brought up by
Eve, the mother of jilts: she cuckolded her husband
with the serpent, then pretended to modesty, and fell
a making plackets presently."

In " Bellamira," Sedley leaned heavily upon Terence
and redeemed his reputation as a wit, which he had lost
with " The Mulberry Garden."   One cannot pass this
comedy by with a simple condemnation of its indecency, and
what is worse, its callousness, for a passage like the following could not be better dramatically and makes one forget
all else.   The contrast between the phlegmatic Merryman
and the tempestuous Lionel, whom he overtakes on the
street, is excellent.

Lionel: I am undone! Ruin'd! I have lost the sight
of this pretty creature, and shall never find her any

more! Which way shall I go? Whom shall I inquire
of? What shall I do, to have a glimpse of her? I
have only this comfort, where-e're she is, she is too
beautiful to be long conceal'd.

Merry (man): Lost! Undone! Beautiful! I am sure
I heard those words plain: He is in love, and after
the manner of that sort of mad men is talking to
himself of his mistress; if he be we shall have fine
work; — he'll commit rape, burglaries, fire houses, or
anything, but he'll have her; and for money, he'll
throw it away like dirt. I pity his father — What's
the matter? You look as if you were drunk.

Lionel: I am worse; I am mad; I am anything; I am
in love.

   * * * * * * * *

Merry: Her age?

Lion: Seventeen.

Merry: I have drunk excellent Hockamore of that age.

Lion: Damn thy dull Hockamore and thy base jaded
palate that affects it; could I but get this divine
creature into my hands, by fraud, force, price, prayer,
anyway so that I enjoy her, I care not.

Merry. Who is she? She may be a person of quality,
and you may bring an old house upon your head.

Lion. 'Tis but a duel or two that way; and if her
relatives be numerous, we'll fight six to six, and make
an end on't.

Merry. What country woman is she?

Lion. I know not.

Merry. Where does she live?

Lion. I can't tell.

Merry. We are upon a very cold scent. Where did
you see her?

Lion. In the streets; with a servant behind her.

Merry. How came you to lose her?

Lion. That's it, I was cursing at, as I met you; nor do I think there is a man whom all the stars conspire against like me. What crime have I committed to be thus plagu'd?

Merry. The stars are pretty twinkling rogues, that light us home, when we are drunk sometimes; but never care for you, nor me, nor any man."

Keepwell is at the mercy of his extravagant mistress Bellamira, who frequently deceives him. A suitor presents her with an orphan for a maid and a eunuch for a page. Lionel, who is in love with Isabella (the maid), disguises himself as a eunuch and manages to rape her. It is discovered that she is a long-lost sister of another of the characters. The latter demands revenge, and Lionel agrees to marry her. Most of the remainder of the plot is concerned with the intrigue by which Keepwell's friends enjoy his mistress, to whom he is passionately attached. There is no limit to the frankness of the dialogue, and the moral standard of the characters may be judged by the lines spoken by Merryman when he is about to make a temporary theft of his friend's mistress. " Well, I am a rogue, to betray my friends thus; but, who'd not be taken off with such a bribe? Besides, in the matter of women, we are all in the state of nature, every man is hard against every man, whatever we pretend or argue." Another bit of dialogue may be given.

Cunningham: He wou'd give me now and then five guineas for a song for her, which I let her know was mine; when I saw her next, we laugh't at the poor fool together — you know he is but a dull silly fellow.

Merryman: And therefore you may very honestly pretend friendship, borrow his money and lie with his mistress.

Cunningham: A pious citizen that goes to church twice
a day, will play the knave in a bargain; a lawyer
take your fee, and for a good sum of money, be absent
when your cause is tri'd; a parson marry you to a
great fortune without a license; we are all rogues in
our way, and I confess woman is my weak side.

This, the Restoration dramatist might say, was satire
against the folly of "keeping." Yes, satire against the
silly dunce, but almost admiration for the false friends
who treacherously take advantage of his confidence and
laugh at him behind his back. This is satire, but satire
which offers no moral excuse for itself. It satirizes a
weakness and defends a meanness. To object that the
characters do not receive poetic justice would be childish;
in fact, to object to anything about Restoration Comedy
on moral grounds is childish; but to defend it as satire
is doubly so.

Of the two plays which remain to us in this group,
neither is so brilliant as the two just discussed, but both
illustrate equally well the moral depravity of the atmosphere. In her exuberant and light-hearted way, Mrs. Behn
committed most of the sins of which Restoration Comedy
can be legitimately accused, but in " The Lucky Chance, or
an Alderman's Bargain," the only one of her plays which
is included in the present group, she is guilty chiefly of
lengthy and elaborate lusciousness, the principal scenes
occurring in bed rooms, and the characters being perpetu-
ally either disrobed or disrobing. It appears that the
indecency of the play had aroused some criticism as coming from a woman, for in the interesting preface Mrs.
Behn maintains her right to be as lewd as her male rivals
in the drama, begging the privilege of her " masculine
part, the poet, to tread in the same paths my predecessors
have so long thriv'd in," and challenging any unbiassed
person who does not know the author, to read the play

and compare it with other comedies of the age, " and if they find one word that can offend the chastest ear, I will submit to all their peevish cavills." Still Genest, the most unsqueamish of clergymen, finds it unusually indecent.

The gallant hero, Gayman, is in love with Julia, the wife of an old alderman. Gayman leads the latter on to gamble until he stakes a night with his wife against money, and loses. Gayman goes to collect his winnings, and she promises to leave the alderman forever. Like all of Mrs. Behn's plays, this one is not repulsive because of the very frankness and lack of pretense. The premise is that, for the man at least, love knows no law, and that love is purely animal. The closing couplet is typical. The alderman and his friend, both of whom have lost their wives to younger men, console themselves thus:

> " That warrior needs must to his rival yield,
> Who comes with blunted weapons to the field."

" The Fortune Hunters: or Two Fools Well Met," by James Carlile, is an excellent example of the type of comedy especially denounced by the Reformers, in which a heartless libertine is rewarded in the end with the hand of a somewhat over-amorous heroine, upon whose fortune he has all along had his eye. Young Wealthy has been disinherited for having stolen a large sum of money from his father. In town he meets his elder brother:

Elder Wealthy: But why have you not ask'd how my father does? What brought us to town, or where you might see us.

Young Wealthy: Why first, I suppos'd he was well, or dead or alive, there is nothing to be got by him. Next, I suppose you came to town for the same reason I stay in town, to whore and drink. Lastly, I thought I might meet you in a bawdy-house.

This promising young man rivals the hero of Sir Fopling
Flutter in the multiplicity of his simultaneous intrigues.
He is supported by a rich widow, is also engaged in the
traditional sport of an amour with a tradesman's wife and,
finally, at his brother's suggestion, undertakes to woo
Marie, the possessor of ten thousand pounds. She, on her
part, has confessed that " the first young gentleman that
I like, (if he have good manners enough to like me) shall
have the spending of this ten thousand pounds of mine,
rather than I'll die of the pip, to leave it to you and your
heirs." Set in pursuit of her, Young Wealthy does not
give up either the widow or the tradesman's wife, for
" 'Tis not like a wise man to leave off one trade, without
a certainty of living better by another." He deceives the
widow to the last and plays a cruel joke on his father, but
when, having won Marie, he says " We will forsake this
hole of sin and sea coal, and make you merry in a better
air. Come, spouse. Your blessing, sir," his father for-
gives him, saying: " Pox take him, he talks as if he had
some grace; he made a long speech too without swearing."

This rapid survey of comedy during the years 1685–9
confirms what has been said in general about Restoration
Comedy. The wild gallant treads a flowery path to fortune, without the slightest regard not merely for decency
but even for fairness, consideration of the rights of others,
or the most rudimentary sense of honor.

I leap now to the year 1696, which alone yields us
thirteen new comedies,[1] because that year includes Cibber's
"Love's Last Shift," which may be correctly called the
first sentimental comedy, since it was the first play to be
recognized by contemporaries as such. Any author might
from time to time drop in expressions which were not
completely in the Restoration tradition, but no previous

---

[1] I have not been able to find *She Ventures and He Wins* mentioned by Genest.

play had struck the audience as establishing a new type.[1]
Cibber, then a young and not very well known actor,
took a conventional plot but gave it a new emphasis, calling upon the audience to delight in the triumph of the
virtuous wife and presenting for their approval a ridiculous masque in praise of marriage. The importance of
the play is purely historic. It is only an experiment and
intrinsically a very bad one at that. The plot concerns
one Loveless, a thoroughly abandoned libertine who has
deserted his wife so long ago as to have forgotten her
completely. She wins him back, not only to love for her
but also to enthusiasm for the marriage state in general,
by becoming his mistress when she discovers that he does
not recognize her as his wife. From every point of view
the play is objectionable. Three-fourths of the dialogue
is as lewd as that of any Restoration play, and the virtuous conclusion reeks with hypocrisy. It is hard to believe
that it was ever taken seriously, but it had a tremendous
success which the author himself [2] attributed to the " mere
moral delight received from its fable."

From now on Cibber was considered, and considered
himself, as one of the reformers of the stage. The following dialogue [3] will illustrate what his contemporaries
thought of his experiment:

Ramble: Ay, marry, that play was the philosopher's
    stone: I think it did wonders.

Sullen: It did so, and very deservedly; there being
    few comedies that come up to't for purity of plot,
    manners and moral."

---

[1] Mr. Allardyce Nicoll in his recently published " A History of
Restoration Drama, 1660–1700 (1923) thinks that he can see ad-
umbrations of sentimentalism in certain comedies produced from
1680 on.

[2] *Apology*.

[3] Gildon. *Comparison between the Two Stages*.

Davies [1] says roundly: " To a player we are indebted for the reformation of the stage. The first comedy, acted since the Restoration, in which were preserved purity of manners and decency of language, with a due respect to the honor of the marriage-bed, was Colley Cibber's ' Love's Last Shift.' " And again he tells us that " The joy of unexpected reconcilement, from Loveless' remorse and penitence, spread such an uncommon rapture of pleasure in the audience, that never were spectators more happy in easing their minds by uncommon and repeated plaudits. The honest tears, shed by the audience at this interview, conveyed a strong reproach to our licentious poets, and was to Cibber the highest mark of honor."

Cibber had evidently been somewhat doubtful as to the success of his attempt, for he had a comic and indecent prologue in which he made fun of the whole thing. His fears, however, were groundless. From what Gildon wrote, it is obvious that the cause of the success lay in the new element, and hence also obvious that if an audience could really be moved to tears by " Love's Last Shift " it was thirsting for sentiment. Collier had not yet spoken, but from the success of Cibber's play it is almost certain that, without Collier, sentimental comedy with its praise of virtue was inevitable. Cibber profited by the lesson of his success, and henceforth shares with Steele the position of premier sentimentalist. He did not, however, like the latter, take a very prominent part in the critical advocacy of the new comedy, though he does so to some extent in his prefaces, and, in the " Apology " (1740), published after his retirement from the stage, he appears everywhere as an exponent of the moral theory of the dramatic function. Here he expresses amazement " that our best authors of that time could think the wit and spirit

[1] *Dramatic Miscellany.*

of their scenes could be an excuse for making the looseness
of them public " and proclaims himself content if his readers will give him no other merit than that of having the
" interest and honor of virtue always in view."

Looking at the other comedies of 1696, we find that
Cibber was not entirely alone, for there are here and
there indications of an inclination to break away from the
old tradition, though this inclination is nowhere sufficiently marked to attract attention, or to rob Cibber of
credit for the perspicacity which led him to invent a new
type of comedy surely predestined to great popularity.
" The Younger Brother " by " the late Mrs. Behn," " The
Mock Marriage " by Thomas Scott, " The Spanish Wives "
by Mrs. Pix, " The Country Wake " by the actor Thomas
Doggett, and " The Husband his own Cuckold " are pretty
well in the old traditions. The latter play, by John
Dryden, Jr., offers opportunity for reflection. In it, Sir
John Crossit discovers that his wife has made an amorous
appointment with a foolish physician. The husband keeps
the appointment in the dark, and leaves scratches on his
wife's face. Angered at the supposed outrage of the physician, she turns upon him the next day and has him driven
from the house. Here we have, if you like, poetic justice
neatly administered, but there is no sentiment whatever.
Had the play been written in 1726 it might have proceeded
thus, but in the end the husband would have explained his
ruse, the wife would have fallen into repentance, promises
would have been given that no indiscretion should be committed in the future, and the curtain would have fallen
upon a scene of reconciliation and tears.

Motteux's flat comedy " Love is a Jest " is neither sentimental nor ingeniously immoral. It hardly makes evidence
one way or the other, except that there is at least no striving after immorality such as one is accustomed to find in

the typical Restoration plays. In the anonymous "The Cornish Comedy " the hero is not particularly scrupulous in his methods, but his love for the heroine is more or less genuine. Neither he nor she indulges in the usual epigrams of inverted morality, and the former actually expresses some scruples of honor. Lord Lansdowne's " The She Gallants " had a rather romantic plot of a deserted heroine who wins back the affections of the hero, and though loose enough in language and incidents had one distinctly sentimental scene where the repentant hero breaks out: " Oh, raise not my confusion with reproaches, so tender and so just: Alas! If you could look into my breast, you would find yourself, if it be possible, enough reveng'd by the shame and remorse that overwhelms me. (Kneeling.) Thus prostrate, the vilest criminals have leave,— to approach the heavens they have offended, etc. etc." There has been no preparation for this, the hero has hitherto shown himself the most confirmed of libertines, but this speech is definitely a foreshadowing of the sort of thing that was to become very common. One of Congreve's heroes could hardly have spoken it.

Dilke's " The Lover's Luck " is the story of a soldier rather than of a wild gallant, and his heroes show some faint shadow of honor. The whole play is at times coarse and always dull, but not particularly immoral, while Mrs. Manley's " The Lost Lover " shows some distinct traces of sentimentality. The hero is a complete cad (which is not unusual even in sentimental comedy), but he tends to be a moralizing rather than a cynical one, indulging in some heroics and exclaiming; " Oh, the curse of lewdness! What woman's fair after we find her faulty " — a completely non-Ovidian and hence non-Restoration idea. He is half-way to becoming a Joseph Surface, a typical product of the eighteenth century, when the libertine had abandoned cynicism and taken to hypocrisy. D'Urfey's unimportant and unexceptionable " Don Quixote Part III " has already been mentioned.

Though "Love's Last Shift " is the only really striking phenomenon of this year, it seems that bits of sentimentalism, or, if you prefer, bits of ordinary human feeling, are creeping in here and there, though the movement was not self-conscious before Cibber's play appeared. It seems, too, that even where sentiment is absent the authors strain less after cynicism and perverted morality, so that the spirit of Restoration Comedy seems more or less on the point of dissolution. It must be borne in mind, however, that such judgments as this should be made with some caution and accepted with more. Beljame, for instance, thinks that " The Way of the World " shows that Congreve was moderating his tone in answer to the moralist, while Whibley [1] takes the same play as the best possible proof that the dramatists cared not a rap for Collier. Still I think that the dramatic production of 1696 does show some tendency to moderate the persistent and cynical lewdness of the typical Restoration plays, and that this fact, since Collier's book did not appear until 1698, is significant.

The nine comedies furnished by the years 1700 and 1701 again show the new and old traits in conflict. The domination of the old school is shown by the fact that illegitimate amorous intrigue still plays an important part; and that whether or not the intrigue is frustrated, the wife's virtue saved, and the wild gallant landed safely in the bonds of matrimony, often depends rather on chance or policy than on the principles of morality.

This latter fact is indeed one of the things which separates Restoration from Sentimental comedy. In the

[1] Cam. Hist., Vol. VIII, Chap. VI.

former, the hero often enough commits matrimony and
the erring wife is often enough erring only in intention,
but the happy conclusions are brought about through the
influence of chance or the direction of prudence rather than
through the workings of moral scruples, and the interest
is centered on the intrigue rather than on the conclusion.
In the Sentimental Comedy, on the other hand, the characters are always being overtaken by remorse or prevented
by scruples. Two contrasting plays will illustrate the
point. For an illustration of the old school take "The
Reform'd Wife" (1700) by Burnaby, which belongs to the
years now under discussion. The epilogue may be noticed
as illustrating the fact that it had become increasingly
necessary to pretend, at least, to morality.

> "Let none hereafter plays ungodly call,
> For this was writ to mortify you all.
> No parson 's here expos'd, no brothel storm'd
> But a kind handsome keeping wife reform'd."

These lines show the need felt to recognize the moral
movement, but if the play was "writ to mortify you all"
then the author proceeded in a strange way. Astrea dislikes her husband, and keeps him at a distance by pretending to dislike all men. She meets Freeman and begins
an intrigue with him, he not knowing that she is the wife
of an old acquaintance, Sir Solomon Empty. The lovers
agree to meet at the house of Clarinda, but she falls in
love with Freeman herself, and he concludes that though
he likes Astrea better, he had rather marry Clarinda's
fortune than remain Astrea's poor lover. Unwittingly he
discovers to Sir Solomon his rendezvous with the latter's
wife. But by Sir Solomon's excitement he suspects the
truth and tells Astrea. They plan that when they meet
she will pretend that there has been a mistake and that

she had never encouraged him. Sir Solomon, in hiding, is taken in by this acted meeting, is convinced of his wife's chastity, and Clarinda and Freeman announce their engagement. It is perfectly evident that the wife's "reform" is merely by necessity, and that the "lesson" of the play, if we must seek it, is prudential rather than moral.

This amoral treatment of the subject may be well contrasted with the treatment of a triangular or rather quadrangular plot in a fully developed sentimental play like "A Wife to be Let" (1723), by the novelist Mrs. Haywood. The prologue expounds that mixture of sentiment and caution which the eighteenth century called virtuous love:

> " Learn, from the opening scene, ye blooming fair,
> Rightly to know your worth, and watch with care;
> When a fool tempts ye, arm your heart with pride,
> And think the ungenerous born to be deny'd:
> But, to the worthy, and the wise, be kind,
> Their cupid is not, like the vulgar's blind:
> Justly they weigh your charms and sweetly pay
> Your soft submission, with permitted sway."

The epilogue sums up the moral thus:

> " . . . the heroine of our play
> Gains glory by a hard and dangerous way;
> Belov'd, her lover pleads — she fears no spy,
> Her husband favors — and her pulse beats high.
> Warm blows his hope — her wishes catch the fire,
> Mutual their flame, yet virtue quells desire."

The beautiful Mrs. Graspall is married to an incredibly avaricious husband. Beaumont, who has deserted his wife Amadea, makes love to Mrs. Graspall. She loves him but will " still hold my honor dearer than my life." Graspall finally offers to sell his wife to Beaumont, who seems to

accept. She rebukes the lover and he protests that he had
no intention of enforcing his bargain. " The flame I feel
for you, is in itself so pure, I grieve it shou'd appear in
any likeness with those unconstant fires which loose desires create; I tremble when I approach you and tho' I'd
forfeit life to touch that hand, so fearful am I to offend,
I dare not ask it." Now it happens that Amadea, his
wife, disguised as a man, has followed Beaumont and
confided in Mrs. Graspall. The latter questions Beaumont as to former loves. The eighteenth century prig
speaks: " I do not deny but that I have met temptations
in my way, which youth and inadvertency, at some un-
guarded hours, have yielded to." She presses him further. He: " Oh Amadea! Now thy image rises to my
view, and brings my broken vows to my remembrance."
Of course Amadea is produced and forgiven. Beaumont:
" Can there be so much generosity in nature! " Complete
reconciliation. This, it would seem, should be enough to
exhaust one's stock of belief in the powers of virtue, but
more is to come. The more complete the orgy of redemp-
tion and reconciliation, the better is the sentimental
dramatist pleased. Mrs. Graspall pretends to have
granted the seeming-man Amadea all that she had refused
to Beaumont. Her husband is distracted, for it is worse
in retrospect than in anticipation. He wishes he were dead.
Now he has been punished enough. Behold! Amadea is
a woman. More raptures. The inconceivable miser becomes yet more inconceivable when we see that he also is
about to reform. So the play ends, and the audience ex-
periences what Steele calls that joy which is too deep
for laughter. Here the wife is kept upon the path of duty,
not as in " The Reform'd Wife " by prudence and the
force of circumstances, but purely through Virtue.

It is useless to comment on the absurdity and unwhole-
someness of such a play as Mrs. Haywood's, or to urge

that the frank cynicism of the Restoration is perhaps truer and consequently more wholesome. We are concerned merely with pointing out the strangeness of a phenomenon. An audience of 1673 liked " The Country-Wife " and an audience of 1723 was expected to endure " A Wife to Let." Mrs. Haywood, in accordance with the movement of the time, gave the superficial appearance of morality and so satisfied the superficial and even, at times, hypocritical rage for the moral.

But it is time to return to the plays of 1700 and 1701 when sentimentalism was still struggling for expression. David Crawford's " Courtship a-la-mode " is not sentimental, but at least the " moral points the right way." D'Urfey's very dull " The Bath, or, the Western Lass " also shows little sentiment except in the somewhat romantic treatment of love. John Corye's " A Cure for Jealousy," however, shows many of the marks of sentimentalism in a plot which is quite old-fashioned in places. Scrapeall is unjustly jealous of his virtuous young wife Arabella, who, though virtuous, roundly tells him of his unfitness for a young wife. He gets the idea that she means to kill him, and hires an assassin to kill her first. The plot is discovered, and he is frightened out of his wits and his jealousy by the appearance of a mock corpse. In a sub-plot, Colonel Blunt, having been driven into the army because his father has refused to support his gay life, returns in disguise and tells his father of the death of his son. The father is stricken with remorse, and there is a sentimental scene of recognition, reunion, and reconciliation. The rakish hero, and some of the incidents, connect the play with the Restoration tradition, but much of the dialogue, by its tendency to serious discussion rather than epigrammatic dismissal of ethical questions, by its romantic love scenes, and especially by its tearful-joyful reconciliation motif, is definitely sentimental.

Similarly, Manning's " The Generous Choice," though the story of a perfect Don Juan, concludes with the hero's reform, and takes much of its point not from cynical laughter but again from sentimental scenes of reconciliation and reformation, and in the end makes its plea to the moralizing taste of the age with the concluding rhymed tag:

> " For what-soe'er delight bad men can find
> In doing wrong, 'tis the unblemished mind
> That makes our lives most sweet,
> Our pleasure most refined."

Whether or not " The Way of the World " (1700) does, as Beljame thinks, show an attempt to give less cause for offense to the moralist, I shall not attempt to decide; but Burnaby's " The Ladies' Visiting Day " complains in the preface: " My care to avoid any thing that might shock the ladies, I perceive has done me no service." Probably he was sincere. He constructed a rather cynical plot in the old style, but no doubt flattered himself that he had at least shown more regard to decency and morality than audiences were accustomed to find in the plays of Wycherley, Dryden, and Mrs. Behn.

Thomas Baker, in the preface to " The Humor of the Age," makes his contribution to the stage controversy. He speaks of those " who bustle mightily for a reformation, and would fain atone their own crimes, by suppressing the vices of others, which they have no pleasure in their taking " ; and continues: " I would not excuse any immorality the stage is guilty of, but when men show so much spleen, as to exclaim against a play, without considering whether the moral of it be virtuous or vicious but because it is a play, an author has not justice done him." " The Humor of the Age " is not very dramatic. It is primarily a series of dialogues discussing and illustrating

contemporary manners. The sinister Railton tries to force
the supposed Quaker Tremilia. Freeman saves her and
falls in love. He offers to marry her in spite of her lack
of fortune. Then she tells him: " Reading and conversation taught me the deceitfulness of men, how many pretended merely for a portion; and that an estate was often
a greater means to ruin a woman than make her happy.
I resolv'd therefore to conceal my fortune, and continue
in this habit, that I might give the world no occasion to
talk or to inquire after me, and either live single, or not
to marry till I found a man whose addresses were out of
pure love." Nothing is more characteristic of sentimental
comedy than this sudden discovery that a disinterested
sacrifice made nobly turns out to be no sacrifice at all.
Poetic justice demands that noble deeds receive proper
payment. Virtue is not its own reward. The hero sacri-
fices material advantages for love, honor, duty or what
not, but always discovers in the end that a sacrifice has
not really been made. Hence the undeniable namby-pam-
byness of sentimental comedy. The moral always seems
to be that nobleness pays; that the best way to look out
for yourself is to appear unselfish, and that the plum will
always drop into your mouth if you appear not to desire
it.

The tone of Baker's satire is gentle rather than misanthropic. Unlike Wycherley, he believed that things could
be improved; and he tried (though he failed) to attain
that sophisticated yet uncynical advocacy of virtue which
made the triumph of the " Spectator." The epilogue concludes:

> " We beg the favors by the fair sex giv'n
> With solemn awe as we petition heaven.
> To please them was the poet's greatest care,
> He thinks in this play, nothing can appear,
> Rude or obscene to grate the nicest ear."

"The Humor of the Age" is an honest attempt to write a moral play, but it will be remembered that one of the charges against the actors when they were arrested included obscene speeches from this play. No reasonable reform would satisfy the reformers. As I pronounce the conclusion of the epilogue, just quoted, innocent, the shade of Collier rises before me and I seem to hear him speak somewhat after the following manner: "What! Petition the fair sex with the solemn awe with which we petition heaven! Thus is God defied, and the flesh-pots given adoration equal to that due to the divine mystery. Under a Christian commonwealth, the lewd poets dare rise to a height of profanity that the Pagans never attained, for they would not have dared pay to a woman the honor due to Jupiter alone."

The group of plays now under discussion shows conclusively that in 1700 and 1701 sentimentalism was making considerable progress, but that it was by no means yet completely triumphant. The best play which appeared in those two years was Farquhar's "Sir Harry Wildair," which is quite in the old tradition and shows its author incapable of treating a romantic scene. In his "A Trip to the Jubilee" (1699) to which the former play is a sequel, he had shown the sinister Lady Lurewell joyfully reunited to her husband, but now she relapses into the character of an unfeeling flirt to accept a large sum of money (which she considers the best love address which she has ever received), and is prevented from fulfilling her part of the bargain only by an unexpected interruption. Farquhar indeed remained true to the old tradition. His two most popular plays, "The Recruiting Officer" (1706) and "The Beaux' Stratagem" (1707), though relatively clean and in so far products of the reformed age, show him a consistent adherent to the old belief that realism and satire, rather than sentiment and morality, were the business of comedy. As long as he and Vanbrugh continued to write successful plays, the triumph of sentimentalism could not be called complete.

On the whole, however, the group of plays just discussed is remarkable both for frequent reference to the necessity for reform and for the evidences of continued development in the direction of sentimentalism. Even where the dramatists were not following the royal road to success which Cibber and Steele were pointing out, they usually avoided the excessive cynicism of Etherege and Wycherley. Between 1696 and this time, the plays of Vanbrugh, in which a good measure of the Restoration thought was mingled with serious discussions of ethical problems and not a little sentiment, had been most successful but had by no means satisfied the reformers. Vanbrugh was denounced (quite unjustly) as more immoral than his predecessors and the continued " reformation " of the stage went on.

Of the plays of the years 1704–5, two are really noteworthy in the development of sentimental comedy, and all the others show some influence from the reform movement, though they are not important. John Dennis was too enthusiastic an admirer of the comedies of King Charles' time not to exclude sentiment from his tragi-comedy " Gibraltar," but he was also too much a believer in the moral end of comedy not to give this one a purpose. Motteux, who tried to pass as a reformer of the stage, gives us " Farewell Folly," a comedy open to little objection either in incident or moral, and concludes thus:

> " Long toss'd in youth, that stormy time of life;
> Our safest port is a kind virtuous wife."

A. Chaves' " The Cares of Love " (1705) is uninteresting
but clean, while Nicholas Rowe's comedy " The Biter "
is one of those plays in which the prevailing perversity and
coarseness of the Restoration has been almost dropped,
though little sentiment has been added. This brings us
to the two important plays of the year, Cibber's " Careless
Husband " and Steele's " Tender Husband."

The great success of both marks an important stage in
the struggle of sentimental comedy for triumph. Both
were conscious attempts to establish a new school. Steele
had already written two moral plays and declared his set
purpose to write innocently. In the preface to " The Careless Husband," Cibber writes significantly as follows:
" The best criticks have long and justly complained, that
the coarseness of most characters in our late comedies,
have been unfit entertainments for people of quality,
especially the ladies." He has waited in vain, he says, for
some one else to take the lead, but is now resolved to
strike the first blow himself. Like its predecessor " Love's
Last Shift," " The Careless Husband " is the story of the
reform of a rake, but it is an infinitely better play. The
former was not only nonsense but hypocritical nonsense,
while the new play was developed with a greater appearance of sincerity, and the reform made probable by preparation from the beginning instead of being unconvincingly tacked on at the end. Sir Charles Easy carries on
amours with both his wife's servant and a certain Lady
Gravairs. Lady Easy knows this, but hides her knowledge. Sir Charles is growing weary of the impertinencies
of his mistress, and one day falls asleep in the servant's
room without his wig. His wife finds him there, and instead of awakening him, simply covers his head. When
he wakes, he realizes what has happened and that his
wife is tender in spite of her knowledge of his unfaithful-

ness. This realization is the last straw, and he goes to seek and find forgiveness from her.

In Steele's play the situation is reversed. The tender husband interrupts a rendezvous which his wife has with a supposed lover whom he has sent to tempt her. A scene of repentance and forgiveness supplies material for sentimentalism. Both of these plays were very successful, and took their place as favorites in the standard repertory of the theater. Since each called attention to itself as departing from the Restoration tradition, success must be interpreted as constituting a substantial triumph for sentimentalism.

The seasons of 1709–10 and 1710–11 together yield only six new comedies. Settle's " City Ramble," the central idea of which is borrowed from " The Knight of the Burning Pestle," is innocent though not sentimental. The two comedies which Mrs. Centlivre produced during the seasons under consideration show her to belong half to the new school and half to the old. Her " Marplot " (published 1711) suggests the old tradition by the way in which the husband is saved from adultery more or less against his will, but " The Man's Bewitch'd " is much cleaner in tone than the Restoration plays and shows definitely the influence of the new tradition. The hero seeks matrimony willingly and not as a last resort. Illegitimate intrigue (the customary parallel to courtship in Restoration plays) is absent, and Shadwell's description of the type, quoted in a previous chapter, would not apply to this play. The names of her characters will serve as well as anything else to show the change in tone. In the old comedies one meets constantly Wildish, Sparkish, Bellamour, etc. In this play appear Faithful, Lovely, and Constant as heroes, and one rubs one's eyes to discover if he has not by chance strayed into " Pilgrim's Progress."

The three remaining plays of this group are definitely and insistently sentimental. Charles Johnson's "The Generous Husband" links itself closely to the new tradition by the importance given to a scene of repentance and forgiveness, but the anonymous "Injur'd Love" is still more striking. Thrivemore has returned from a voyage on which he was reported dead, to find that his former love Charmilla is a widow and about to enter into a marriage of convenience with Rashlove, who, believing his wife unfaithful, had left her to die on a desert island from which she has escaped and followed him disguised as a man. Of course Thrivemore wins back Charmilla, and Rashlove's wife proves that his suspicions of her are unfounded. At this discovery he breaks out: "With surprise and joy, ecstasy and wonder, my soul as by meeting torrents tost leaves me not calm enough to consider whether I dream or wake."

Charles Shadwell's "The Fair Quaker of Deal" won a permanent place in the dramatic repertory. It is a typical sentimental comedy in that all the bad characters are about to receive poetic justice but are reprieved on a promise of reform, and in that the last scene consists of an orgy of benevolence and happiness. Captain Worthy, landing from a voyage to claim his faithful Quaker, Dorcas (imagine a Quaker heroine in a Restoration play!), overhears a plot on the part of the foppish Lieutenant Mizen to steal her for her money. He concocts a plan and writes a false note of encouragement purporting to come from her, but sends a disguised street-walker to take her place. A similar trick is played on another rake. Then Dorcas' sister makes advances to Worthy. Instead of treating her as a wild gallant would have done, he says, somewhat in the vein of Joseph Surface: "Madame, I know my own unworthiness too well to believe you are in earnest; but were it so, my honor tells me I must not be so base to wrong your sister." In revenge she writes a forged letter to Dorcas, saying that Worthy is married to some one else. Dorcas swoons, but is revived to discover the imposture. Now the two rakes enter with their disguised wives. They are dismayed on hearing the truth, but Worthy tells them he can relieve them if they will provide for the women so as to enable them to lead honest lives. The rakes agree and say moreover that they will reform themselves also. Worthy then tells them that they were married by a bogus parson and that the whole scheme was concocted to encompass their reform. It is significant that this play became one of the most popular of the new pieces, and that to it Cibber attributes a considerable share in the financial success of the company which played it. By this time sentimentalism was well on its way to the domination of the English stage.

Dramatic production during these years was languishing in quantity as well as quality. The seasons of 1714–15, 1715–16, and 1716–17 saw only six new comedies, including the highly indecent "Three Hours after Marriage," which was so promptly and crushingly damned. Needless to say, Addison's "The Drummer" was free from offense. It complains:

" To long has marriage in this tasteless age.
With ill bred raillery supplied the stage,

and attempts thus to rebuke a stock scene with the double charge of immorality and bad taste, two criteria which were coming to be regarded as supreme. Mrs. Davys' "The Northern Heiress" boasts that "it is free from the three grand topics on which most of our modern comedies are founded, viz: obscenity, faction and a general contempt of religion." It is indeed, like Christopher Bullock's

" Woman is a Riddle," innocent enough and certainly dull. " The Artful Husband," attributed to William Taverner, achieved success by borrowing from Shirley still another story of the wife reformed of her errors; and Charles Johnson, with " The Country Lasses," showed that it was possible to avoid both the virtues and the vices of Restoration Comedy and still be mildly amusing without falling into the worst excesses of sentimentalism. In this play Hartwell and Modely find their horses lamed in the country. They mistake two ladies, Flora and Aura, for country wenches, and persuade them to find shelter. In the manner of the usual wild gallant they make love and propose that the girls become their mistresses. Flora presents to Hartwell a serious statement of the reasons why it would be unwise for her to do so, and he marries her. Modely, however, scoffs at him and tries to force Aura. In a Restoration Comedy she might have remonstrated, but at worst would probably have only called him a gay dog, and considered the incident merely as a tribute to her attractiveness. Here she slaps his face and calls for help. Freeman, a country gentleman, arrives and denounces Modely in good round terms. The latter puts up the customary excuses of the Restoration hero — it is a custom — he loves all women — and so forth and so forth. Instead of applauding this as an expression of liberal philosophy, and pronouncing Modely a witty and charming young man, Freeman tells him: " You have broke every virtue, and yet impudently imagine you are in the character of a gentleman," thus merely reproducing Steele's remark that the famous hero of " Sir Fopling Flutter " was considered a type of the gentleman though he broke all the laws of gentility. The significant fact is that the audience of 1715 was taking pleasure in seeing the conventional morality upheld, just as the audience in 1685 had taken pleasure in seeing it scoffed at.

To show that by 1725, the upper limit of this study, the transformation of comedy was practically complete; that in spite of sporadic reversions to type like the " Beggar's Opera," the plays of Fielding, and the burlesques which led to the passing of the licensing Act of 1737, the brilliant perversity of the old comedy had almost ceased to exist, and that sentimentalism had become the prevailing spirit, it will only be necessary to glance rapidly at the twelve new comedies which appeared during the seasons 1719–20 to 1725–6 inclusive.[1]

Several of the plays of this period, including by far the most noteworthy, Steele's " The Conscious Lovers," reek with sentiment, and not one is in the old spirit of cynical abandon. The two which come nearest to the Restoration spirit are Griffith's " Whig and Tory " (1720), which, without being particularly indecent, is not sentimental or moralizing, and Mrs. Centlivre's " The Artifice " (1722). Mrs. Centlivre is hardly a sentimental dramatist. Her personal predilections are for the good old days of Mrs. Behn; but she knows that a bit of morality pleases her generation, and so she adds a dash of maple sugar to the spice, following the old tradition of making a hero a wild gallant constantly engaged in dodging husbands and repulsing mistresses, but satisfying the new taste by taking on a moral conclusion. Face to face with a cast-off mistress, the hero offers her a one-third share in his affections, and she refuses. Then with that strange susceptibility to conversion which began to manifest itself in rakes about the year 1700, he is about to turn honorable when she tells him that, anticipating no such conclusion, she has just given him poison. The fear of matrimony is allayed by the prospect of death, and he agrees to atone for past sins

---

[1] *A Wife to be Let* has already been discussed. I have not been able to find *The Impertinent Lovers* mentioned but not seen by Genest.

by marrying her. Of course the draught turns out not to be
fatal and the couple are left to live happily ever after, or at
least as happily as the reader can imagine them to have.
The prologue calls attention to the noble example proclaiming:

> "You tender virgins and neglected wives,
>   For you, she all her artifice contrives."

Richardson was by no means the first to consider marriage
to a rake a suitable reward for virtue, for the history of
sentimentalism is full of such artifices.

Smythe's "The Rival Modes," Sturme's "The Compromise," and Odingsell's "The Capricious Lovers" are completely innocent and terribly dull; while Thomas Southern
boasts (perhaps not wholly justifiably) of his "Money the
Mistress" that "'tis fram'd on the model of Terence, and
as comedies ought to be, not to do harm; the characters
in nature, the manners instructive of youth, and at least
becoming sixty and six, the age of the writer. I have
punish'd infidelity in the lover and falseness in the
friends." Leigh's "Kensington Gardens" again presents
the heroine who conceals her fortune in order to be sure
that she is loved for herself alone; and the concluding tag
adds another voice to the chorus which was endeavoring to
drown in a praise of matrimony the cynical views which
the Restoration wit had expressed of this subject. It runs:

> "Let roving minds, vain empty joys pursue,
>   And court loose pleasures only, cause they're new:
>   Let others by vile arts their ends obtain,
>   And try by falsehoods their desires to gain:
>   Man's chiefest bliss, this night's success does prove,
>   Is truth, and constancy, and virtuous love."

In "The Bath Unmask'd" Odingsell registers a sort of
general protest against the conventional stage morals of

the Restoration which he embodies in the person of Pander, while he takes as his hero a very sedate young man in whom love has not only ceased to be animal but has grown more or less into that " esteem " of which we hear so much in the eighteenth century. " Virtue is the incentive of love," says he; and when Pander expresses a seventeenth-century commonplace thus: " Constancy is a crying sin against the law of nature, because it tends to monopoly, which robs others of that perfection which each has an equal right to," the virtuous hero is content to let who will be clever and replies only: " This is villainous scandal, and I'll not believe it." In the end he slights his former mistress (in the most innocent sense, of course) to marry her younger sister because the former has imbibed too much *esprit* from Pander. Yet Congreve was still alive.

Similarly, Welsted's " The Dissembled Wanton " presents the hero as prig rather than the hero as rake. When it is suggested that he appear, for strategic purposes, to make love to some one not the object of his affections, he replies: " Make love to one I have no love for, nor any desire to obtain! Will that be honorable, dear Severne? I may possibly win the young lady's affections." Wishing to try the virtue of the object of his heart, he proposes an irregular union. And she, planning to escape somehow, agrees on the condition that he tell her the truth about a rumor which credits him with an amour with another woman. Of course the rumor is calumny, but the young man, far from being enthralled as a Restoration hero would have been with the idea of having his mistress without the necessity of submission to the matrimonial yoke, is appalled by her too great generosity and exclaims: " Fall'n from her bright orb of innocence, and her great soul level'd with vice," and again: " Oh, virgin honor! Oh, spotless virtue. Have you a real being or do you subsist only in sound?" One wonders what one of Mrs. Behn's heroines would have said to such a lover.

Steele's "The Conscious Lovers" I have left to the last. It assumes a position of primary importance because of the extraordinary success which it achieved, and because the author evidently intended it to be a telling blow against the old comedies. The play is too well known to require an elaborate discussion. The hero Bevil, a kind-hearted gentleman and romantic lover, is intended to be a sort of a model gentleman of the new and reformed school; and the prologue, written for a performance of the play at the College at Dublin, shows that he was thought of as a sort of contrast to the hero of Sir Fopling Flutter, the model gentleman of the old school. The plot, taken from Terence, involves the familiar situation of the discovery of a long-lost daughter, and concludes with a scene of tender and almost tearful joy such as the sentimentalist liked to offer instead of a comic dénouement. Dennis, Steele's inveterate enemy, makes fun of the care which the latter took to insure the success of this crowning effort and final plea for the new comedy. Advertisements, he says,[1] have been sent to newspapers, saying that in the opinion of excellent judges the comedy then in rehearsal is the best that ever came upon the English stage; and he remarks that "His play has traveled as far as Edinburgh northward, and as far as Wales westward, and has been read to more persons than will be at the representation of it, or vouchsafe to read it, when it is published." Indeed, as early as 1720, Steele had spoken in "The Theater" of "a friend of mine who has lately prepared a comedy according to the just laws of the stage," and in "Mist's Weekly Journal" (Nov. 18, 1721) it is noted that "Sir Richard Steele proposes to represent a character upon the

[1] *A Defense of Sir Fopling Flutter.*

stage this season that was never seen there yet; his Gentleman has been two years a dressing, and we wish he may make a good appearance at last." [1]

Steele took care that " The Conscious Lovers " should be understood to be not merely a play but also one more protest against the Restoration Comedy; for he prefaced it with a discussion in which he declared that its " chief design " was to be an innocent performance, and boasted of its ethical purpose by writing: " The whole was writ for the sake of the scene of the fourth act, where Mr. Bevil evades the quarrel with his friends." Its importance as a triumph for sentimentalism was recognized by Dennis, who directed pamphlets against it; by Benjamin Victor, who befriended it; and by George I, who gave Steele a handsome present in recognition of the play's service in contributing to the reform of the stage. Its success was immense, as it not only had a long initial run, but became a favorite piece in the standard repertory, thus showing that popular favor had swung definitely to the sentimental drama. It may indeed be taken as marking the final victory of the new type. As the survey of comedy from 1720 to 1725 has shown, sentimentalism now dominated the stage.

The method which we chose to select plays for comment has its disadvantages. It has necessitated the mention of many pieces of little importance, and the omission of some intrinsically good ones by Farquhar, Vanbrugh, and Mrs. Centlivre, but it has achieved our immediate purpose in demonstrating the steps by which a change came over English dramatic writing. Emphatically, a marked change did take place, beginning just before Collier's attack on the stage, and continuing until it had transformed the prevailing tradition. Of course it was not abrupt. Congreve

[1] G. A. Aitken. Introduction to Mermaid ed. of Steele's Plays.

did not immediately cease to be Congreve, and the old school did not immediately cease to have followers, yet the change was, as such things go, rather surprisingly rapid. As early as 1696 there could be observed some tendency to moderate the tone of comedy. The authors were, perhaps, not quite so anxious to be indecent, and their heroes were probably not quite so hard or so base. Certainly such a change is observable shortly after 1696, and it progresses until by 1725 indecency was the exception rather than the rule, and the rake had ceased to be the model of perfection. The new elements of sentiment, emotion, and conscious moralizing had also entered, and gradually became more and more prominent until the typical play was more likely to be idealistic, moralizing, and lachrymose than cynical, perverse, and intellectual.

It must not be forgotten, however, that though new plays had ceased to follow the old tradition, still the old ones continued to be popular. The number of new plays produced per year was usually not very large, and the actors were forced to depend upon a tried repertory to which new plays were added as soon as they were shown to have an abiding popularity. The new theories concerning propriety, though they influenced so markedly the new dramatic output, did not prevent the continued popularity of the best of the old plays. The following table will illustrate this fact by showing the number of performances of certain popular plays which occurred during representative seasons of the first quarter of the eighteenth century. From it, it will be seen that while such sentimental plays as "Love's Last Shift," "The Tender Husband," "The Careless Husband," and "The Fair Quaker of Deal" established themselves in lasting favor, nevertheless such plays as the lascivious "The Rover" of Mrs. Behn, Crown's "Sir Courtly Nice" (for expressions in which the actors had been arrested), "Sir Fopling Flutter" (Steele's *bête noir*) as well as other typical Restoration plays continued to be popular.[1]

Season	1704–5	1709–10	1714–15	1719–20	1724–25
Number of Performances during Season (Approximate)					
Amphytrion.............	3	3	0	3	1
Careless Husband........	16*	3	4	4	6
Committee..............	7	4	3	9	7
Constant Couple.........	2	5	6	4	6
Fair Quaker of Deal......	..	15*	0	4	3
Love for Love...........	3	8	2	6	4
Love in a Tub..........	5	0	1	0	0
Love's Last Shift.........	1	2	4	3	5
Man of Mode...........	3	3	3	3	3
Old Bachelor...........	3	3	4	4	6
Plain Dealer...........	3	0	0	0	0
Recruiting Officer........	..	8	3	6	6
Relapse................	3	2	6	0	7
Rover.................	3	5	1	5	4
She Would if She Could...	3	1	1	1	1
Sir Courtly Nice.........	3	4	2	2	3
Squire of Alsatia........	4	0	1	3	4
Tender Husband.........	6*	2	2	3	3

* Indicates Premier Performance.

[1] A complete theatrical record for this period has never been published. This table is compiled from a manuscript calendar which is almost complete. It was made by Frederick Laterille and bequeathed to the British Museum. It is no doubt only approximately correct, but it is suggestive.

CHAPTER IX

THE THEORY OF SENTIMENTAL COMEDY

WHILE the controversy over the purely moral aspects of the drama was going on, general literary criticism was continuing to develop in the different directions indicated in a previous chapter, and was constantly increasing in bulk and prominence. The great achievements of the period — such as Congreve's discussion of the Pindaric Ode, Addison's criticism of Paradise Lost and Chevy Chase, and the Shakespearian scholarship of Rowe, Pope, and Theobald — are well known, but there was restless critical activity in other fields. Spenser was edited, and ballads were collected. Translations from the French continued to appear, while Dennis, Gildon, and others wrote additional heavy treatises. But here once more we are concerned only with pointing out the greatly increasing interest in literary criticism which reveals itself in the abundance of trifling catch-penny publications as well as in those serious works which have found a place in literary history. Popular literary biography began with a series of last wills and testaments satirized by Addison.[1] "There is," he says, "a race of men lately sprung up — whom one cannot reflect upon without indignation as well as contempt. They are our Grub-street biographers, who watch for the death of a great man like so many undertakers, on purpose to make a penny of him. He is no sooner laid in his grave, but he falls into the hands of an historian; who, to swell a volume, ascribes to him works which he never

[1] "The Freeholder" No. 35. April 20, 1716.

wrote, and actions which he never performed; celebrates virtues which he was never famous for, and excuses faults which he was never guilty of. They fetch their only authentic records out of Doctors Commons, and when they have got a copy of his last Will and Testament, they fancy themselves furnished with sufficient materials for his history." These little books deserve Addison's contempt, but they illustrate the growing public interest in literature. Pamphlets on individual plays continue to appear, and journalistic criticism takes a more and more prominent part. In the journal " The Freeholder " we have a number of dramatic reviews not differing much in scope or character from the criticisms with which one is familiar today.

Criticism had established with literature a rapport which made the controversy concerning the moral function of the stage more rapidly effective. It is not to be understood, of course, that the drama would not have changed without criticism. The change was inevitable, since it was part of a great movement expressing itself everywhere in life. Still the existence of a rapport between literature and a criticism whose fundamental tenets played into the hands of the moralist made it possible for the drama to respond much more readily to popular demands than would otherwise have been possible. Nor is it probable that, without criticism, the new drama would have taken just the form which it did. As has already been pointed out, Restoration Comedy could have been purified without the addition of the sentimental element, but this and the other distinguishing characteristics of the Sentimental Comedy were encouraged by the development of their theoretical basis in criticism. The Elizabethan drama was of spontaneous growth, with no theory behind it. Every feature of the Sentimental Comedy, on the other hand, was sup-

ported by critical dogmas which developed along with it.
Perhaps its own essential badness would have condemned
it to an early death had not criticism " proved " that it was
good.

An interesting illustration of the influence of criticism
on popular taste may be seen in the case of Addison's
"Cato," the success of which has always seemed rather
strange to modern readers. It is not a good play. Nor
is it the sort of thing that the English public has ever
taken to naturally. Its success has been partially explained on the basis of its supposed application to the
politics of the day, but this is not all. It was a success
also because it fulfilled the requirements set by the now
popular criticism for a good tragedy. That it should please
was secondary. A tragedy, said the critics, must be regular, and, above all, must be instructive — must be a sugar-
coated pill of philosophy. These conditions " Cato "
fulfilled, and consequently it was incumbent upon the
public to be pleased. As one writer in discussing this play
put it,[1] " the rules and what pleases are never contrary to
each other." " Cato," he adds, is consonant with the rules
and so if it does not please this is the fault of the spectator
and not of the piece. At least five separate pamphlets
were called forth by the play.[2]

Dennis, it is true, wrote against it but he never thinks
of questioning the rules. He attacks " Cato " on the
grounds that it does not satisfy critical requirements.

[1] *Cato Examined.* Anon. 1713.
[2] *Remarks upon Cato*, etc. By Dennis. 1713; *A Vindication of
the English Stage, exemplified in the Cato of Mr. Addison.* Anon.
1713; *Cato Examined.* Anon. 1713; *Mr. Addison turn'd Tory . . .
wherein it is made to appear that the Whigs have misunderstood
that author in his tragedy . . . to which are added, some cursory
remarks upon the play itself.* Anon. 1713; *Observations upon Cato.*
[W. Sewell] 1713.

Love should not have been introduced; and, above all, it fails because it does not satisfy the requirements of poetic justice. It shows Cato a blameless man brought to a tragic end, and therefore has an immoral tendency, because people should be taught that the virtuous are rewarded.

All this seems far enough from a modern attitude towards literature; but it will help to make clear the importance which critical theory had in moulding popular taste of this period. The hack writer George Sewell wrote a pamphlet called " A Vindication of the English Stage Exemplified in the Cato of Mr. Addison," in which his enthusiasm cannot contain itself within the limits of prose and ends with a burst of verse as follows:

> "Britons, with lessen'd wonder, now behold
> Your former wit, and all your bards of old;
> Jonson out-vi'd in his own way confess,
> And own that Shakespeare's self now pleases less."

An Elizabethan audience would not have been so fooled. It would have recognized immediately the lifelessness of " Cato " and there would have been an end of it; but to the Queen Anne audience it had been demonstrated by logic absolute that " Cato " was a good play and therefore must be admired.

A sufficient number of quotations from prologues, epilogues, prefaces, and dedications was given in the preceding chapter to illustrate how self-conscious was the movement for a reformed drama, and how constantly the playwrights appealed to their audience to note that the play about to be presented or read complied with the new ideas of stage morality and hence had a right to favor. I wish now to examine the theory of sentimental comedy as expounded by its practitioners.

Cibber, no doubt, was the first to seize the idea of the

practical value of sentimentalism, and since " Love's Last
Shift" came before the Collier controversy, it is evident
that the need which Cibber met could not be directly
traced to Collier, but that it existed before Cibber and
Steele made their successful efforts to meet it. Throughout
his long career Cibber never ceased to preach as well as
practice the principles of the new drama, and he was constantly pointing out that his plays were conscious attempts to meet its demands. He proclaimed that " The
Careless Husband " was written in answer to " the best
criticks," who " have long and justly complain'd, that
the coarseness of most characters in our late comedies have
been unfit entertainments for people of quality, especially
the ladies." He adds: " I was long in hopes, that some
able pen (whose expectation did not hang upon the profits
of success) wou'd generously attempt to reform the town
into a better taste, than the world generally allows 'em:
But nothing of that kind having lately appear'd, that
wou'd give me an opportunity of being wise at another's
expence, I found it impossible any longer to resist the
secret temptation of my vanity, and so ev'n struck the first
blow myself." " A play without a just moral," he says
elsewhere,[1] " is a poor and trivial undertaking; and 'tis
from the success of such pieces, that Mr. Collier was furnish'd with an advantageous pretense of laying his un-
merciful axe to the roots of the stage." Accordingly,
" The Lady's Last Stake " has a moral, the evil of gam-
bling; and the purpose of the play, he declares, is answered
if one person is reformed. Similarly, " The Non-Juror "
is an attempt to remove prejudice and to show " what
honest and laudable uses may be made of the theater,
when its performances keep close to the true purposes
of its institution "; and as for the " Provok'd Hus-

[1] Dedication to *The Lady's Last Stake.*

band," " the design of this play [is] chiefly to expose, and
reform the irregularities that, too often break in upon
the peace and happiness of the married state." In com-
pleting Vanbrugh's posthumous fragment " The Provok'd
Husband," he assures us that Vanbrugh himself had been
convinced of the error of his former ways, and intended
this play to be strictly moral — even to go so far as to
show the erring wife banished from her home. However,
finding this too severe for comedy, Cibber has fallen back
upon the device of repentance and reform and given the
play a happy ending. Of Vanbrugh himself he says:

> " At length, he own'd, that plays should let you see
> Not only, what you are, but ought to be;
> Tho' vice was natural, 'twas never meant
> The stage should shew it, but for punishment."

To Steele, however, belongs whatever credit may attach
to the position of foremost theoretical advocate of the new
comedy. His exposition encouraged its development, and
to him we must turn for its most complete apologia. He
too was perfectly conscious of his purpose and set himself
definitely to his task. Nor did he regard himself as an
innovator. He acknowledged his debt to Collier, of whom
he proclaimed himself " a great admirer," [1] and in the prologue to the " Lying Lover " he recognized the spirit of his
age and asked for favor:

> If then you find our author treads the stage
> With just regard to a reforming age.

He wished simply to throw his influence on the side of a
movement whose existence he recognized.

His first play, " The Funeral," is hardly a sentimental
comedy, but in each of the others he proclaims his prevailing intention. " The Lying Lover " was an attempt

[1] *Mr. Steele's Apology for Himself and his Writings.* 1714.

to write comedy " which might be no improper entertainment in a Christian commonwealth." In " The Tender
Husband " he was careful, he says, to avoid everything
that might look " ill-natured, immoral, or prejudicial toward what the better part of mankind holds sacred and
honorable; " while as for " The Conscious Lovers," " the
chief design of this was to be an innocent performance."
So firmly did he believe that the fundamental function of
the drama was instruction that he had no objection to a
state censorship even though that censorship were conducted from a political standpoint. It ought to be the
aim of every government, he says, to see that public
spectacles are agreeable to the law, religion, and manners
of the country in which they are produced and to take
care that their teaching is in agreement with the government's policy. When he petitioned King George for a
theatrical patent, he based his claim upon his position
as a reformer. " Your petitioner," he says, " by writing the
comedy of ' The Conscious Lovers,' has found by experience that more regular and virtuous entertainment would
take place, if he had duration of time in which to establish rules and make contracts accordingly." [1]

There was no doubt as to his fitness for the task which
he set himself. If the stage was to be " reformed," it
must be through the leadership of some one who had the
sympathy of the cultured and liberal part of mankind. The
theater-going public must be met half-way. Collier had
been an excellent awakener, but his extreme views made

[1] British Museum. Add. Mss. 32, 685. It is to be noted that
Steele had no conception whatever of the value of that critical
spirit which is generally supposed to be the chief virtue of modern
literature. To him, morality, religion, and policy were simple
things concerning which there could be no legitimate difference of
opinion, and his idea of a perfect dramatic literature was one
completely orthodox in all particulars.

him useless except as an agitator. Over him Steele had an immense advantage. In the first place, being a wit, a dramatist, and a man of letters, Steele belonged to the class he was attacking, and was not, like Collier, a complete outsider and hence at a tremendous disadvantage. Secondly, being a man of the world, he could differentiate between those things which practically all decent men would agree in considering objectionable and those things which could offend only fanatics like Collier, Bedford, and the rest. Accordingly, when he makes an attack on a play he chooses one obviously corrupt like "Sir Fopling Flutter," instead of confusing the issue by exercising ingenuity to find offense in doubtful instances. All this was necessary. The early eighteenth century was a reforming age, but it was also a polished age; and the time was past when people were willing to follow the leadership of pedantic Puritans of the type of Gosson and Prynne. Steele's generation was opposed to the licentiousness of the court of Charles II, but it had no intention of being dragged back into fanaticism. Prynne and Gosson could cause the theater to be closed, but they could not modify the Elizabethan drama. By establishing a rapport between esthetics and morality in criticism, Cibber, Steele, and others were able to produce a new comedy.

At least from the time of the performance of "The Lying Lover" to that of "The Conscious Lovers," Steele kept up a constant propaganda in favor of the reformed stage by writing plays which illustrated what he demanded and by publishing in his periodicals little articles in which he praised or blamed current dramatic works in accordance with his principles, and unobtrusively laid down and defended the theoretical basis of sentimental comedy. Quotations from the "Spectator" have a double significance. They show, on the one hand, how Steele was, in a measure, leading public opinion. On the other hand, since the paper was so enormously popular, he must have been, when he was not leading, at least giving expression to ideas already half formulated in the minds of his readers. Though he did not initiate either the moral movement or the idea of sentimentality, yet his contemporaries as well as subsequent generations were accustomed to look at him as the center of influence. Cibber testifies to his success, saying that scarcely a member of the theatrical company had not been improved by "The Tatler" and that "many days had our house been particularly fill'd by the influence and credit of his pen." [1] According to Gay,[2] he was the first to show that "anything witty could be said in praise of the marriage state," or that "devotion or virtue were anywhere necessary — to the character of a fine gentleman." [3]

Steele was not without some opposition. The old comedy had a violent supporter in John Dennis, who came into ill-tempered conflict with him; but the greatest member of the old school, Congreve, retired from dramatic writing and remained respected but silent. Congreve was a genius and he was not opposed to decency, but he had too keen an insight not to be conscious of the absurdities into which the new style comedy was drifting, and he was too much of an artist not to regret them. He realized that he was out of the spirit of the times, and hence he held his peace. One wishes that he had written fully what he thought, but we must be content with a sentence, which, however, reveals much. To Joseph Kealley, Esquire, of Dublin, he writes from London on December 9, 1704: "Cibber has produced a play [no doubt the wonderful

---

[1] *Apology.*

[2] *Character of Steele.* 1729.

[3] See also Steele's discussion of plays in *Town Talk*. Nos. 1, 2, 6 (1714).

" Careless Husband "], consisting of fine gentlemen and fine conversation altogether; which the ridiculous town for the most part likes; but there are some that know better." [1] Congreve had outlived his age, but he knew how to keep silent.

It is to the " Discourse upon Comedy in reference to the English Stage " (1702), by Farquhar, the last of the old school, that we must look for the best exposition of the principles of Restoration Comedy. He finds in his unhappy age that poor comedy is attacked on all sides. The scholar calls out for decorum and economy, the courtier for wit and purity of style, and the citizen for humor and ridicule, while the clergy damns the theater for immorality. However willing he may be, the unfortunate poet cannot please all. If he sets out to write according to the rules, he will bore his audience so completely that it will seek other amusements among the masks of the pit; and so " tho' the play be as regular as Aristotle, and modest as Mr. Collier cou'd wish, yet it promotes more lewdness in the consequence, and procures more effectively for intrigue than any Rover, Libertine, or old Batchelour whatsoever."

Lay aside the rules, he says, and look at the institution of comedy. He defines it as a " well-fram'd tale handsomely told, as an agreeable vehicle for counsel and reproof," which seems conciliating enough to Dennis, Steele, and their like; but let us note his application. He finds that Congreve's " Old Bachelor " has an excellent moral. " Fondlewife and his young spouse are no more than the eagle and cockle; he wanted teeth to break the shell himself, so somebody else run away with the meat — here are precepts, admonitions and salutary innuendos for the ordering of our lives and conversations couch'd in the allegories and allusions." In other words, says Farquhar, the

[1] *Literary Relics. George Monck-Berkley.*

moral is that if an old man marries a young wife he must not be surprised if she is unfaithful to him. Truly this is a moral, but not one which would have pleased Steele, who would have been more anxious to reprove the moral delinquency of the wife. Yet the fable does carry a lesson. It does illustrate forcibly a truth. The best Restoration comedies, such as those of Wycherley and Congreve, do this constantly. They are not moral in the sense of striving much to raise the ethical standard, but like all good art they give information concerning the life which they depict and to that extent are instructive in worldly wisdom. But with such instruction Steele was not satisfied. Like Collier and the other moralists he wanted the drama to teach an ideal. Wycherley and Congreve were wise men. They understood the life of their time, they knew a good deal of human nature, and they illustrated its principles in the actions of their characters, but they made no attempt to improve it. As the author of the " Letter to Mr. Congreve, etc." points out, the real moral of " Love for Love " is contained in the tag:

> " The miracle today is, that we find
> A lover true: Not that a woman's kind."

This is indeed a pointed truth and hence in one sense a genuine moral. Farquhar was making a plea for the recognition of the value of such worldly instruction. When he says that comedy teaches, it is evident that he does not mean that it teaches abstract virtue, but merely that it teaches prudence or, to put it more broadly, *savoir vivre*.

Steele insisted that literature should inspire a desire for ideal excellence, a thing which Restoration Comedy had never attempted and which, indeed, Sentimental Comedy, as anyone who will read it may see, failed lamentably to accomplish. It wished to express an idealism, but it did not succeed in embodying that idealism in any form capable of appealing to a sophisticated generation. Two centuries have agreed that Restoration Comedy could not be expected to elevate human nature in any way, but have recognized its success within the limits which it proposed itself. Sentimental Comedy attempted, perhaps, a nobler task, but it failed because of an error in method. Anxious to recommend virtue, it insisted that virtue be given material success and that, concretely, the honorable young man should infallibly marry an heiress. But in so doing it produced plays which were false comedy because they were false to life. Neither the old comedy nor the new can be said to have taught virtue, the first because it did not make virtue attractive, and the second because, not content with making virtue attractive, it insisted on making it necessarily successful. Since every one recognized the *non-sequitur* of this relationship which the dramatist had established between uprightness and success, no one was edified.

Let us turn now to a consideration of Steele's theory of the drama.

The most obviously just charge that could be brought against Restoration Comedy was that it introduced what Collier called "smut." The Restoration audience liked it, and the poorer writers used it as their chief stock in trade, while even the best fell back upon it occasionally. Collier said that the dramatist used smut "as the old ones did machines to relieve a failing invention."[1] And Steele follows him.[2] Most writers, he says, have fallen back upon it occasionally, and he observes that "it is remarkable that the writers of least learning (Mrs. Behn and Mrs. Pix) are best skilled in the luscious way." He himself

[1] *Short View.*
[2] *Spectator*, No. 51.

wishes first of all to be innocent. In the dedication to
" The Tender Husband " he writes to Addison: " I should
not offer it to you — had I not been careful to avoid everything that might look ill-natured, immoral, or prejudicial
to what the better part of mankind holds sacred and honorable." And he was not averse to revising even his own
works on the basis of his severe principles. A letter in
" Spectator " 51 calls attention to the following speech from
" The Funeral ":

> Campley: Oh, that Harriot! To hold these arms about
> the waist of the beauteous, struggling, and at last
> yielding fair! "

In the next edition the latter part of the speech was forthwith expunged as being too " luscious."

The plea of the old dramatists had been that while of
course they represented vice on the stage, comedy was by
definition a picture of faulty people, and their characters
were held up to scorn rather than admiration. Sometimes
such a plea was justified, but often, if made, it was obviously insincere, for much of the comedy dialogue consists
in nothing more than a flouting of all the principles of
conventional morality. Steele, like Collier, felt that smut
was not permissible under any circumstances, and of course
he rejected the insincere protestations of the dramatists,
recognizing that, for all they might say, the perverted ingenuity of their characters represented too often the opinions of themselves and their audience. In " Spectator " 525
he writes: " Indeed, if I may speak my opinion of a great
part of the writings which once prevailed among us under
the notion of humor, they are such as would tempt one to
think there had been an association among the wits of
those times to rally legitimacy out of our island," but as
for himself, " I must confess it has been my ambition, in
the course of my writings, to restore, as well as I was able,
the proper ideas of things."

The quotations just given represent the opinion of Steele, not only upon the subject of smut, but also upon the kindred subject of the bad man as hero or central character. According to him, what one sees on the stage one tends to imitate. If the characters talk smut, then the spectators will talk smut; and if the central character is immoral, then the spectators will tend to be immoral. The defense of the old dramatist was the same in both cases. Comedy must represent people as they are. Indelicacy is common in contemporary life, therefore it must be common on the stage. Many prominent men in life are bad, therefore many heroes are bad. The dramatist must not be taken to approve of all that he shows. The fact that his characters talk smut does not mean that he approves of smut, and when he makes a bad man a central character he intends the picture to be satiric and the audience to avoid the faults which are exhibited.

Simple natures, however, have a not wholly unfounded distrust of satire, which is indeed a dangerous weapon. Whatever may be its purpose, it too often, as Dryden said of his " Limberham," expresses the vices which it satirizes. Steele would have no misunderstanding possible. There must be no doubt as to what the dramatist intends. In " Spectator " 446 he writes: " Whatever vices are represented upon the stage, they ought to be so marked and branded by the poet, as not to appear laudable nor amiable in the person who is tainted with them. But if we look into the English comedies above mentioned, we would think they were formed upon a quite contrary maxim, as if this rule, though it held good upon the heathen stage, was not to be regarded in Christian theaters." It is not hard to understand Steele's protest. When the dramatists drew a glittering picture of the young rake resplendent in his vices, satire was often far from their minds; but to insist, as Steele did, that all satire should be perfectly obvious so

that not even a Collier could misunderstand it as he had
misunderstood Vanbrugh's picture of the absurd Lord
Foppington, is to rob satire of its effectiveness; and so
while Steele's requirements might make for morality, they
could hardly make for subtlety, and as a matter of fact the
typical Sentimental Comedy is childishly transparent.

If, said Collier and after him Steele, the Restoration
dramatists intended their pictures of young men about
town as satires, then they had been misunderstood, for
these heroes were commonly regarded by the audience as
models of perfect gentility. "The truth of it is," said
Steele,[1] "the accomplished gentleman upon the English
stage, is the person that is familiar with other men's
wives, and indifferent to his own; as the fine woman is
generally, a composition of sprightliness and falsehoods —
I have often wondered that our ordinary poets cannot
frame to themselves the idea of a fine man who is not a
whore-master, or a fine woman that is not a jilt." All
this, he said, repeating in more moderate language what
Collier had said before him, caused great mischief. The
frequent reflections on love and marriage which had been
heard from the mouths of the characters of comedy were
responsible for a great deal of the corrupt sentiment which
prevailed upon these subjects; for whatever the dramatist
might pretend as to satire, "It is not every youth that
can behold the gentleman of the comedy represented with
a good grace, leading a loose and profligate life, and condemning virtuous affection as insipid, and not be made
secretly emulous of what appears so amiable to a whole
audience." This evil was to be corrected in two ways:
first, by seeing that the bad man achieved failure and not
success in the end, and second, since the audience persisted
in regarding dramatic types as examples for imitation, by

[1] *Spectator,* 446.

presenting for such imitation images of virtue instead of profligacy.

Both of these suggestions ran counter to certain ideas long prevalent. As far back as Jonson poetic justice had been looked upon as somewhat out of place in comedy, and the point had been brought up in the course of the Collier controversy. The purpose of comedy, said Drake,[1] is, indeed, to instruct by example; but it proceeds by showing what should be avoided rather than what should be imitated. And there must be no examples except for caution. Vanbrugh had expressed the same idea more fully.[2] He has drawn, he says, the fine gentleman as he appears in life. He has laid open his vices as well as his virtues, and it is the business of the audience to observe where the gentleman's flaws lessen his value, and to see how much finer a thing he would have been without them.

In theory, Vanbrugh was nearer right than Steele or Collier. Comedy must present real and not ideal characters, but Restoration Comedy had not fairly laid open virtues and vices. It had too often covered the faults of its gallant heroes or represented vices so amiably that they seemed virtues. A great drama might have been made by throwing, as Vanbrugh suggests, the faults of a character in relief by placing them side by side with his virtues; but this the Restoration drama had not often done. In disgust with the dramatic product of the preceding age, Steele threw overboard its whole method, sound as it was, and attempted to found a new comedy on an impossible principle. The ideally virtuous hero whom he wished to set up must always appear as a perfect monster.

Disgusted as he was with the actual dramatic product of the Restoration period, Steele was in no mood to con-

[1] *Ancient and Modern Stages Surveyed.* 1699.
[2] *Short Vindication,* etc.

sider the soundness of its theory. In numerous papers in
the "Spectator" he attacked the old plays violently and laid
down the theory of a new sort of comedy, while in his
plays he illustrated how this theory might be put into
practice. When engaged on the destructive side, he wisely
picked out " Sir Fopling Flutter " as the particular object of
his wrath. It was a play of long-continued popularity,
and as he said, regarded as a type of genteel comedy. Yet
it was one of the very worst, and pretty well justified his
definition of it as a perfect contradiction of good manners,
good sense, and common honesty. The hero, as he says, is
a direct knave in his dealings and often a clown in his
language. He tries to marry his friend to a girl whom
he hopes afterwards to make his mistress, and he not only
deserts but reviles those women who have been foolish
enough to listen to his love-making in the past.

Dennis, a staunch upholder of the old comedy, wrote
" A Defense of Sir Fopling Flutter " in reply to Steele
who, he says, admits that it represents nature but "nature
in its utmost corruption and degeneracy." " But," Dennis
continues, " can anything but corrupt and degenerate
nature be the proper subject of ridicule? and can anything
but ridicule be the proper subject of comedy "? For
nearly half a century, he says, judges praised Sir Fopling
because it was found to " answer the two ends of comedy,
pleasure and instruction." Steele says that Dorimant is
not a fine gentleman. He was, says Dennis, a fine gentleman according to the idea of the time, as is proved by the
fact that he was so regarded. Steele, he says, in supposing
that the hero of this play is held up for imitation, shows
simply that he knows nothing of the rules of comedy, the
purpose of which is not to set up patterns of perfection
but to picture existing follies which we are to despise,
and to show that being done upon the comic stage which

ought never to be done upon the stage of the world. Here
again Dennis was right so far as theory was concerned.
He put his finger upon the danger of Steele's comedy,
which lay in the fact that by proposing examples of virtue it was likely to cease to be either realistic or funny. But
in the case of the particular example, " Sir Fopling Flutter,"
Steele was right. Dennis failed to see that in fact
Etherege's comedy failed as lamentably as Steele's to live
up to the rule which he was laying down; for its rakish hero
was presented in such a way that his vices seemed virtues
and he was indeed proposed and taken as an example of
the perfect man of pleasure. Steele saw all this perfectly
and he turned again to Etherege's play as the most effective contrast for his own plays.

In an epilogue written for " Measure for Measure " he
says the nation is corrupt:

> " Else say, in Briton why shou'd it be heard,
> That Etheredge to Shakespeare is preferr'd?
> Whilst Dorimant to crowded audience wenches,
> Our Angelo repents to empty benches:
>
> *   *   *   *   *   *   *   *
>
> The perjur'd Dorimant the beaux admire;
> Gay perjur'd Dorimant the belles desire:
> With fellow-feeling, and well conscious gust,
> Each sex applauds inexorable lust.
> For shame, for shame, ye men of sense begin,
> And scorn the base captivity of sin:
> Sometimes at least to understanding yield
> Nor always leave to appetite the field;
> Love, glory, friendship languishing must stand,
> While sense and appetite have sole command;
> Give man sometimes some force in the dispute,
> Be sometimes rational, tho' oftener brute."

And another time he represents the ghost of Sir Fopling
Flutter as appalled by the popular success of the more

virtuous hero of "The Conscious Lovers." The ghost speaks: [1]

"Ladies, ye stare as if ye knew me not —
What! Can Sir Foppling be so soon forgot?
There was a time, when Dorimant and I,
Won every heart, and reign'd in every eye;
Till this new sot, this moralizing fool,
Had turn'd the theater into a school:

*   *   *   *   *   *   *   *

Oh gentle George, if he had studied thee,
He wou'd have learnt to lard his comedy:

*   *   *   *   *   *   *   *

His hero too — oh, 'tis a faithful swain,
As ever sigh'd upon Arcadian plain;
Loving and eke belov'd, of youth and beauty,
Yet wants to reconcile his love and duty,
Oh! Etheridge, bard of easy, luscious vein,
Where are the heroes, of thy happy reign?
Old Roman heroes famous for undoing,
Who rais'd their characters on rape and ruin!
Thy Dorimant with nobler maxims blest,
Had made right use of innocence distressed;
Superior to reproach of guilt, or shame,
Had first enjoy'd and then despis'd the dame;
While thou his waste of fortune to repair,
Had crown'd his virtues with some wealthy fair.
Rise, mighty shade, nor let this upstart drone,
This puling moralist, usurp thy throne;
Once more assert thy juster empire here,
Till then, I take my leave — adieu mes cheres."

There was no danger that the audience would fail to realize the difference between the new comedy and the old.

The theories expressed in the quotation just given demand a modification of the Restoration tradition in two

[1] Prologue to *The Conscious Lovers* when played before the gentlemen of the College of Dublin, 7th March, 1722.

ways: first, by the elimination of over-frankness whatever
its purpose; and second, by the introduction of the ideal
hero as a foil to the imperfect one. In making these demands, however, Steele expressed nothing that was not
implicit in Collier. Like Collier, he had pointed out that
that old comedy was smutty and blasphemous, and that
the audience had taken as models for imitation characters
who were by no means perfect.

Steele's original contribution consisted in the introduction of the element called sentiment, which, though new
in theory, was no invention of his. Cibber had stumbled
upon it in 1696, and the success of his play had shown
that it appealed to an actual appetite of the audience.
Steele saw in it a useful element to replace the salt which
he extracted from the old formula, and proceeded to give
it a theoretical defense.

Sentiment was totally out of place in Restoration Comedy with its fondness for a hard, intellectual and cruel
attitude. Comedy had concerned itself with the crimes
and follies of mankind, and regarded emotional idealism,
if existent, as at least outside its sphere of hard realism.
Drake [1] had put the case clearly when in speaking of
Etherege's " The Comical Revenge " he had said: " These
scruples of honor, and extravagancies of jealousy and despair are unnatural on the comic stage," and again: " however brave and generous in action it appear, consider'd
simply in itself, it is a trespass against justice and propriety of manners in that place " (i.e., in comedy). But
to make a place in comedy for ecstasies of jealousy and
despair, and for scenes illustrating heroism and the principles of honor, was exactly the aim that Steele had.
" Anything," he wrote, " that has its foundation in happi-

[1] *Ancient and Modern Stages Surveyed.*

ness and success must be allowed to be the object of
comedy; and sure it must be an improvement of it to
introduce a joy too exquisite for laughter." [1]

Persuasive as this plea is, it contains the fatal germ of
half of what is bad in Sentimental Comedy. When comedy left the path of laughter to seek sentiment, it went
down and down until it not only ceased to be funny but
became maudlin. One does not know what to think of an
audience that would weep over " Love's Last Shift " or
" The Conscious Lovers." But we are told that audiences
did so, and in referring to a performance of the latter
play Steele writes: " I must, therefore, contend that the
tears which were shed on that occasion flowed from reason
and good sense, and that men ought not to be laughed
at for weeping till we are come to a more clear notion
of what is to be imputed to the hardness of the head and
the softness of the heart." Modern criticism has decided
that the softness which results in such tears as these lies
in the head.

The device of the eleventh-hour or fifth-act repentance
became popular because it so perfectly fitted the requirements of the new comedy. The well-known difficulty of
devising intrigue for a perfect character was avoided by
making him fallible at first and perfecting him at the end
by means of remorse and repentance. Thus plot-making
was made easier, and in addition a splendid opportunity
was given for the introduction of tender scenes of forgiveness and reconciliation which were redolent with that joy
too deep for laughter. As is the case with all the devices
of Sentimental Comedy, Steele gave this one a theoretical
defense; and in the preface to " The Lying Lover " he gives
the moral of his action. Speaking of his hero, he says:
" Thus he makes false love, gets drunk, and kills his man;

[1] Preface to *The Conscious Lovers*.

but in the fifth act awakes from his debauch, with the
compunction and remorse which is suitable to a man's
finding himself in a gaol for the death of his friend, without his knowing why. The anguish he there expresses, and
the mutual sorrow between an only child and a tender
father in that distress, are, perhaps, an injury to the rules
of comedy, but I am sure they are a justice to those of
morality."

This is but another illustration of the fact that Sentimental Comedy was not a spontaneous expression but a
machine-made product constructed in accordance with
definite rules. As such, it became necessarily stereotyped
and artificial, and the late-reform motif was so obviously
a mere convention that, as Fielding protested, the heroes
were often notorious rogues and the heroines abandoned
jilts during the first four acts and became respectively
worthy gentlemen and women of virtue at the end for no
other reason than that the play was drawing to a conclusion. It is as natural, he said, for stage rogues to repent
in the last act of a play as for real ones to be seized
with remorse in the last hour of their lives.[1]

Steele thought he had found in Latin comedy a justification for his theory that laughter was not the chief business
of comedy. In " Spectator " 502 he discusses the question in
connection with a play of Terence. " There is," he says,
in ' The Self-Tormenter ' a perfect picture of human life
but nothing to raise a laugh." He notes that the famous
phrase " Homo sum," etc. is said to have created instanta-
neous applause in the Roman theater, but regrets that it
would not have done so had the words been spoken on an
English stage; for an English audience cares nothing for
the truths of simple human nature but prefers to laugh at
what is directly against common sense and honesty. Ac-

[1] *Tom Jones.* Book VIII, Chap. 1.

cordingly, when Steele determined to write a final illustration of all his theories, he went to Terence for the plot of
" The Conscious Lovers." And he took care to warn the
public long beforehand that it was to see not merely a
play but an illustration of all that the stage, henceforth,
should aim to be. How carefully he advertised it in advance has already been shown in Chapter VIII.

The play was to make its principal appeal not to the
sense of the comic but to more serious emotions. Its
chief aim was to be innocent and to instruct by presenting
a picture of the perfect gentleman. The plain tendency
of such a comedy to upset the long-established but dying
English tradition was recognized immediately; and a little
controversy raged around it. Dennis, especially, attacked
it violently in " Remarks on the Conscious Lovers " (1723).
Whatever one may think of Dennis, he showed considerable penetration and a tendency to go directly to the root
of the matter. Even before the appearance of " The Conscious Lovers " he had recognized Terence's weakness on
the comic side,[1] and in the pamphlet just referred to he
goes immediately to the point. Steele had said that his
chief design was to write an innocent performance. Dennis
thereupon points out that, while innocence may be a good
beginning, it is hardly a satisfactory chief design. He
points out so well the fact that Sentimental Comedy is
bad Comedy because it is not comedy at all that it is
worth while to quote him:

" When Sir Richard says, that anything that has its
foundation in happiness and success must be the subject
of comedy, he confounds comedy with that species of
tragedy which has a happy catastrophe. When he says,
that 'tis an improvement of comedy to introduce a joy too

[1] *Original Letters*, etc. 1721.

exquisite for laughter, he takes all the care that he can to show that he knows nothing of the nature of comedy. . . . When Sir Richard talks of a joy too exquisite for laughter, he seems not to know that joy, generally taken, is common like anger, indignation, love, to all sorts of poetry, to the epic, the dramatic, the lyric; but that that kind of joy which is attended with laughter, is a characteristic of comedy; as terror or compassion, according as the one or the other is predominant, makes the characteristic of tragedy, as admiration does of epic poetry.

"When Sir Richard says, that weeping upon the sight of a deplorable object is not a subject for laughter, but that 'tis agreeable to good sense and to humanity, he says nothing but what all the sensible part of the world has already granted; but then all the sensible part of the world have always deny'd, that a deplorable object is fit to be shown in comedy. When Sir George Etherege, in his comedy of ' Sir Fopling Flutter,' shows Loveit in all the heights and violence of grief and rage, the judicious poet takes care to give those passions a ridiculous turn by the mouth of Dorimant."

The newspaper " The Freeman's Journal " attacks the play twice, and on the first occasion devotes nearly three columns to it.[1] It finds,[2] as a modern reader must find, that the hero is so perfect as almost to suggest burlesque, and justly enough complains of the play: " there are more tears than laughter produced by it." Like Dennis, too, the critic of this newspaper sees the weakness of sentimental comedy when he writes:

" We are told after, that anything that has its founda-

[1] November 14, 1722.
[2] November 28, 1722.

tion in happiness and success, must be allow'd to be the
subject of comedy; here we are equally at a loss in our
critic as in our comedian —

"For it is indisputably true, that some instances of
success and happiness may be of a kind too elevated, and
by consequence, very improper for comedy.

"We are likewise in very moving terms instructed, that
tears, which were shed in the case of the father and
daughter, flow'd from reason and good sense. It seems
that crying as well as laughing are marks of a reasonable
nature, and ought to specially enter the definition of a
man."

Sentimental comedy was not good comedy for the simple reason that it was not comedy at all; and it was not
good drama because of its artificiality and falsity. But
there was no doubt as to the popular success of "The
Conscious Lovers." It triumphed in spite of its plain
tendency, which Dennis and others pointed out, to upset
the comic tradition; and its triumph was a triumph for
the type. After it, plays like those by Fielding were only
sporadic anachronisms. There were protests, such as that
voiced by parson Adams when he remarked slyly that
Steele's play contained some things almost solemn enough
for a sermon, or when Fielding wrote the still more
delightful scene in "Tom Jones" where the puppet show
is performed "with great regularity and decency," being
only the fine and serious part of "The Provok'd Husband"
"without any low wit or humor, or jest, and performed
by a man whose discourse is only the necessity of rational
entertainment and the duty of every puppet-show to aim
chiefly at the improvement of the morals of the young."

It was not until the time of Goldsmith and Sheridan
that an effective protest was set up, and even those two
writers by no means immediately killed the tradition, as

the complaints of Hazlitt will show. The triumph of sentimental comedy was the triumph of morality and criticism over wit. Certainly morality was more powerful than criticism, but morality was backed by the efforts of the most influential dramatic critic of the time. From the old criticism he took the idea of the moral end of literature and made this idea dominant in his theories; but he was careful, also, to give a critical justification, to all the new elements which were introduced so that his audience might indulge their moralistic tendencies with the further satisfaction of feeling that they had the support of critical theory.

So just are many of the charges brought against Restoration Comedy, and so persuasive are Steele's pleas for a comedy which would substitute ideals for cynicism, and human emotion for heartless laughter, that if one reads only the criticism and does not taste its fruit, one is inclined to sympathize wholly with the reformers. But one has only to read a few of the comedies of the early eighteenth century to see how completely they failed, not only to embody ideals, but to achieve readability. Naturally one asks why.

Primarily, they were failures because their authors refused to recognize that a comedy cast in a realistic mould must make some attempt to be true to actual character and events. An ideal world may be made convincing if the scene is laid in far-off time, or perhaps on the coast of some unknown Bohemia, but if the action of a play takes place in a contemporary drawing-room, it must bear some sort of resemblance to what really takes place in such a drawing-room. One can learn no lesson from the high tone and the romantic nobility exhibited by the perfected heroes of Steele or Cibber because one sees that they bear no relation to the life which the comedy of manners pretends to depict. It is all very well to show the magnanimous hero rewarded in the end by the discovery of unexpected wealth in the possession of his true love; but it gives no impulse to imitation, because the reader knows that though he may behave as nobly as the hero he has no reason to expect a similar prize, there being no connection between virtuous action and fortuitous reward.

In other words, the whole theory of poetic justice, if interpreted as childishly as the eighteenth century interpreted it, is wrong. If men are to be encouraged to seek virtue, one must show its real rewards by picturing the inherent beauty of uprightness or the self-satisfaction of conscious rectitude. But this the sentimentalist was not content to do. He insisted on showing that virtue paid in the material sense; and he made material prosperity its reward, though all the world knew that such was not necessarily the case. Over all the drama of the period there is the taint of falsity in language and sentiment, for the dramatists did not believe the truth of what they were writing. Under this tradition wit died, for the basis of wit is a realization and recognition of the contrast between ideals and reality, while the sentimentalist insisted upon their identity. The new dramatist was so afraid of reality that he could never give it the opportunity of a jest, and pungent observation disappears in false and complacent morality. Humor comes to be considered as " low," and Fielding asks in vain what his contemporaries mean, pointing out that at any rate they have succeeded in banishing all humor from the stage and have made the theater as dull as a drawing room.[1]

The Restoration comic dramatist, on the other hand, was right in theory. He saw that a comedy of manners must represent to a considerable extent the actual manners of

[1] *Tom Jones.* Book V, Chap. 1.

its time, that it must be allowed a certain freedom of satire, and that its action should be regulated to a considerable extent by an observation of what actually takes place in society. He distributed rewards and punishments not according to any ideal system of morality but according to probability, and realized that to be convincing he must be worldly. He saw the fallacy of the perfect monster as hero, and realized that characters must be presented with their beauties and blemishes in conflict and that he must, in a word, show life rather as it is than as it ought to be, and must rather depict than ignore vice. But sound as it was in theory, Restoration Comedy has shocked all succeeding generations; partly because it mirrored Restoration life, which itself would have shocked all subsequent generations, but partly also because the sound method of comedy was perversely used. The men who wrote the plays were men of their age, and they shared its vices. Sometimes they cynically pandered to a corrupt taste which they did not wholly share, as in the case of Dryden; while sometimes they were repulsive only because they carefully expressed that cynical idea of life which they held but which the bulk of their subsequent readers has not shared.

But the remedy for this was not to be found in a new type of comedy. There was no reason why a comedy open to no reasonable objection on the moral ground might not have been written in the old style. There was nothing essentially vicious in the model. We may conceive that if society purified itself the drama would have purified itself also. It would have continued to mirror real life, but as real life became less brutal than Restoration life the reflection of it would have been less revolting, and a Wycherley born in the latter eighteenth century would not have been the same as a Wycherley of the

seventeenth. A start toward a better comedy had been
made by Vanbrugh. In spite of some freedom, there is
nothing that need shock a sophisticated reader in " The
Relapse," though there is much in Etherege, for instance,
to shock any reader. But such a development was not
to be. The self-conscious moral movement, and the
simultaneous development of sentimentalism, practically
killed comedy.

This study has taken us over a wide field both of time
and of subject matter — over too wide a field, perhaps, to
be adequately examined in a single book. But such a com-
prehensive survey was necessary if anything was to be
added to the understanding of the phenomenon whose
ending was Sentimental Comedy — a phenomenon often
observed, but never adequately explained, and concerning
which there has been the widest possible difference of
opinion. I hope that I have been able to make clear what
happened, when it happened, and, to some extent, why it
happened. Certainly the movement cannot be said to have
had any single cause. It is not true that it was the
direct result of the Collier controversy, nor is it true that
Collier had no influence upon it. Still less is it true that,
as Mr. Bernbaum in his " Drama of Sensibility " seems
to imply, the movement was not fundamentally the result
of the moral badness of Restoration writers, but simply
the result of the development of a sentimental view
of life. It was the result of many causes interacting upon
one other, and like any important intellectual movement
it was too complex ever to be fully explained. But
by examining the drama itself, the social life which it re-
flects, the movement for general reform, specific attacks
on the stage, and the development of criticism, we get a
truer idea of the phenomenon than would have been pos-

THE THEORY OF SENTIMENTAL COMEDY

sible if we had confined our attention to any one of these departments. At least we can see what happened.

In the beginning a leisure class, relieved from adversity and artificial restriction, plunged into dissipation, and developed a comedy which reflected its life and expressed its ideals, embodying all its wit, cynicism, and perversity. As the reaction died away and life returned to something more like normal conditions, comedy continued to picture the social life of the time which had given it birth; and by the latter part of the seventeenth century was already somewhat of an anachronism following rather a tradition than expressing the idea of the new generation which had grown up and taken its place in the theater. A general movement for reform predisposed the public to receive favorably the violent but pointed attacks of an able fanatic; and it awoke violently to the realization that popular comedy did not express the ideals of its age. Finally, criticism, just establishing a rapport with popular literature, evolved a set of critical theories based partly on old and partly on new ideas, which encouraged and, to some extent, directed the development of a new comic tradition more closely suited than the old to the taste of its generation.

Thus the question with which we started, " To what extent was Collier responsible for the development of sentimental comedy? " is seen to be an extremely complicated one, and one which is perhaps unanswerable. No man and no argument can control the course of events. A man and his arguments are merely a crystallization of the spirit of the age; and the man leads only in the sense of taking people where they want to go, for arguments are the result of opinions rather than opinions the result of arguments. Since all the characteristics of the movement were discernible before Collier wrote, he cannot be said to be responsible for it. On the other hand, since it became considerably accentuated immediately after the appearance of his book, and since Steele, its principal protagonist, acknowledged himself as Collier's follower, the latter must have been, at least, the most effective mouthpiece of the opposition. He formulated the argument which was the result of the opinion of his time, and he led the people where they were ready to go. Without him, Restoration Comedy would have died of its own accord; but he hastened its death. He produced Sentimental Comedy not more than Rousseau produced the French Revolution; but like Rousseau he made a movement articulate. And as Rousseau's is the name most closely associated with the French Revolution, so justly enough that of Collier is the one most closely associated with the literary triumph of morality and dullness.

Bibliography

Some Critical Works Published between 1660 and 1700

It was thought advisible to add this bibliography which is, so far as I know, the only one which has been compiled, as an illustration of Chapter III. It is not continued beyond 1700 as there is a bibliography to W. H. Durham's "Critical Essays of the Eighteenth Century." I include biographies of literary men and in general any "books about books" in this list.

(F. Kirkman.) Tom Tyler and his wife. — Together with an exact catalogue of all the plays that were ever yet printed. The second impression. 1661.

Richard Flecknoe. Loves Kingdom — With a short treatise of the English Stage. 1664.

Letters upon several occasions; written by and between Mr. Dryden, Mr. Wycherley, Mr. ——, Mr. Congreve, and Mr. Dennis. Published by Mr. Dennis. 1666.

The Works of Mr. Abraham Cowley. (With Sprat's "Life.") 1668.

Richard Flecknoe. Sir William Davenant's voyage to the other world: with his adventures in the poet's Elyzium. A Poetical Fiction. 1668.

(F. Kirkman.) Nicomede — Together with an exact catalogue of all the English stage-plays printed. 1671.

(R. Rapin.) Reflections upon the use of the eloquence of these times. 1672.

(R. Rapin.) A Comparison between the eloquence of Demosthenes and Cicero. Translated out of the French. 1672.

George Villiers, Duke of Buckingham: The Rehearsal. 1672.

(Richard Leigh?) The Censure of the Rota on Mr. Dryden's Conquest of Granada. 1673.

A description of the Academy of the Athenian Virtuosi with a discourse held there in vindication of Mr. Dryden's Conquest of Granada; against the author of the Censure of the Rota. 1673.

Mr. Dryden vindicated, in a reply to the Friendly Vindication of Mr. Dryden. With reflections on the Rota. 1673.

Remarks on the humors and conversations of the town. 1672.

Remarks upon Remarks, or a vindication of the conversations of the town. 1673.

Animadversions on two late books.— One called— Remarks etc. The other called Reflections on Marriage etc. 1673.

R. Rapin. The comparison of Plato and Aristotle — translated from the French. 1673.

(Dryden, Shadwell, and Crown.) Notes and observations on " The Empress of Morocco." 1673.

Raillery a la mode considered etc. 1673. (The British Museum has a copy with a title page dated 1663. This is probably an error as the book is entered in the Term Catalogues in 1673.)

R. Rapin. Reflections on Aristotle's Treatise of Poesie. (Translated by Thomas Rymer.) 1673.

(E. Settle.) Notes and observations on The Empress of Morocco revised. 1674.

R. Flecknoe. A treatise of the sports of wit. 1675.

Edward Phillips. Theatrum Poetarum.— with some observations and reflections upon many of them, particularly those of our nation. Together with a prefactory discourse of the poets and poetry in general. 1675.

W. Williams. Poetical Piety, or poetry made pious. 1677.

T. Rymer. The tragedies of the last age considered and examined by the practice of the ancients and by the common sense of all ages. 1678.

Reflections upon ancient and modern philosophy — translated out of the French by A. L. 1678.

(Thomas Durfy) The Fool turned critic. A Comedy. 1678.

The Refined Courtier, or a correction of several indecencies crept into civil conversation. 1678.

J. Davies. Instructions for history — out of the French. (of R. Rapin.) 1680.

Genuine Remains of Samuel Butler. (Printed in 1759 but written before 1680.)

(J. Puleney.) A treatise of the loftiness or elegency of speech. Written originally in Greek — and now translated out of the French etc. 1680.

Wentworth Dillon, Earl of Roscommon. Horace's Art of Poetry made English. 1680.

(Mulgrave and Dryden?) An essay upon Satyre. 1680.

T. Hobbes. The art of rhetoric. 1681.

John Sheffield, Earl of Mulgrave. An essay upon poetry. 1682.

Some instructions concerning the art of oratory. 1682.

Hedelin, Archbishop. The whole art of the stage — written in French — and now made English. 1684.

(Soame and Dryden.) The art of poetry — made English. (From Boileau.) 1683.

(Shadwell?) Some reflections on the pretended parallel in the play The Duke of Guise. 1683.

John Dryden. Of dramatic poesie. 1684.

T. Creech. The Idylliums of Theocritus, with Rapin's discourse of pastorals. Done into English. 1684.

Mixed essays upon Tragedies, Comedies, Italian comedies, English comedies and operas. Written originally in French by Sieur de Saint Evremond. 1685.

(W. Winstanly.) The lives of the most famous English poets — from the time of King William the Conqueror to the reign of his present Majesty, King James II. 1686.

Miscellanea: or various discourses. Written originally by Sieur de St. Evremond and made English by F. Spence. 1686.

M. Clifford. Notes upon Mr. Dryden's poem in four letter — To which are annexed some reflections upon The Hind and the Panther. By another hand. 1687.

(E. Settle.) Reflections on several of Mr. Dryden's plays. Particularly the first and second parts of the Conquest of Granada. 1687.

Spenser Redivivious. Containing the first book of the Fairy Queen, his essential design preserved, but his obsolete language and manner of verse totally laid aside — By a person of quality. (Contains a critical preface.) 1687.

(Tom Brown.) The reason of Mr. Bays' changing his religion. 1688. To Poet Bavius. (Against Dryden.) 1668.

G. Langbaine. Momus Triumphans; or the plagiaries of the English stage. 1688.

The man of honor. (Concerning Dryden.) 1688.

The modest critic; or remarks upon the most eminent historians — By one of the Port-Royal. 1698.

(Tom Brown?) The Reason of Mr. Joseph Haines the player's conversion and re-conversion. 1689.

The late converts exposed: Or the reason of Mr. Bays' changing his religion — part the second. 1690.

Sir William Temple. Miscellanea, the second part. 1690.

Wit for money, or poet Stutter (Durfey). A dialogue — containing reflections on some late plays, particularly on Love for Money, or the Boarding School. 1691.

A search after wit, or a visitation of the authors. 1691.

G. Langbaine. An account of the English dramatic poets. 1691.

The art of pleasing conversation. Written by Cardinal Richelieu. 1691.

A letter to Mr. Durfey occasioned by his play called The Marriage-Hater Matched. (Prefixed to the play.) 1692.

Poeta Infamis; or, a poet not worth hanging. 1692.

(Charles Gildon?) Miscellaneous poems upon several occasions; consisting of original poems by the Duke of Buckingham, Cowley, Milton, Prior, etc. — with an essay upon satyr by M. Dacier. 1692.

Thomas Rymer. A short view of tragedy. 1693.

John Dennis. The impartial critic, or some observations upon a late book, entitled, A Short View of Tragedy. 1693.

John Dennis. Miscellanies in verse and prose. 1693.

(R. Rapin.) Mr. Rapin's reflections on Aristotle's treatise of poesie — Made English by — Mr. R. to which is added some reflections on English poetry. 1694.

(J. Wright.) Country conversations. 1694.

(P. Motteux.) The Works of F. Rabelais — with a large account of his life. 1694.

Edward Phillips. Letters of state written by John Milton — to which is added an account of his life. 1694.

(Charles Gildon.) Miscellaneous letters and essays, on several subjects. — By several gentlemen and ladies. 1694.

(T. Taylor.) Monsieur Rapin's comparison of Thucydides and Livy. Translated into English. 1694.

(L. Echard.) Plautus' comedies, Amphitryon, Epidicus, and Rudens, made English, with critical remarks upon each play. 1694.

Sir Thomas Pope Blount: De re poetica. 1694.

Monsieur Bossu's treatise of the Epic Poem — to which are added an essay upon satyr, by Monsieur D'Acier; and a treatise upon pastorals, by Monsieur Fontanell. 1695.

The Miscellaneous works of Charles Blount, esq. — To which is prefixed the life of the author, and an account and vindication of his death. 1695.

A reflection on our modern poesie, an essay. 1695.

Letters upon several occasions; written by and between Mr. Dryden, Mr. Wycherley, Mr. Congreve, and Mr. Dennis. (Contains Congreve's " An Essay Concerning Humor ".) 1696.

John Dennis. Remarks on — Prince Arthur, an heroic poem — and — several new remarks upon Virgil. 1696.

A letter to the Duke of Vivone by — Monsieur Boileau. Translated by T. Check esq. Monsieur Boileau's speech to the Academy. Translated by Mr. Dennis. 1697.

Familiar Letters. (Rochester, Otway, Katherine Phillips and others.) 1697.

Money masters all things: — To which is added — a satyr on Mr. Dryden, and several other modern translators etc. 1698.

(Charles Gildon.) The lives and characters of the English dramatic poets; — First begun by Mr. Langbaine; improved and continued down to this time, by a careful hand. (1698).

Luke Milbourne. Notes on Dryden's Virgil. 1698.

Verdicts of the learned concerning Virgil's and Homer's heroic poems; with regular and irregular thoughts on poets and orators. 1698.

An essay upon sublime style, translated from the Greek of Longinus, the rhetorician; compared with the French of the Sieur Boileau-Despreaux. 1698.

(John Toland.) A Complete collection of the historical, poetical and miscellaneous works of John Milton — To which is prefaced the life of the author. 1698.

(J. Wright.) Historia Histrionica: An historical account of the English stage — In a dialogue of Plays and Players. 1699.

(John Toland.) Amyntor; or a defense of Milton's life. 1699.

Sir Richard Blackmore: A Satyre against wit. 1700.

A satyr upon a late pamphlet, entitled, A Satyr Against Wit. 1700.

Discommendatory verses, on those which are truly commendatory, on the author of the two Arthurs, and the Saytr Against Wit. 1700.

Samuel Wesley: An epistle to a friend concerning poetry. 1700.

A new session of the poets, occasioned by the death of Mr. Dryden. 1700.

Poetae Brinnicae. A poem satirical and panegyrical upon the English poets. 1700.

Homer and Virgil not to be compared with the two Arthurs. 1700.

The polite gentleman. 1700.

Familiar and courtly letters, written by Monsieur Voiture — To
which is added, a collection of letters of friendship, and other
occasional letters, written by Mr. Dryden, Mr. Wycherley,
Mr. ——, Mr. Congreve, Mr. Dennis, and other hands. 1700.
John Toland. The Oceana of James Harrington and his other
works — with an exact account of his life prefixed. 1700.
Edward Bysshe. The art of English poetry. 1700(?) 1702(?)

The Collier Controversy

I have attempted to make this bibliography as nearly complete
as possible. Some years ago a tentative one was published in
"Notes and Queries" and Dr. Johannes Ballein in his "Jeremy
Colliers Angriff auf die Englische Buhne" gives a much more
extensive one. Mine contains more items than either. Three
disagreements with Dr. Ballein may be noted and defended.

He records one title, "Hell upon Earth" and in the text says:
"Gegen die Buhne gerichtet ist dagegen das anonyme Hell upon
Earth, or The Language of the Play-House. Diese Schrift, die
ich ebenfalls nicht habe sehen können, wird von W. C. Ward in
seiner Ausgabe von Vanbrugh's Werken citiert und erschein nach
ihm 2–3 Jahre nach dem Sturm, d. h. also wohl 1705 or 1706."

Ward's statement is: "The anonymous author of a pamphlet
published two or three years later, under the edifying title of
Hell upon Earth or the Language of the Play-House, makes the
mournful admission that the horrid comedy of Love for Love,
the Provok'd Wife, and the Spanish Fryar, are frequently acted
in all places to which the players come." I have been able to
find no such pamphlet but the title is given in some editions of
Bedford's "Evil and Danger of Stage Plays " to a section of
that work. Ward's pamphlet is probably Bedford's "Evil and
Danger of Stage Plays" and Ballein's bibliography is wrong in
assuming a separate and unproduceable pamphlet.

But why did W. C. Ward give the title "Hell upon Earth,"
and why did he call it anonymous? An examination of one copy
of the "Evil and Danger of Stage Plays" in the British Museum,

reveals a mystery. After an elaborate title page "The Evil and Danger of Stage Plays etc." come five sheets "To the Reader," then a table of contents, then a page one, nearly half of which is taken up with the heading "The Evil and Danger of Stage Plays." Next comes a second page one, identical with the first in text and key words at the bottom, but differing in that it is headed "Hell upon Earth; or the Language of the Play-House."

Another copy of "The Evil and Danger" in the British Museum does not show this peculiarity as it has only the first page one. But in it, as in the other, page 204 contains the quotation given by Ward. Hence it is obvious that the pamphlet he quotes is identical with "The Evil and Danger." But did he simply copy this heading in the British Museum copy instead of the title page, and, furthermore, call it anonymous, or does there some-where exist a separate and anonymous edition of this pamphlet called "Hell upon Earth etc.", and is the British Museum copy a composite of the two different editions? That there should actually have been two editions is less likely, from the fact that the work is not a pamphlet in size, but a book of over 200 pages.

As to the second disagreement, Ballein quotes the following from the dedication to "An Act at Oxford" (1704): "The viewer, (who wishes her majesty, the same place in the throne she has in his dictionary), drew the proclamation against irreligion, and her regulation of the theaters as imperfect as his works; therefore on the fast day out comes his supplemental pamphlet to rectify the government's omission with the same modesty he formerly absolv'd it traytors." Then Ballein comments:

" Mit was für einer Schrift haben wir in diesem " Supplemental Pamphlet " zu tun? Zunächst könnte man sich versucht fühlen, an Colliers Dissuasive zu denken. Aber bei dem " Supplemental Pamphlet " handelt es sich ganz augenscheinlich um eine am Fasttag neu herausgekommene Schrift, während Mr. Colliers " Dissuasive " schon drei Wochen früher erschienen und in den berechtigten Kreisen jedenfalls schon vor dem Fasstage verbreitet und gelesen worden war. Auch weist die Bezeichnung " Supplemental Pam-phlet " darauf hin, dass bereits eine andere Schrift Colliers vorangegangen war. Und endlich ist seine " Dissuasive " durchaus nicht gegen irgendwelche " Omissions of the Government " gerichtet. Es wird zwar von dem Widerstand der Bühne gegen alle bishörigen Massregeln gesprochen, aber die Regierung wird mit keiner Silbe wegen irgendwelcher " Ommissions " getadelt. Auch

von den andern genannten Schriften durfte keine in Betracht
kommen: denn erstlich erscheinen sie anonym, was bei der Frage
stehen allem Anschein nach nicht der Fall war, und sodann stimmen
auch sie inhaltlich nicht zu Backers Angaben. So durfen wir wohl
annehmen, dass wir es hier mit einer neuen, wahrscheinlich verlorenen
Schrift Colliers zu tun haben."

Here, Bellein has, I think, quite unnecessarily hypothecated a
lost pamphlet, where there is no reason to suspect it ever existed.
Baker (the author of " An Act at Oxford ") does not use the words
"Supplemental Pamphlet" as a title, but only means "another
pamphlet by Collier." As Ballein himself points out earlier, the
" Daily Courrant " for the day following the storm advertises Collier's
" Dissuassive " for sale, and notes that on the fast day thousands
of pamphlets were given away. No doubt Baker got one. If he
received Collier's " Dissuasive," then, when it was being advertised
in the newspapers, he did not observe whether it was published
that day or three weeks before. There is little doubt that it
was the " Dissuasive " that he referred to as the Supplemental
Pamphlet. Ballein's objects that it is not directed against Anne,
but this is not to the point. Baker in the preface calls attention
to the fact that Collier is not loyal to his sovereign. What he
means is " Anne has just ordered a reform of the theater. Every
good subject will have confidence that she will do all this, but if
that non-juror Collier comes out with his Dissuasive he implies
that the Queen does not know her business." The German scholar
has, apparently (to revive the old story), evolved the book instead of the camel out of his inner consciousness. Such subjective
bibliography is not likely to please anyone but the compiler.

As to the third disagreement, Settle's " The City Ramble " was
printed without a date, and, owing to Settle's unpopularity, without his name. Ballein feels that the reference in it to Collier is so
direct that the play must have appeared earlier than August 17,
1711, which is the date Genest gives it. Ballein finds support for
his belief in Baker's " Companion to the Play-House " which in
one place gives the date as 1699, and then in another place leaves
the play undated. The unsupported statement of an eighteenth
century bibliography is not worth much, and a glance at contemporary newspapers will reveal several advertisements like the
following: " Never acted before. At the Theater-Royal and Drury
Lane, this present Friday, being the 17th of August, (1711) will
be presented a new comedy call'd ' The City Ramble '; or ' A Play-
House Wedding.' " This same paper for August 21st, adds " This

play is sold by J. Knapton at the Crown in St. Paul's churchyard and B. Lintott Nado's Coffee-House, Temple Bar." The British Museum copy has " as it is acted at the Theater-Royal," so, since there does not seem to me to be any strong internal evidence to show that the play might not have been written and first performed in 1711, I see nothing but the unsupported statement in an eighteenth century bibliography to support the unlikely theory that it was printed long after it was acted, and must conclude that 1711 is the proper date for the play.

* Indicates that I have not read or seen the work in question.

Animadversions on Mr. Congreve's late answer to Mr. Collier. In a dialogue between Mr. Smith and Mr. Johnson. 1698.

Baker, Thomas. An Act at Oxford. 1704.

Bedford, Arthur. The evil and danger of stage-plays showing their natural tendency to destroy religion, and introduce a general corruption of manners; in almost two thousand instances, taken from the plays of the two last years, against all the methods lately used for their reformation. 1706.

Bedford, Arthur. The great abuse of music. 1711.

(Bedford, Arthur?) A second advertisement concerning the profaneness of the play-house. 1705.

Bedford, Arthur. Serious reflections on the scandalous abuse and effects of the stage: in a sermon — preached — in the city of Bristol. 1705.

Bedford, Arthur. A serious remonstrance in behalf of the Christian religion, against the horrid blasphemies and impieties which are still used in the English play-houses . . . Shewing their plain tendency to overthrow all piety . . . from almost seven thousand instances, taken out of the plays of the present century. 1719.

Bedford, Arthur. The evil and mischief of stage playing: a sermon preached — in the city of London. 1730. (Second edition 1735.)

Bourbon, Armand, Prince de. The works of the most illustrious and pious Prince of Conti. — Translated from the French.

*Bossuet, J. B. Maxims and reflections on plays. (A translation.) 1699.

(Tom Brown.) The Stage-beau tossed in a blanket: or, hypocrycy a la mode; exposed in a true picture of Jerry . . . , a pretending scourge to the English stage. 1704.

*Burridge, R. Scourge for the play-house, or the character of the English stage. 1702.

Cibber, Colly. Love makes a man. 1701.

Collier, Jeremy. A short view of the immorality and profaneness of the English stage, together with the sense of antiquity upon this argument. 1688. (3rd. edition 1698. 4th 1699.)

Collier, Jeremy. A defense of the short view of the immorality and profaneness of the English stage — Being a reply to Mr. Congreve's Amendment. — And to the Vindication of the author of The Relapse. 1699.

Collier, Jeremy. A second defense of the short view — Being, a reply to a book, entitled, The Antient and Modern Stages Surveyed. 1700.

Collier, Jeremy. Mr. Collier's dissuasive from the play-house, in a letter to a person of quality, occasioned by the late calamity of the tempest. 1703.

Collier, Jeremy. Mr. Collier's dissuasive from the play-house etc. — To which is added, a letter written by another hand; in answer to some questions sent by a person of quality. 1704.

Collier, Jeremy. A farther vindication of The Short View — in which the objections of a late book, entitled A Defense of Plays, are considered. 1708.

*Concio Laici, or the lay man's sermon. (Cited in Bedford's Evil and Danger.)

The conduct of the stage considered. Being a short historical account of its origin, progress, various aspects, and treatment in the Pagan, Jewish and Christian world. 1721.

Congreve, William. Amendments of Mr. Collier's false and imperfect citations &c. from the Old Batchelor, Double Dealer, Love for Love, Mourning Bride. By the author of those plays. 1698.

A defense of dramatic poetry. 1698.

Drake, J. The ancient and modern stages surveyed. Or Mr. Collier's view of the immorality and prophaneness of the English stage set in a true light. 1699.

Esther; — A sacred tragedy. — With a dedication to the Lord Archbishop of York. (From Racine.) 1705.

Caffaro, Father. Beauty in distress. A tragedy, written by Mr. Motteux. With a discourse of the lawfulness and unlawfulness of plays, lately written in French by the learned Father Caffaro, Divinity Professor at Paris. Sent in a letter to the author by a divine of the Church of England. 1698.

Defoe, Daniel. The Pacificator. 1700.

Dennis, John. The person of quality's answer to Mr. Collier's letters: containing a defense of a regulated stage. (In " Original Letters.") 1721.

Dennis, John. The stage defended — Occasioned by Mr. Law's late pamphlet. 1726.

Dennis, John. The usefulness of the stage to the happiness of mankind, to government and to religion. 1698.

Durfey, Thomas. The campaigners: or, the pleasant adventures at Brussels. A comedy: With a preface upon a late reformer of the stage. 1698.

Dryden, John. Fables: (Preface.) 1700.

*Feigned Friendship, or the mad reformer. n. d. cir. 1700.

*Field, John. A humble supplication to the Queen and parliament to suppress play-houses and bearbaiting. 1703.

Filmer, Edward. A defense of plays — wherein is offered the most probable method of reforming our plays. With a consideration how far vicious characters may be allowed on the stage. 1707.

Heydegger's letter to the Bishop of London. 1724.

The immorality of the English pulpit as justly subjected to the notice of the English stage, as the immorality of the stage is to that of the pulpit. In a letter to Mr. Collier. 1698.

Law, William. The absolute unlawfulness of the stage-entertainment fully demonstrated. 1726.

Law Outlawed: — Together with an humble petition to the governors of the incurable ward of Bethlem to take pity on the poor distracted authors of the town, and not suffer 'em to terrify mankind at this rate. Written at the request of the orange-women. 1726.

(Gildon, Charles.) Phaeton — A Tragedy — With some reflections on a book called, A Short View etc. 1698.

*A letter to A. H. Esq. 1698.

A letter to Mr. Congreve on his pretended amendments, &c., of Mr. Collier's Short View etc. 1698.

(Josiah Woodward?) A letter to a lady concerning the new playhouse. 1706.

*A new project for regulating the stage, by John Dennis and Charles Gildon. (A satire.) 1720.

*Oldmixon, John. Reflections on the stage, and on Mr. Collier's defense of the Short View. 1699.

A collection of the Occasional Papers for the year 1708. (Contains a paper " Of Plays and Masquerades.") 1708.

*Reflections on the stage, and on Mr. Collier's defense of the Short View. 1699.

*A refutation of the apology for the actors. 1703.

A representation of the impiety and immorality of the English Stage, with reasons for putting a stop there to. and some questions addressed to those who frequent the play-house. 1704.

A seasonal apology for Mr. H(eide)g(ge)r. 1724.

Settle, E. The Citty-ramble: or, A play-house wedding. A comedy. 1711.

Some considerations about the danger of going to plays. In a letter to a friend. (In "The Occasional Paper" Number 9.) 1698. (Reprinted 1704).

Some remarks upon Mr. Collier's defense of his Short View of the English Stage, &c. In vindication of Mr. Congreve. In a letter to a friend. 1698. Some thoughts concerning the stage. In a letter to a lady. 1704. The stage acquitted. Being a full answer to Mr. Collier. 1699. The stage condemned. 1698.

Stage Plays justly condemned. 1720.

The stage vindicated: a satyr. By I. H. Esq. (In "The Muses Mercury" for July, 1707.)

Vanbrugh, John. A short vindication of The Relapse and The Provoked Wife. 1698.

(Gildon, Charles?) A vindication of the stage, with the usefulness and advantages of dramatic representations, in answer to Mr. Collier's late book. 1698.

Visits from the shades: or, dialogues serious, comical, and political. Calculated for these times — Jo. Hains' ghost and the reforming Mr. Collier.

Modern Works Relevant to the Subject
of the Present Study

PREPARED BY PROFESSOR G. S. ALLEMAN, *Rutgers University*

Abbreviations. ELH: ELH, a Journal of English Literary History; JEGP: Journal of English and Germanic Philology; MLN: Modern Language Notes; PMLA: Publications of the Modern Language Association of America; PQ: Philological Quarterly; RES: Review of English Studies.

THE COLLIER CONTROVERSY

Anon., Representation of the Impiety and Immorality of the English Stage (1704) and Anon., Some thoughts Concerning the Stage (1704). Introduction by Emmett L. Avery. Augustan Reprint Society, Series Three, No. 2, 1947.

Ballein, Johannes. Jeremy Collier's Angriff auf die englische Bühne [Marburg dissertation]. Marburg, Elwert, 1910.

Blackmore, Sir Richard. Sir Richard Blackmore's "Essay upon Wit" (1716) and Joseph Addison's "Freeholder, No. 45" (1716). Introduction by Richard C. Boys. Augustan Reprint Society, Series One, No. 1, 1946.

Dennis, John. The Critical Works of John Dennis, ed. Edward Niles Hooker. Baltimore, Johns Hopkins Press, 1939–43.

Heldt, W. "A Chronological and Critical Review of the Appreciation and Condemnation of the Comic Dramatists of the Restoration and Orange Periods." *Neophilologus*, VIII (Oct., 1922; Jan. and Apr., 1923), 39–59, 109–128, 197–204.

Krutch, Joseph Wood. "Government Attempts to Regulate the Stage after the Jeremy Collier Controversy." *PMLA*, XXXVIII (March, 1923), 153–74.

Letter to A. H. Esq.; Concerning the Stage, A (1698) and The Occasional Paper: No. IX (1698). Introduction by H. T. Swedenberg, Jr. Augustan Reprint Society, Series Three, No. 1, 1946.

Ressler, Kathleen. "Jeremy Collier's Essays." *Seventeenth Century Studies*, Second Series, by Members of the Graduate School, University of Cincinnati, ed. Robert Shafer, pp. 179–285. Princeton, Princeon University Press, 1937.

Rose Anthony, Sister. The Jeremy Collier Stage Controversy 1698–1726. Milwaukee, Marquette University Press, 1937.

Strachey, [Giles] Lytton. "Congreve, Collier, Macaulay and Mr. Summers." Portraits in Miniature, pp. 40–49. New York, Harcourt, 1931.

Symons, Julian. "Restoration Comedy. (Reconsiderations II.)" Kenyon Review, VII (Spring, 1945), 185–97.

Wells, Staring B., ed. A Comparison Between the Two Stages: a Late Restoration Book of the Theatre. "Princeton Studies in English," 26. Princeton, Princeton University Press, 1942.

White, Arthur F. "The Office of Revels and Dramatic Censorship during the Restoration Period." Western Reserve Bulletin, new series, XXXIV (Sept. 15, 1931), 5–45.

Wood, Frederick T. "The Attack on the Stage in the XVIII Century." Notes and Queries, CLXXIII (Sept. 25, 1937), 218–22.

HISTORY AND CRITICISM OF DRAMA, GENERAL

Agate, James, ed. The English Dramatic Critics; an Anthology. London, Barker, 1932.

Avery, Emmett L. "A Tentative Calendar of Daily Theatrical Performances, 1660–1700." Research Studies of the State College of Washington, XIII (Dec., 1945), 225–83.

Bartholomew, A. T. "The Restoration Drama, III." Cambridge History of English Literature, ed. A. W. Ward and A. R. Waller, VIII, 202–223, 490–500. New York, Putnam, 1912.

Beljame, Alexandre. Le Public et les hommes de lettres en Angleterre. Paris, Hachette, 1897.

Durham, William H., ed. Critical Essays of the Eighteenth Century, 1700–1725. New Haven, Yale University Press, 1915.

Ellehauge, Martin. English Restoration Drama; Its Relation to Past English and Past and Contemporary French Drama from Jonson via Molière to Congreve. Copenhagen, Levin & Munksgaard, 1933.

Gray, Charles Harold. Theatrical Criticism in London to 1795. "Columbia University Studies in English and Comparative Literature," 101. New York, Columbia University Press, 1931.

Miles, Dudley Howe. The Influence of Molière on Restoration Comedy. "Columbia University Studies in English and Comparative Literature" [25]. New York, Columbia University Press, 1910.

Nettleton, George Henry. "The Drama and the Stage." Cambridge

History of English Literature, ed. A. W. Ward and A. R. Waller, X, 75–103, 479–500. New York, Putnam, 1913.

—— English Drama of the Restoration and Eighteenth Century (1660–1780). New York, Macmillan, 1914.

Nicoll, Allardyce. *A History of Early Eighteenth Century Drama, 1700–1750.* Cambridge, Cambridge University Press, 1925.

—— A History of Restoration Drama, 1660–1700. Cambridge, Cambridge University Press, 1923.

Praz, Mario. "Poets and Wits of the Restoration." *English Studies.* X (Apr., 1928), 41–53.

—— "Restoration Drama." *English Studies*, XV (Feb., 1933), 1–14.

Schelling, Felix E. "The Restoration Drama, I." *Cambridge History of English Literature*, ed. A. W. Ward and A. R. Waller, VIII, 131–65, 472–82. New York, Putnam, 1912.

Smith, Dane Farnsworth. Plays about the Theatre in England [1671–1737]. New York, Oxford University Press, 1936.

Spingarn, J[oel] E., ed. Critical Essays of the Seventeenth Century. Oxford, Clarendon Press, 1908–9.

Thorndike, Ashley H. English Comedy. New York, Macmillan, 1929.

Whibley, Charles. "The Restoration Drama, II." *Cambridge History of English Literature*, ed. A. W. Ward and A. R. Waller, VIII, 166–201, 482–90. New York, Putnam, 1912.

Wilcox, John. The Relation of Molière to Restoration Comedy. New York, Columbia University Press, 1938.

Wilson, John Harold. The Influence of Beaumont and Fletcher on Restoration Drama. "Ohio State University Contributions in Language and Literature," 4. Columbus, Ohio State University Press, 1928.

COMEDY OF MANNERS AND THEORY OF COMEDY

Archer, William. The Old Drama and the New. Boston, Small, Maynard [1923].

Bateson, F[rederick] W. English Comic Drama 1700–1750. Oxford, Clarendon Press, 1929.

Bentley, Eric Russell. "The Views of Mr. Symons." *Kenyon Review*, VII (Summer, 1945), 477–80.

Crawford, Bartholow V. "High Comedy in Terms of Restoration Practice." *PQ*, VIII (Oct., 1929), 339–47.

Dobrée, Bonamy. Restoration Comedy 1660–1720. Oxford, Clarendon Press, 1924.

Draper, John W. "The Theory of the Comic in Eighteenth-Century England." *JEGP*, XXXVII (Apr., 1938), 207–223.

Gibbs, Anthony. Restoration Comedy. London, Hutchinson, 1939.

Houghton, Walter E., Jr. "Lamb's Criticism of Restoration Comedy." *ELH*, X (Mar., 1943), 61–72.

Hughes, Leo. "Attitudes of Some Restoration Dramatists toward Farce." *PQ*, XIX (July, 1940), 268 87.

Knights, L. C. "Restoration Comedy; the Reality and the Myth." *Scrutiny*, VI (Sept., 1937), 122 43. Reprinted in L. C. Knights, *Explorations; Essays in Criticism*, pp. 149–68. New York, Stewart [1947].

Lynch, Kathleen M. The Social Mode of Restoration Comedy. "University of Michigan Publications, Language and Literature," 3. New York, Macmillan, 1926.

Mignon, Elizabeth. Crabbed Age and Youth; the Old Men and Women in the Restoration Comedy of Manners. Durham, N. C., Duke University Press, 1947.

Montgomery, Guy. "The Challenge of Restoration Comedy." *California Publications in English*, I (1929), 131-51.

Nicoll, Allardyce. *The Theory of Drama*. New York, Crowell [1931].

Noyes, George Rapall. "The Development of English Comedy of Manners." *Representative English Comedies*, ed. Charles Mills Gayley and Alwin Thaler, IV, 538-48. New York, Macmillan, 1936.

Palmer, John. The Comedy of Manners. London, Bell, 1913.

Perry, Henry Ten Eyck. The Comic Spirit in Restoration Drama. New Haven, Yale University Press, 1925.

Snuggs, Henry L. "The Comic Humours; a New Interpretation." *PMLA*, LXII (Mar., 1947), 114–22.

Stoll, Elmer Edgar. "The 'Beau Monde' at the Restoration." *MLN*, XLIX (Nov., 1934), 425–32.

——— "The 'Real Society' in Restoration Comedy; Hymeneal Pretenses." *MLN*, LVIII (Mar., 1943), 175–81.

Trevelyan, G. M. " 'Artificial' Comedy." [London] *Times Literary Supplement*, correspondence, Jan. 5, 1928, p. 12. [Discussion continued by Basil Williams, Jan. 12, 1928, p. 28; Elmer Edgar Stoll, Mar. 1, 1928, p. 150; G. M. Trevelyan, Mar. 8, 1928, p. 170; T. A. Lacey, Mar. 15, 1928, p. 188.]

Williams, Edwin E. "Dr. James Drake and Restoration Theory of Comedy." *RES*, XV (Apr., 1939), 180–91.

SENTIMENTAL DRAMA

Bernbaum, Ernest. The Drama of Sensibility; a Sketch of the History of English Sentimental Comedy and Domestic Tragedy 1696–1780. "Harvard Studies in English," 3. Boston, Ginn, 1915.

Cox, James E. The Rise of Sentimental Comedy. Springfield, Mo., Drury College [author], 1926.

Croissant, De Witt C. "Early Sentimental Comedy." *Essays in Dramatic Literature; the Parrott Presentation Volume,* ed. Hardin Craig, pp. 47–71. Princeton, Princeton University Press, 1935.

Edmunds, James M. "An Example of Early Sentimentalism." *MLN,* XLVIII (Feb., 1933), 94–97.

Nolte, Fred O. The Early Middle Class Drama, 1696–1774. "New York University Ottendorfer Memorial Series of Germanic Monographs," 19. Lancaster, Pa., Lancaster Press, 1935.

Stroup, Thomas B. *"The Princess of Cleve* and Sentimental Comedy." *RES,* XI (Apr., 1935), 200–203.

Waterhouse, Osborn. "The Development of English Sentimental Comedy in the Eighteenth Century." *Anglia,* XXX (1907), 137–72, 269–304.

Williams, Stanley T. "English Sentimental Drama from Steele to Cumberland." *Sewanee Review,* XXXIII (Oct., 1925), 405–426.

Wood, Frederick T. "The Beginnings and Significance of Sentimental Comedy." *Anglia,* LV (July, 1931), 368–92.

—— "Sentimental Comedy in the Eighteenth Century." *Neophilologus,* XVIII (Oct., 1932; July, 1933), 37–44, 281–89.

BIBLIOGRAPHY

Harbage, Alfred. Annals of English Drama, 975–1700. Philadelphia, University of Pennsylvania Press, 1940.

N[icoll], A[llardyce]. "The Drama." *Cambridge Bibliography of English Literature,* ed. F. W. Bateson, II, 395–402. New York, Macmillan, 1941.

Paine, Clarence S. The Comedy of Manners (1660–1700); a Reference Guide to the Comedy of the Restoration. Boston, Faxon, 1941. Reprinted from *Bulletin of Bibliography,* XVII (1940–1942), 25–27, 51–53, 70–72, 97–99, 116–17, 145–48.

Woodward, Gertrude L., and James G. McManaway, eds. A Check List of English Plays, 1641–1700. Chicago, Newberry Library, 1945.

Index

"Absalom and Achitophel" (Dryden), 30, 106

"Academy of the Athenian Virtuosi, A Description of the," 62, 66

"Account of Rise and Progress of Religious Societies . . . , An" (Woodward), 159, 160

"Account of the English Dramatick Poets, An" (Langbaine), 63

"Act for the more effective suppressing profaneness . . . , An," 167

Actors, arrested: trials, 169 ff.; prosecution stopped by Anne, 176; Tate's proposal for regulating, 177

Adams, parson, 252

Addison, Joseph, 63, 67, 219; on poetic justice, 81; adopted pseudo-classical theory re purpose of drama, 146; reply to Blackmore's attack on wit, 156; criticism: satire, 228; reason for success of "Cato," 230; attacked, 230 f.

Adultery, 36

"Advancement and Reformation of Modern Poetry, The" (Dennis), 60

"Adventures of Five Hours, The" (Tuke), 15

"Amendments to Mr. Collier's

false and imperfect citations . . ." (Congreve), 122

"Amphytrion" (Dryden), 111, 122

"Anatomist or Sham Doctor, The," 171

"Angliae Notitia . . ." (Chamberlayne), 161

Animadversion on Mr. Collier's . . . (Congreve), 10n

"Animadversions upon Mr. Congreve's late answer to Mr. Collier, etc.," 125

Anne, Queen, witnessed plays only when performed at court, 28n; trend toward reason and morality in age of, 154, 156; proclamations, 166; support of Societies for Reformation, 167; stopped prosecution of actors, 176; earnest desire to regulate stage, 178, 190; order re licensing plays, 183; against complete suppression of stage, 185

"Apologie for Poetrie, An" (Sidney), 50, 73

"Apology" (Cibber), 204

Arber, Professor Edward, quoted, 36

"Arcadia" (Sidney), 74

Aristocracy, *see* Upper class

Aristotle, 10n, 54, 57, 68, 72, 77, 89, 107, 108; view of tragedy,

tion ,31; an act for suppressing, 167

"De Causa Dei" (Wycliff), 138

"Defense" (Sidney), 74; *see also* "Apologie for Poetrie, An"

"Defense of Dramatic Poetry, A," 94

"Defense of Plays" (Filmer), 74

"Defense of Sir Fopling Flutter, A" (Dennis), 244

"Defense of the Short View, etc., A" (Collier), 125

Defoe, Daniel, 131, 189; middle class found voice in newspaper of, 153, 157; on wit, 155; attitude toward theater, 158; on unfulfilled promise of reform, 188

Dekker, Thomas, 59

Dennis, John, 24, 32, 56, 65, 70, 76, 155, 178, 215, 228; as a critic, 60; view re proper method of comedy, 77; on poetic justice, 79 f., 82; unsuccessful as dramatist, 86; basis for defense of stage, 127; on storm of 1703 and the theater, 128; moral but anti-ascetic philosophy, 136; attack upon authority of the Fathers, 138; on relation of state and the theater, 142; pseudo-classical theory re purpose of drama adopted, 146; attitude toward doctrine of poetic justice, 147; criticism of Steele, 224, 225, 236, 250; criticism of Addison, 230; defense of old comedy, 236, 245

"De Re Poetica" (Blount), 60, 64

"Description of the Academy of the Athenian Virtuosi, A," 62, 66

"De Spectaculis" (Tertullian), 137

"Devil of a Wife, The" (Behn), 196

Dialogue, 8 f.; witty, between flirting couple, 15 (*see also* Wit); Congreve's, 22; Fletcher, 75

"Discourse of the English Stage" (Flecknoe), 55, 74

"Discourse upon Comedy in reference to the English Stage" (Farquhar), 237

"Discoveries" (Jonson), 51

"Dissembled Wanton, The" (Welsted), 223

Doggett, Thomas, 170, 171, 205; theatrical patent received by, 189

"Don Quixote . . ." (D'Urfey), 111, 118, 169, 207

Dorset, Earl of, 65, 66, 180

Dorset Garden Theater, 128, 180, 181, 183

"Double Dealer" (Congreve), 104, 169

Drake, James, on poetic justice, 81; noblemen in comedy, 145; purpose of comedy, 243; jealousy and despair in comedy, 247

Drama, change in method from satiric to sentimental, 53; written according to rules, 56 ff.; distrust of all plays, 90; opinions expressed 1660-98, 92 ff.; discrepancy between theory and practice, 100; may stimulate rational passions and pride,

"Mock Astrologer, The" (Dryden), 43, 105
"Mock Marriage, The" (Scott), 205
Molière, 4, 68, 94, 107; debt of Restoration Comedy to, 22; influence in establishing poetic justice, 82
"Momus Triumphans" (Langbaine), 63
"Money the Mistress" (Southern), 222
"Monitor" (Tate and others), poetical, 165
Morality, controversy over questions of, 149; teaching of, the purpose of literature, 72 ff.; audience's pleasure in seeing, upheld, 220; triumph over wit, 253; see also Reform movement; Sentimental comedy
Moral test as applied to comedy, 40 ff., 74 ff.
"Morning Ramble, The" (Payne), 20, 31
Motteux, P., 32, 63, 135, 205, 215
"Mourning Bride, The" (Congreve), 119, 123
"Mulberry Garden, The" (Sedley), 19, 65, 197
Mulgrave, Earl of, 34, 61; quoted, 62, 85; attacked Rochester's tragedy as obscene, 87

Nabbes, Thomas, 10, 11
Newcastle, Duchess of, 36
"New Session of the Poets, A," 64
"News-Letter," 169
Newspapers, middle class found voice in, of Defoe and Tutchin, 153, 157

Nichols, John, 150
Nicoll, Allardyce, 203
Nobility, indignities offered to, in drama, 82, 84, 144; discussion aroused by Collier's defense of, 145; see also Court
"Non-Juror, The" (Cibber), 232
"Northern Heiress, The" (Davys), 219

Oates, Titus, 34, 35
Obscenity, of Wycherley's plays, 46; a fault of taste, 84, 110; in Dryden, 85; in playwrights' language, 104; in Vanbrugh's play, 188; in Cibber's first sentimental comedy, 203
"Observator, The," 167
"Ode to Mistress Anne Killegrew" (Dryden), 122
Odingsell, Gabriel, 222
"Of Dramatick Poesie" (Dryden), 58
"Of Humor in Comedy" (Congreve), 86
"Of Modern Comedies"(Wright), 97
"Of Plays and Masquerades," 157
"Old Bachelor, The" (Congreve), 106, 125, 237
Oldfield, Mariah, 175
Oldham, John, 96
"Old Troop, The" (Lacy), 19
"On the Evil of Corrupt Communication" (Tillotson), 95
"Ordinary, The" (Cartwright), 10
Origen, 141
"Othello" (Shakespeare), Rymer's attack on, 83

Ovid, 23, 139
Oxford, Earl of, 32

"Pacificator, The," 155
Pack, George, 171
Pagan attitude toward the theater, 89
Palmer, John, 75
Pamphleteers, opinions of, on stage, 121-43; summarized, 143; discussion as to whether contemporary comedies were evil, 143
Parker, Archbishop, 138
"Parson's Wedding" (Killigrew), 11
Passions, rational exercise of, 136
"Pastime of Pleasure" (Hawes), 50
Paul, St., 141
Payne, Nevil, 20
Pepys, Samuel, 15, 27, 31, 33, 36; shocked at immorality of court, 93
"Person of Quality's Answer etc." (Dennis), 178
Philipps, Edward, 63
Philosophers, contempt of ancient, for pleasure, 89; objections of pagan, to stage, 137 ff.
"Pilgrim, The" (Dryden), 121, 122
Pinkman, William, 176
Pix, Mary, 205, 239
"Plain Dealer, The" (Wycherley), 46, 98
Plato, 72, 78, 89, 139; support of doctrine of poetic justice, 81
Plautus, 105
Players, see Actors
"Play-House, The. A Satire"

(Gould), 13, 95, 96; excerpts, 96
"Play-House to Let" (Davenant), 22
Plays, see Comedy; Drama; Tragedy
Playwrights, see Dramatists; Restoration dramatists; Sentimental dramatists
Pleasure, contempt of, 89
Plutarch, 72
"Poems on State Occasions," 37
"Poeta Infamis . . . ," 63
Poetic Justice, doctrine of, developed by Rymer, 56, 77; roots, 78; violation of laws of, 79; a cardinal doctrine, 81; Platonists' support of, 81; plays important part in Collier controversy, 82; idea becoming more generally accepted, 107; doctrine the easiest solution of stage reform, 147; eighteenth-century interpretation, 254
"Poetics" (Aristotle), 54, 72
Poetry, verse satire, 64; chief end of, 73 ff.; satire on, 154
Poets, justification of, 72, 73; duty to instruct, 99; betray religion, virtue, and their own art, 99; in pay and under control of State, 100; see also Dramatists
Politics, 34
Pope, Alexander, 55, 57, 154, 228; quoted, 70
Portsmouth, Duchess of, 29
"Post Boy Rob'd of his Mail, The" (Gildon), 64
Powell, John, 175
Prefaces, critical, 58, 59

and recognized, 17; Charles II and his court, 24 ff.; men of the, gentlemen in everything except essentials, 30; debauchery, 31; tone of books, 36; made critic a recognized figure, 51; polish and sophistication, 153; reaction against the physically and politically destructive moral anarchy, 156

Restoration Comedy, Collier controversy, ix, 24, 49, 89-149, 256 (*see further under* Collier, Jeremy); development of the tradition, 1-23; comedy of manners, 2, 6 f., 10 ff., 24, 254; cynicism, 2, 18, 19, 22, 45, 255; types of characters, 4, 7; development, 6 ff.; defined, 6; cultivated society, 7; relationship between Jonson and, 7; wit: dialogue, 8; realism, 9; studies of low life, 10; historical study: moral atmosphere, 12 ff.; Dryden first to seize completely the essentials of, 15, 17; best possible general title, 16; spirit developed and recognized, 17; study of evolution of type, 18, 257; later plays, 19; most powerful, 21; literary influences, 22; and society, 24-47; a faint representation of actuality, 24; took tone from Charles and his court, 28, 153; brutality, 34; inevitable characteristics, 39; chief end, 43, 55, 99; growing importance of literary criticism, 48-71 (*see also* Literary criticism); first critical prefaces, 51, 54, 58, 59;

effect of criticism, 71; moral test as applied to, 75; influence of idea of poetic justice, 77 ff., 107, 147 (*see also* Poetic justice); a school of debauchery, 107; represents heroes as debauched and also as attractive, 113; pamphleteers' discussion of, 143 ff.; full of abuses, 147; merits purely intellectual, 154; onslaught on, 89-149; gradual displacement, 195; survey of 1685-89, 196-202; defense of, on ground of satire, 200; survey of 1696, 202-7; on point of dissolution: survey of 1700–1701 shows new and old traits in conflict, 207 ff.; Steele's protest against, 217, 224, 225; brilliant perversity almost ceased, 221; change inevitable: part of great movement expressing itself everywhere in life, 229; could have been purified without sentimentalism, 229; unfit for people of quality, 232; success within limits which it proposed itself, 239: failure to make virtue attractive: smut, 239; flouts principles of morality, 240; bad man as hero, 241; had not fairly laid open virtues and vices, 243; emotional idealism outside its sphere of hard realism, 247; right in theory, 254; has shocked all subsequent generations, 255; remedy, 255; *see also under names of Restoration dramatists, e.g.,* Congreve; Wycherley

Restoration dramatists, aim and

"Stage Condemn'd, The" (Ridpath?), 94, 140
State, attitude toward the stage, 140
Steele, Sir Richard, 4, 29, 63, 67, 127, 220, 221; influence in establishing sentimental tradition, 52; protagonist of stage reform, 49, 75, 119 f., 258; extension of poetic justice to comedy, 78, 82, 147; allegiance to orthodox criticism, 86; agreement with Collier, 116; adopted pseudo-classical theory re purpose of drama, 146; plan to moralize wit, 154; criticism of Fletcher, 156; theatrical patent granted to, 185, 180; petition for power to reform theater: license revoked, 190; moral play written by, 195; position of premier sentimentalist shared with Cibber, 204; declared purpose to write innocently, 216; departure from Restoration tradition, 217; blow at old comedies, 224; foremost theoretical advocate of new comedy, 233 ff.; attitude toward state censorship, 234; idea of perfect dramatic literature, 234n; helped to establish rapport between esthetics and morality in criticism, 235; belief that literature should inspire a desire for ideal excellence, 238; theory of the drama, 239 ff.; attitude toward smut, 240; on vices upon stage, 241, 242; belief that satire should be perfectly obvious, 241;

would eliminate subtlety, 242; attempted to found a new comedy on an impossible principle, 243; epilogue for "Measure for Measure," excerpt, 245; Prologue demanding modification of Restoration tradition, 246; sentiment introduced but not invented by, 247; on joy in comedy, 248; on fifth-act repentance, 249; one can learn no lesson from heroes of, 253
Stillingfleet, Bishop, 160
Stoicism, 89
Storm of Nov., 1703, 128
Sturme, John, 222
Suckling, Sir John, 64
"Sullen Lovers, The" (Shadwell), 3, 20
Sunderland, Earl of, 181, 182
Swift, Jonathan, quoted, 70

Tacitus, 78
Talk, enjoyment of, 8
Taste, influence of critical theory in moulding popular, 230
Tate, Nahun, 165; proposal for regulating stage and players, 177
"Tatler, The," 164, 165, 236
Taverner, William, 220
Temple, Sir William, 28, 36, 64, 67
"Tender Husband" (Steele), 216, 217, 226, 234, 240
Tenison, Archbishop, 177n, 187
Terence, 105, 224, 249, 250
Tertullian, 137
Theater, controversy over Collier's attack upon, ix, 24, 49, 92; one instance of a sovereign